Fields in Vision

Fields in Vision offers a comprehensive and analytical study of the international phenomenon of television sports coverage. Garry Whannel considers the historical development of sport on television, the growth of sponsorship and the way that television and sponsorship have reshaped sport in the context of the enterprise culture.

Drawing on archival research, Whannel first charts the development of the BBC Outside Broadcast department and the growing battle for dominance between BBC and ITV, showing how sponsorship and the rising power of sports agents began to transform sport – not only in the UK but across the world – in the 1960s. He goes on to examine the implications of this vast and escalating global network during the 1980s by analysing the central role that stars and narratives began to play in television sport, presenting case studies of major challenges such as Coe versus Ovett, Decker versus Budd and so on. His study also takes into account one of the more indirect, but no less significant, results of international televised sport – the rise of popular fitness chic and the workout boom of the 1980s.

Fields in Vision explains the development of television sport by linking its economic transformation with the cultural forms through which it is represented, offering a study encompassing not simply the sports world, but our relationship with television and the media industries as a whole.

Garry Whannel is a Senior Lecturer in Sports Studies at Roehampton Institute.

Communication and Society
General Editor: James Curran

Fields in Vision

Television sport and cultural transformation

Garry Whannel

London & New York

First published 1992
by Routledge
11 New Fetter Lane, London EC4P 4EE

Simultaneously published in the USA and Canada
by Routledge
a division of Routledge, Chapman and Hall Inc.
29 West 35th Street, New York, NY 10001

© 1992 Garry Whannel

Set in 10/12 pt Times by Florencetype, Kewstoke, Avon
Printed and bound in Great Britain by
T J Press (Padstow) Ltd, Padstow, Cornwall

British Library Cataloguing in Publication Data
A CIP catalogue record for this book is available from the
British Library.

Library of Congress Cataloging in Publication Data
Whannel, Garry.
    Fields in vision : television sport and cultural transformation /
Garry Whannel.
        p.   cm.
    Includes bibliographical references.
    1. Television broadcasting of sports – Great Britain – History.
2. Sports – Great Britain – Marketing. 3. Sports – Social aspects –
Great Britain – History. 4. Corporate sponsorship – Great Britain –
History.   I. Title.
GV742.3.W47 1992
070.4'49796'0941 – dc20   91-47903

ISBN 0 415 05382 X
ISBN 0 415 05383 8 (pbk)

For Nicky

Contents

Illustrations

Acknowledgements

Thanks are due first of all to Richard Johnson and Stuart Hall for their patient and invaluable advice during the long years I spent struggling to finish a thesis. The project first took shape in the context of analysis of popular television by the Media Group at the Centre for Contemporary Cultural Studies (CCCS) between 1979 and 1981 and discussion and debate with Hazel Carby, Dorothy Hobson, Adam Mills and Michael O'Shaughnessy. I am grateful also to Roy Peters, Ian Connell, Dave Morley and Charlotte Brunsdon. The work of Paddy Scannell and David Cardiff on the BBC was a great source of inspiration, and both gave me invaluable advice on broadcasting research. Michele Shoebridge of the Sport Documentation Centre, Neil Somerville and John Jordan at the BBC Written Archives Centre and staff at the Sports Council Information Department all took time to explain their filing systems to me, for which many thanks. I am doubly grateful to the BBC Written Archives Centre for their permission to quote from archive sources. The analysis of the Moscow Olympics was aided by a collaboration with film-maker Gabrielle Bown, which gave us both access to many hours of video material.

Earlier versions of sections of this book have appeared in article form, and I would like to thank the following for permission to re-use some of this material: E. and F.N. Spon for 'The unholy alliance: notes on television and the re-making of British sport', *Leisure Studies* 5, 1986; Michael Green and CCCS for 'Narrative and television sport', in *Sporting Fictions* (edited by Jenkins and Green) 1982; the Leisure Studies Association for 'Sit down with us: TV sport as armchair theatre', in *Leisure and the Media* (edited by Sue Glyptis) 1983; 'Televising sport: the archaeology of a professional practice', in *Leisure: Politics, Planning, People. Volume 5: The Media and Cultural Forms*, 1986; and 'Building our bodies to beat the best: sport, work and fitness chic', in *Leisure, Labour and Lifestyles: International Comparisons. Volume 12: Sport in Society: Policy, Politics and Culture* (edited by Alan Tomlinson) 1990; and Edward Buscombe and the British Film Institute (BFI) for 'Grandstand, the sports fan and the family audience', in *Popular Television in Britain: Studies in Cultural*

History (edited by J. Corner) 1991.

Paddy Scannell, Graham Murdock, John Clarke, Michael Jackson and James Curran all read and commented on draft versions of sections, and if I'd accepted all their advice it probably would be a much better book. Adrian Metcalfe (Channel 4), Gary Frances (Thames), Harold Anderson (BBC) and Tony McCarthy (LWT) were kind enough to explain aspects of the production practices of television to me. In the course of a different (uncompleted) project several independent producers were good enough to allow me to watch them at work, so thanks to Derek Brandon, Phil Pilley, Des Bradley, Elaine Watts, Brian Venner and Mike Mansfield.

My understanding of television coverage of sport was also aided by work on several television documentaries and discussion with Susan Boyd-Bowman, Michael Jackson, Mike Dibb and Cary Bazalgette. Special thanks are due to Taylor Downing and David Edgar of Flashback Television. Working on their series of documentaries on the Olympic movement has been not only extraordinarily interesting, but also great fun. Meetings of the BFI group that planned two weekend events on sport also combined insight and pleasure, thanks to Philip Simpson, Christine Geraghty, Tana Wollen, Tim Cornish, Alan Tomlinson and Nicky North. The work of John Clarke and Chas Critcher has constantly provided me with a frame of reference, and my own work on television sport has been greatly sustained by the Leisure Studies Association, and by contact with its members.

Alan Tomlinson heroically not only read the whole of a late draft, but, unprompted by me, also sub-edited, corrected my punctuation and spelling, and cut out all the etceteras. I could not have finished without technological assistance from Apple computers, and the more human assistance of Huw Price and Steve Morrisby at Bidmuthin. Marta Wohrle of *Broadcast* and Andrew Shields of *Sport and Leisure* have been kind enough to offer me money to write about television sport on occasion. James Curran, Rebecca Barden and Jane Armstrong have helped make the production process as smooth as possible. Lastly, special thanks to Michael Jackson, Nicky North and Alan Tomlinson, who all gave much support, encouraged me to finish it, and are probably hoping that, now it's over, I'll find something else to talk about. It's a team game, Brian.

Abbreviations

AAA	Amateur Athletic Association
ABA	Amateur Boxing Association
ABC	Associated Broadcasting Company
ABC (USA)	American Broadcasting Company
ACTT	Association of Cinematograph and Television Technicians
AELTC	All-England Lawn Tennis Club
AFL	American Football League
APA	Alan Pascoe Associates
APCS	Association for the Protection of Copyright in Sport
AR	Associated Rediffusion
ARA	Amateur Rowing Association
ARD	Arbeitsgemeinschaft der offentlichrechtlichen Rundfunkanstalten der Bundesrepublik Deutschland (Consortium of Chartered Broadcasting Companies of the Federal Republic of Germany)
ASA	Amateur Swimming Association
ATV	Associated Television
BAAB	British Amateur Athletic Board
BAPU	British Athletics Promotion Unit
BBBC	British Boxing Board of Control
BBC	British Broadcasting Corporation (note: before 1927 it was the British Broadcasting Company)
BFI	British Film Institute
BSB	British Satellite Broadcasting
CBS	Columbia Broadcasting System
CCCS	Centre for Contemporary Cultural Studies
CCPR	Central Council for Physical Recreation
CNN	Cable Network News
CTelP	Controller of Televised Programmes (BBC)
CU	Close-up
DG	Director General (BBC)
DTel	Director of Television (BBC)

EBU	European Broadcasting Union
EOC	Equal Opportunities Commission
ETTA	English Table Tennis Association
FA	Football Association
FIFA	Federation of International Football Associations
FL	Football League
GLC	Greater London Council
GRA	Greyhound Racing Association
HMSO	Her Majesty's Stationery Office
HOB	Head of Outside Broadcasting
IAAF	International Amateur Athletic Federation
IAC	International Athletes Club
IBA	Independent Broadcasting Authority
IMG	International Management Group
IOC	International Olympic Committee
ISL	International Sport and Leisure
ITA	Independent Television Authority
ITC	Independent Television Commission
ITCA	Independent Television Companies Association
ITV	Independent Television
LS	Long shot
LTA	Lawn Tennis Association
LWT	London Weekend Television
MCC	Marylebone Cricket Club
MCI	Merchandising Consultants International
MS	Medium shot
NBC	National Broadcasting Company
NFL	National Football League
NOC	National Olympic Committee
OB	Outside Broadcast
OFT	Office of Fair Trading
OU	Open University
PMG	Postmaster-General
RFU	Rugby Football Union
SCAAA	Southern Counties Amateur Athletic Association
STAC	Sports Television Advisory Committee
TAC	Television Advisory Committee
TCCB	Test and County Cricket Board
TWI	Trans World International
WAAA	Women's Amateur Athletic Association
WCT	World Championship Tennis

Chapter 1

Sport, television and culture

'The commercialisation of the Olympic Games will never be tolerated. They will remain the only sports event in the world where there is no advertising in the stadia or on the athletes' vests.'

(Juan Antonio Samaranch, President of the International Olympic Committee, 1981)

'You paid $225 fucking million for these Games. You put on what the fuck you want, Roone. Don't listen to that schmuck [Samaranch]. You do what you want. You paid the goddamn money.'

(Film producer David Wolper, talking to Roone Arledge, President of ABC News and Sports; quoted in Reich 1986: 124)

At a sport event one day in 1986 I found myself sharing a lift on three separate occasions with, respectively, Sebastian Coe, Gina Lollobrigida and a tap dancer dressed as a moose. Over 1000 journalists and 55 camera crews were covering the event although there was no sport to be seen. It was the meeting of just 92 powerful people who comprise the International Olympic Committee (IOC) and the major item on the agenda was the selection of a city to host the 1992 Olympic Games. It was the intense lobbying and campaigning that brought moose, Coe and Lollobrigida, along with the world's press and hundreds of the most powerful and influential figures of world sport, to Lausanne, the headquarters of the IOC. As the Olympic movement has been transformed by the forces of television, sponsorship and globalisation, the vivid intensity of the tensions between tradition and modernity, amateurism and professionalism, and nationalism and individualism, has been plain to see. This book traces these tensions as they have been played out in British television and sport sponsorship, in the recent history of athletics, and in the Olympic Games and the World Cup.

What is so important about television sport that it warrants a whole book? There is a lot of it, over 2000 hours a year, not including the satellite channels; and while it's not all wildly popular it is watched by significant numbers, and, on major occasions like the Cup Final or the Olympic Games, by as much as half the population. Television sport is by any standards a component of popular culture and to understand it better is to understand more about the culture in which we live.

In that it chooses particular sports and gives us a particular view of them, television must inevitably affect the ways in which we see and understand sports. Moreover, the coverage is not simply concerned with sport; it inevitably also continually makes implicit and explicit statements, in words and pictures, about our sense of nation, of class, of the place of men and women, our relation to other nations and so on. Think how many stock stereotypes of foreigners (temperamental Latins, happy-go-lucky West Indians, dull but efficient Germans, faceless factory-bred East Europeans) have unfolded partly around images of sport.

Second, television, in association with sponsorship, has been responsible for changing the face of sport in the last 25 years. You only need to think of the rise of snooker, one-day cricket, shirt advertising in football or the decision to stage the next World Cup in the USA. These changes are evident not only at the elite levels. Organisers of the smallest local competition or league now seem convinced that nothing can be accomplished without sponsorship. In a very real sense sport has become a branch of the advertising and public relations industries.

I like sport and it has given me some treasured memories – seeing golfer Harold Henning get a hole in one in 1963, Fulham beat Liverpool 2–0 at Craven Cottage in 1966, Crystal Palace clinch the Second Division Championship in 1979, Dave Moorcroft beat Sydney Maree over 3000m in 1982, and Ian Botham get his 355th and 356th Test wickets at the Oval to become the greatest taker of Test wickets of all time in 1986. I also like television sport and have many more golden memories as a result, but they're probably similar to yours. One interesting effect of the vivid full-colour realism of television is that after a while you begin to be unsure about which events you saw in the flesh. Sport has also, increasingly, made me angry – sitting in crowds of people wearing cheap cardboard hats to advertise a building society, watching interminable award ceremonies staged for the benefit of sponsors, or watching cricket amongst sales executives so saturated with corporate hospitality they have difficulty focusing on the game. As this is a fairly dispassionate and analytic book, neither pleasure nor anger are given full rein – I am saving that indulgence for a subsequent project. I began studying television sport in 1978 as an embryonic PhD thesis, which I eventually finished in 1987. During this time both my children were born, both my parents died, Mrs Thatcher came to the throne, Fulham went down to the Third Division and Seb Coe, Alex Higgins, Martina Navratilova and Ian Botham all had their golden days.

While it's possible to debate whether the changes wrought by television and sponsorship are good or bad, it's more relevant to try and understand the conventions of television, how they emerged, and how television, as an economic reality and a set of aesthetic conventions, has intervened in and transformed the cultural practices of sports. That, in short, is the intention of this book.

QUESTIONS OF SPORT: THEORY AND ANALYSIS

The English Idea of Sport is such that the English do not like pro-fessional professorial discourses on sport.

(Conservative Minister for Education, 1958;
quoted in McIntosh 1952: 281)

I am not sure how professorial or professional my discourse is, but one of its intentions is to examine and challenge this suggestion that sport should not be open to analysis. Sport occupies a major place in English cultural life. It provides many of the major national ritual occasions of public life; indeed, our concepts of nation and our concepts of sport are closely linked. Politicians have traditionally made extensive use of sporting metaphors: 'keeping a straight bat', 'playing the game', 'all pulling together', are phrases etched into the social and political fabric. Morality too draws upon concepts of fair play developed around ideologies of sport (see McIntosh 1979). This centrality is typified by the FA Cup Final, an event that manages to be a popular celebration with strong working-class roots, a shared national ritual and a constructed link between royalty and popular culture, all in one (see Masterman 1980, and Colley and Davies 1982).

Television has become central to the prominence of sport. Major sport-ing occasions draw enormous television audiences, sometimes over half the population. Television has in turn become a significant source of revenue for a variety of sports. More importantly, television coverage has opened the way to much larger earnings for sport in the form of sponsorship. In becoming central to the world of sport, television has also transformed that world. Relatively obscure sports have gained huge new followings. The popularity of show jumping, snooker and, to a degree, darts has been boosted dramatically. Conversely, sports with high participation rates (squash, angling, badminton) have been adversely affected by their appar-ent unsuitability for television. For most of us, for most of the time, sport is television sport.

For television itself, sport has become very important. At times of major events like the Olympic Games, it has a unique ability to win and hold large audiences even well outside normal peak viewing hours. To offer high-quality sport coverage has become important to the prestige of broad-casting organisations, as the battles over television rights to football demonstrate. And, despite the publicity given to the financial struggles over football contracts, sport as a whole is still a source of very cheap programming, compared with other programme forms.

Despite the centrality of television sport, and the growth of media studies and cultural studies in the last 15 years, until recently there has been little detailed analysis. The pioneering study of football edited by Edward Buscombe (1975) and other work in this era were heavily influenced by film theory, as was parallel work in France (Daney 1978, Telecine 1978), and concentrated on close textual analysis along with consideration of political and ideological signification (see also Peters 1976, Nowell-Smith 1978). The influence of Buscombe can also be detected in North America during the 1970s, alongside more traditional forms of content analysis (see *Journal of Communication*, summer 1977, special issue on media sport, and Real 1975). But further developments were slow and spasmodic (see Birrell and Loy 1979, Clarke and Clarke 1982, Whannel 1982, Bown 1981) and only in the last few years has the field been more thoroughly explored. Alongside Barnett's (1990) study of British television sport, there is a range of North American studies (Rader 1984, Chandler 1988, Wenner 1989a, Cantelon and Gruneau 1988, Gruneau 1989, Real 1989), the rapid growth of cultural studies in Australia during the 1980s has spawned several studies of media sport (see Lawrence and Rowe 1987, Rowe and Lawrence 1989, Goldlust 1987), and Critcher (1987) has reviewed the emergent field.

I think there are three sets of questions to consider:

1 How are television's representations of sport organised? What are the characteristic forms in which material is organised, and what cultural and ideological themes are in play?
2 What production practices and professional ideologies underlie such representations, and how, historically, were they formed? What was the institutional base for the formation of these practices, and what relationship could be seen between practices and texts?
3 What are the cultural and economic relations between television and sport, and how, if at all, has television transformed sport? What relationship is there between the cultural and economic level in this particular instance?

Texts and practices

During the 1970s work on the media was handicapped by the emergence of two distinct paradigms, which became artificially distanced by their separate theoretical bases. On the one hand, a rich tradition of text analysis drawing on the insights of structuralist analysis and semiology produced a reified view of the text as the privileged object of analysis from which everything else can be read (e.g. Heath and Skirrow 1977). On the other hand, an equally rich tradition of investigation of the structures and practices of television production tended to see programmes themselves as relatively unproblematic consequences of production practices, economic relations or the intentions of producers (e.g. Elliott 1972). The effects of this divergence have persisted and continue to mark media and cultural analysis in the postmodern era. Angela McRobbie has recently drawn attention to the way some New Times analysis has tended to celebrate consumption, whilst severing it from the context of social practices, whereas some neo-Marxist critiques of postmodern theory advocate a return to reductionist analysis (McRobbie 1991). David Morley warns of the need to steer between the dangers of an improper romanticism of consumer freedoms on the one hand and a paranoiac fantasy of global control on the other (Morley 1991). This study investigates texts, institutions and economic relations in order to see what relationships can be established between them. It attempts to avoid both the idealisation of texts, and the reduction of texts to a mere effect of their process of production.

The character of the institutions of media production, the economic relations within them, and the tendency towards concentration, integration and diversification have been well explored (e.g. Murdock and Golding 1974, 1977). But without an adequate methodology of content analysis and a sufficiently sophisticated model of the process of determination, this area of work always contained the danger of reducing programmes to a mere effect of the economic relations underpinning their production.

The elaboration of the encoding/decoding model (Hall 1973) promised to resolve some of these problems, in that it introduced the question of language and convention while retaining and offering a way of examining the question of determination. As Morley characterised it, the model posits a flow in the communication chain between a sender and a receiver, two points with their own structure, different and yet linked. Mechanisms or forms are needed to unify them, this being a complex, not a simple unity. The production of a meaningful message is always complex and contradictory; and the process of reading is complex – a range of readings is always possible. In short, the message is a structured polysemy, but with particular elements structured in dominance (Morley 1980).

In focusing on television representations I am drawing upon the encoding/decoding model of communications. But the need to conceptualise the relation between television and sport as both cultural and economic in turn raises questions about the use of this model. Stuart Hall's elaboration of the model roots encoding and decoding in the frameworks of knowledge, relations of production and technical infrastructure in which each takes place. It thus allows a relation to be made between representations, and the production practices, professional ideologies and institutional structures that support and produce representations.

It has been argued that work that remains within a determinations problematic is on inherently unstable ground. The task of maintaining the two ends of the chain – relative autonomy, and determination in the last instance – is an ill defined one for which there is no adequate methodology. Consequently the analysis is always likely to drift either towards reductionism or towards an unacknowledged total autonomy of the cultural level. Coward argued that much work of the Centre for Contemporary Cultural Studies (CCCS) was prone to a reductionist tendency, and was too class rooted, at the expense of the structuring effects of gender difference (Coward 1977). Chambers and others replied that the work of CCCS remained rooted in a determinations problematic, and, in rejecting some of the implications of psychoanalytic theories of the production of human subjectivity, warned of the dangers of unprincipled eclecticism (Chambers *et al.* 1977).

By contrast others criticised Hall, not for reductionism, but for neglect of the economic level. Murdock and Golding claim that, in Hall's work, a brilliant analysis of the cultural sat upon an undeveloped analysis of the economic base, and they, and Garnham, both argued that Hall overemphasised the role of the state and underemphasised capitalist entrepreneurship (see Murdock and Golding 1977, and Garnham 1977 and 1979).

These were relevant criticisms, particularly in terms of sport. Much of Hall's work on television was focused upon areas of news and current affairs. In this area of television it can be argued that, while the marketplace and economic relations do not play a central role, the state, via the statutory instruments governing broadcasting, and the consequent conventions of impartiality, neutrality, objectivity and balance, is crucial in establishing and constraining the formal conditions of the production of television journalism.

However, when one examines popular television, it is arguably the case that, while the role and effect of the state are somewhat less crucial, the significance of economic relations becomes considerably greater. The production of entertainment is both a cultural–ideological and an economic practice. While recognising the relative autonomy of the cultural level, it is vital also to identify all the ways in which the nature of the economic relations underpinning cultural production constantly sets limits and exerts pressures (R. Williams 1973).

Hall's subsequent (1977) development of the encoding/decoding model expanded upon the role of the field of representations from which encodings are selected. More recently, Angela McRobbie (1991) has called for a return to integrative modes of analysis which track the social and ideological relations which prevail at every level between cultural production and consumption. This means examining all of those processes which accompany the production of meaning in culture, not just the end product. Following this, this book situates television sport in the context of the field of representations upon which it draws. It also examines the economic substructure of the relation between television and sport, as a determinant both upon the pro-televisual sporting event and upon the practices, ideologies, forms and content of television sport coverage itself.

Fields of struggle

Questions concerning the relation between television and sport focus on the problem of transformation, and draw upon debates about the cultural nature of sport itself. Critical analyses of sport have tended to a striking one-dimensionality (see Hoch 1972, Vinnai 1976, Brohm 1978). Sport has been characterised as a distraction, a new opium for the masses, a form of bread-and-circus, a position that tends to undervalue the force of sport as the site of a set of ideologies with their own effectivity. Ideological analyses of sport have tended to present it as an unmediated and uncontested form of dominant ideology, in which no meanings are contradictory, or the subject of struggle. More economistic analysis has suggested that sport is just another form of capitalist business. Clearly to some degree, and increasingly so since the sponsorship boom, this is true. Yet an important feature of the development of sport has been the tension between the amateur paternal benevolence of traditional sporting organisations and the rising power of capitalist entrepreneurship. Similarly, analyses that emphasise the relation between sport and the state, while of great interest, do not take sufficient account of the strong element of voluntarism in the formation and development of English sport. What many of these analyses lacked was a space for the rather complex relations between structures of control and lived sporting cultures. Only recently have developments in the history and sociology of sport begun to explore such complexities more fully.

Historians and sociologists traditionally ignored sport or regarded it as merely epiphenomenal. Only in the last decade has British sport history begun to develop at a more rapid pace (Mason 1980, Holt 1989, Jones 1986, 1989, Mangan 1981, Mangan and Park 1986, Mangan and Walvin 1987). Similarly, it's only in the last ten years that Dunning's (1971) collection of sport sociology has been significantly added to. The growth of cultural studies has provided an impetus (see Tomlinson 1981a,b) as has the work of the Leisure Studies Association, especially through the collections of papers from the international conferences in 1986 and 1990 (see also Horne, Jary and Tomlinson 1987).

Within this body of work some have emphasised the role played by class relations, gender relations, and the cultural and ideological field – a necessarily complex and contradictory one – through which such relations are re-worked (see Gruneau 1983, J.A. Hargreaves 1982, Clarke and Critcher 1985, and J.E. Hargreaves 1986). Critcher (1986) and Tomlinson

(1989) have reviewed radical and mainstream traditions within leisure studies. Gramsci's concept of hegemony has been of considerable influence on this work. The concept suggests that a dominant class must constantly work not merely to engineer consent, or simply to ensure its legitimacy, but also to become an active leading force, so that subordinate groups come to assent, to approve of and give some degree of support to its project. Thatcherism, for example, clearly attempted to construct a new hegemony around its key themes, but never fully succeeded. Hegemony is not so much a state as a process, never finally achieved, but constantly being struggled over, a contestation that marks both cultural and economic levels. Applied to cultural analysis Gramsci's concept of hegemony suggests that popular culture is best understood, not as simply imposed from above, or generated from below, but as a field of struggle between dominant and subordinate groups.

If media study has been beset by a separation between institutional analysis and textual analysis, there are two key oppositions within cultural studies that have arguably had both positive and negative effects. The first is between the model of culture as imposed from above and the model of culture as generated from below, while the second is that between culturalism and structuralism as apparently incompatible epistemological bases. In approaching popular culture, Bennett rejects both imposed-from-above and generated-from-below models as inadequate, proposing instead the conceptualisation of popular culture as a field of struggle in which neither the state, capitalist cultural production, nor the people can simply dominate and control meaning. Rather there is a continual process of contestation over the ground on which meanings are produced (Bennett 1981).

Cultural study is of course the product of two distinct traditions. The stress in Hoggart on the meanings embedded in ordinary everyday working-class life, in Williams upon structures of feeling, and upon culture as a whole way of life, and the insistence in E.P. Thompson of this as also a whole way of struggle, are together a crucial foundation for work in what has become termed the 'culturalist' tradition (Johnson 1979a). The appropriation of Saussurian linguistics in order to elaborate a theory of visual language by Barthes and others, and the model of ideology offered by Althusser have in turn transformed theories of meaning production (Hall 1977, Coward and Ellis 1977).

Both traditions have also produced problems. Culturalism, it is argued, lacks a systematic theory of the reproduction of human subjectivity through language and ideology. Structuralism, in that it tends to eliminate consciousness and agency, consequently finds it hard to conceptualise struggle adequately (Thompson 1978, Johnson 1979b). It is no surprise, therefore, that Gramsci's concept of hegemony increasingly appeared appealing as an apparent resolution of the difficulty of forging an adequate synthesis of two productive but seemingly incompatible paradigms (Hall 1980).

This study follows Bennett and others in conceptualising popular culture as neither imposed from above nor generated spontaneously from below. It sees sport as another site upon which rests a field of struggle over meaning. This struggle takes place within the terms of that broader struggle of the dominant group to become hegemonic and the response of subordinate groups to that process. Like all forms of popular culture, sport and its representations also constitute an interface between the common-sense of everyday language and the more organised discourse of political discussion. The representations of sport inevitably draw upon elements of common-sense, and articulate these elements in the form of more organised and coherent ideological combinations.

Richard Gruneau (1983 and 1988) and John E. Hargreaves (1986) have produced accounts of the relation of sport to hegemonic struggle, and their work has been further debated by Ingham and Hardy (1984), Parry (1984) and Whitson (1983b and 1986). Hargreaves argues that, in general, sports are more determined than determining, but, as sport has become more important as a component of the national culture, it has hence become more important to hegemony.

The most significant way in which sport was shaped by the hegemonic struggle was as a culmination of class and cultural struggles of the nineteenth century. The last quarter of the nineteenth century was a crucial formative period for the institutions of British sport. In this period the majority of British sports for the first time acquired national governing bodies and national competitions. Even those sports which had had governing bodies since the eighteenth century (e.g. golf, cricket, horse racing) were significantly restructured during this period. It was the dominant class, the Victorian bourgeoisie, that was able to utilise its cultural, social, educational and political power to dominate these institutions. Crucially it was specifically the men of this class that played this dominant formative role, laying down the structure of British sport after their own interests – rooted in class privilege, class exclusiveness and patriarchy.

In the last 20 years sport would appear to have undergone a similar transformation. So the questions concern the extent to which this can be seen in hegemonic terms. To what extent in Britain does sport play a significant role in the construction of concepts of national unity? Does it provide a set of rituals that offer a national unity apart from, and hence over and above, the narrow divisions of party politics and thus provide one base for the construction of the imaginary coherence of nation?

In what ways do the cultures of sport contribute to the strata of common-sense and to that continual process of treading and retreading whereby the ground of common-sense yields up more systematised popular ideological elements? There is the concept of fair play and sportsmanship, the stress on youth and fitness, the supporting role of the family, and the necessity of dedication and hard work. There is the centrality of national belongingness and the apparent naturalness that patriotism acquires. Most significant of all, perhaps, are the implicit assumptions about natural abilities that underpin and feed into the marking of gender difference, and also racial difference.

So sport can clearly be examined in terms of ideological elements and their articulation. The more central issue for this study is the way in which these various ideological elements are present/absent in television sport coverage and the ways in which particular combinations are articulated.[1]

Part I

Institutions, practices and economic relations

Chapter 2

National events and the authority of the BBC

I have never attempted to conceal my belief that Wimbledon treated us generously. I assumed it was the deliberate policy of an amateur sport towards a public service.

> (Seymour Joly de Lotbiniere, head of BBC Outside Broadcasting Department [1935–1954] quoted in Briggs 1979: 859).

That year, what with Hillary and Tensing climbing Everest, England regaining the Ashes, and Gordon Richards winning the Derby, it really did seem for a time that some benevolent force was trying to cheer us all up.

> (Black 1972a: 169)

The BBC monopoly of broadcasting between 1922 and 1955 was a crucial factor in the development of television sport. The coverage of major sporting occasions both reinforced and to a degree reconstructed a calendar of principal events that came to constitute the sporting year. At the same time, major state occasions were also relayed by the BBC. The BBC's identity as an institution was shaped by its close relation with the major national rituals, both of state and of sport. Consequently in 1955, when ITV was founded, the BBC had many in-built advantages in the ensuing competition over sport coverage. It was a more prestigious institution, it already had national coverage, facilities and technical resources, production and technical expertise, contacts in the sport world, and long-term exclusive contracts with major sports. The dominance of the BBC in this field meant that its practices of production set the standard, and the two systems are more notable for similarities than for differences.

The earliest years of radio broadcasting were characterised by tensions between broadcasting, the press and the entertainment business, as the BBC sought to establish itself (Wedlake 1973: 168). The entertainment and sport businesses were suspicious of the new competitor, the newspapers and news agencies were worried at the threat to their dominance of news, and particularly hostile to the broadcasting of sports results and running commentaries. The Post Office got a substantial portion of its revenue from press telegrams and was inclined to support press interests (Wedlake 1973: 171–2). The deadlock became an issue for the forthcoming Crawford Committee on Broadcasting (Briggs 1961: 262–7). During the period 1922–26, then, there was a rather uneven development of sport broadcasting. The institution was shaping itself, the technology of outside broadcasting was being constructed, while the opportunity to broadcast sport was still severely limited.

Following the Crawford Report (1925) the company became a public corporation, and the deadlock with sporting and entertainment interests was broken. For the first time the BBC was able to broadcast proper commentaries on sport, and in the first year of the Corporation there were outside broadcasts (OBs) of the Grand National, the Boat Race, the Inter-Varsity Sports, Rugby Union, amateur golf, and Wimbledon. Gerald Cock had been appointed Director of Outside Broadcasts in 1925, and achieved much with meagre staffing. In 1927 he had only one programme assistant and even by 1934 only five (Briggs 1965: 81). Despite the limited staffing, these years saw a rapid exploration and development of the technology and subject matter of outside broadcasting. The first commentators had to be trained, and conventions of commentary developed – the BBC acquired its first purpose-built Outside Broadcast lorry in 1928; the lip microphone was introduced in 1933. The range of sports and events covered was slowly expanded.

During the 1930s, television was emerging from experimentation. In 1935, Gerald Cock moved from being Head of Outside Broadcasts to be Head of the new Television Service, to be launched in 1936. His successor as Head of Outside Broadcasts was S.J. de Lotbiniere, who was to pioneer many of the conventions of sport broadcasting and became known as the architect of commentary. Like radio before it, television notched up a series of notable 'OB firsts' – Wimbledon, the Derby, the Cup Final, etc. (Snagge and Barsley 1972: 66, Briggs 1965: 659).

Among its many effects upon the BBC, the Second World War temporarily halted the growth of sport broadcasting. A case was made for maintaining and expanding outside broadcasts, on four grounds. These were that OBs added greatly to the variety of broadcast material; that they gave the public 'a reassuring impression of normality'; that there was as much virtue in actuality as ever; and that OBs dealing with topicality gave an impression of BBC resourcefulness and vitality.[1] While there was to be much OB material during the war, debate took place within the BBC about the place of sport, and particular concern was taken over the broadcasting of racing results. In the event a whole new variety of OB programmes, broadcast from factories and other similar locations, was to emerge. Workers' Playtime, Factory Canteen, Works Wonders, and Ack-Ack Beer-Beer were all developed to serve the needs of morale. The war caused a six-year interruption in the development of television. When television resumed in 1946 it would soon become more than merely the junior partner. Television came to dominate the BBC and, until challenged from 1955 by ITV, the whole field of broadcasting.

NATIONAL OCCASIONS

When ITV was launched in 1955, one major advantage the BBC had was its high level of cultural prestige. In its tradition of broadcasting major sport events, it had turned these events into national occasions in a new sense. The Boat Race, the Grand National, the Cup Final and the Derby had become shared national rituals, extended by broadcasting to a much wider public. The BBC was therefore a central part of the apparent importance of these events. The Corporation was also strongly identified with the state through its broadcasting of major occasions of state and Crown. It saw itself as, and to a large extent was seen by the audience as, the 'natural' place for major national events. The more recent intransigence of the BBC during the alternation debate (see Chapter 4) must be seen in this context. It was this particular prestigious position within the national cultural field that formed the bedrock upon which the BBC sustained its phrase, 'BBC for Sport'.

There is a recognisable sporting calendar, a list of major events that most people could identify. This list is characterised by its static and recurrent nature, rooted in tradition (see Peters 1976), the same events appearing year after year at the appropriate time. There is nothing natural or given about this calendar; it is constructed and determined by a set of factors – the history and organisation of sport, its coverage in the press and broadcasting, and the nature of sporting practices in the education apparatus.

The field of sport has to take account of, and is in part structured by, the popularity of events, their financial viability and the intentions and plans of various governing bodies – events have been sustained by governing bodies for the sake of tradition, after their popularity has been eroded or financial base weakened. Equally, events have emerged and grown considerably in popularity before becoming inscribed in the calendar of major events. The external influence of the press upon this calendar can be considerable. The apparatus of education also has its effects – the shared experience of public school and university men producing among other things a particular hierarchy of importance. The significant thing about the BBC's own particular construction of this field is the cultural power which it has to reinforce, reproduce and redefine the calendar of major sporting events.

This is not of course to say that the BBC selection is merely a result of personal preference, although, particularly early on, this undoubtedly had its effects. There were many other factors at play: availability, technical feasibility, cost, assumptions about audience, etc.

They also selected from a pre-structured field of events – their own hierarchy in part merely reproduced an existing hierarchy. The BBC's particular hierarchy, however, soon became invested with an authority and 'official' character. In this sense the association of the BBC with major occasions becomes important. While the BBC has always trodden very warily through the minefield of political controversy, it has been able to advance much more confidently into those 'neutral' non-political state events, particularly those associated with the monarchy. Indeed its coverage of these occasions has transformed the relation of royalty and the people, carrying the voice of monarchy into the home. So major sport occasions and major state occasions entered into everyday life in a new, more intimate way, both framed by the experience of listening to broadcasting provided by the BBC. Events like the Cup Final, the Boat Race and the Grand National 'became for the first time, truly national events to which the whole country could listen'.[2]

Just as sporting events became in this sense national events, so state occasions became national events in a new way, through the same channel. The monarchy became more accessible and their broadcasts helped establish the popularity of the medium. Scannell and Cardiff refer to such occasions as 'ritual expressions of a corporate national life'.[3] Because both sport and state occasions were handled by the same department, Outside Broadcasts, the production practices and codes and conventions for the two developed in close harmony. The very popularity of these events gave them an important role in the development of broadcasting. When television was relaunched after the war, it was the large audiences wanting to see major events that helped to spread the popularity of the new medium. In particular, the Coronation in 1953 triggered off a boost in set ownership. It marked the point at which television overtook radio as the primary medium of public communication (see Black 1972a: 167).

The BBC was not unaware of the value of the authority and prestige that attached to it in these fields and was not slow to attempt to capitalise in the period after 1955 when it had a competitor. Its publicity and handbooks have always given prominence to its coverage of major events. It is, then, not surprising that the BBC has come to play such a major role in the construction of that hierarchical organisation of sporting events, the annual sporting calendar. Once the restrictions on outside broadcasts were lifted, it is remarkable how quickly the BBC was to establish some of the major events of its sporting calendar. In 1927, the first year of the Corporation, there were commentaries on the Boat Race, the Grand National, a football cup tie, Wimbledon tennis, a rugby international, and an eye-witness account of a Test Match. By 1930, six of the events later singled out in the Postmaster-General's 'non-exclusivity' arrangement (the Boat Race, Test Matches, Wimbledon, the Cup Final, the Grand National and the Derby) were being covered every year on the radio.[4] The non-exclusivity agreement, ironically designed to protect the BBC from competition by ITV, designated these six events as national events. Neither broadcasting organisation was allowed to obtain exclusive rights on them. The dominance of these events in the sporting year must at the least have been heavily reinforced by their dominance in the BBC's year, and their consequent transformation into shared national rituals. When television began, it too was quick to appropriate this same calendar and five of the six events listed above were televised between 1936 and 1938. Television's construction of the sporting year was affected to a much greater degree by the resistances of promoters to television. The Grand National was not televised until 1960.

The construction of this calendar has two aspects – foregrounding the more important events and marginalising others. It could be argued that the Boat Race, Rugby Union and Inter-Varsity Sports events have been given much greater apparent importance by broadcasting than their general popularity would warrant. It is reasonable to speculate here that the class and educational background of many BBC staff at this time had its effects – see, for example, the autobiography of Captain H.B.T. Wakelam, the first commentator (Wakelam 1938). John Snagge has said that 'from the BBC point of view the Boat Race has always been regarded as one of the key fixtures of the year. Maybe that's partly because so many BBC men have been to one or other of the two universities' (Snagge and Barsley 1972: 77).

On the other hand, certain sports have always been more popular than their broadcasting exposure would lead one to think. Swimming, fishing, speedway, greyhound racing, and even football were by no means as high on the BBC priority list as their social popularity might suggest that they should have been. The major events in athletics and golf were, for a long time, outside the pantheon. Greyhound racing remained absent from the television screen during the height of its popularity, because of a wartime ban, and did not appear until 1953.

Indeed the debate over greyhound racing provides a revealing insight into BBC attitudes. Greyhound racing was hugely popular during the 1940s and early 1950s. In 1951 there were around 210 licensed tracks attended by 200,000 people a week. Taxes (entertainment, bookmakers' and tote turnover) on greyhound racing yielded over £8.5m. Attempts were made to get permission to televise greyhounds by the television OB Manager Orr-Ewing[5] and by Television Controller Collins,[6] but this was regularly refused. Head of OB de Lotbiniere complained that the ban was harming relations with the owners of White City, Wembley and Harringay, venues of many televised events,[7] and proposed screening three races a year 'to keep the greyhound racing world quiet'.[8]

The main arguments concerned the undesirability of encouraging betting, that greyhound racing was not a national sport, and that it provided bad broadcasting (!). It was stated that no sport had a right to be broadcast; the BBC must use its discretion. Greyhound racing had an 'anti-social character'. It was 'not a desirable or sociologically useful sport and broadcasts would lower BBC standards'.[9] A counter-argument that greyhound racing was 'part of the working man's entertainment and a sport that has come to stay' was offered. Eventually in 1953 the Board of Governors agreed to permit coverage of three races, providing no results appeared in the News![10]

Significant in the debate is the way that class and cultural assumptions are crucial, whilst unspoken – most of the objections to greyhound racing also apply to horse racing. Many of the features of the Reithian BBC are exemplified here. The objection to betting is rooted in a moral paternalism. The concept of a national sport illustrates the way the BBC's cultural paternalism was reinforced by its own social authority to define the nation. The idea that greyhound racing provided 'bad' broadcasting suggests that professionalism in broadcasting characteristically takes the form of an elitist arrogance towards popular taste, although it should be noted that on this issue the Governors and not the producers were invoking broadcasting standards. Finally, the invocation of 'sociologically useful' suggests a commitment to social engineering. Clearly we have here four related forms of displacement of class distinction. The debate doesn't mention the most significant reason for the different treatment of the two major occasions for gambling (horse and greyhound racing) – their class composition. Whilst the culture of horse racing includes both workers and aristocrats, greyhound racing is decisively a lower-class culture only and hence morally bad, nationally insignificant and sociologically useless.

Just as during the 1930s the BBC built up its roster of main sport events, it was also establishing a range of major state events. While it always trod very cautiously around political life, the more de-politicised state occasions were an OB staple from the earliest days. Armistice Day at the Cenotaph, Trooping the Colour, the Lord Mayor's Show and the Royal Command Performance were part of the annual round, along with some of the more ritualised political occasions, such as the Prime Minister's Guildhall speech. Irregular occasions like royal comings and goings, weddings and funerals were also given much space, and one of the most popular of broadcasts was the Christmas Message, entirely a product of broadcasting.

When television re-started in 1946, the course of its struggle with the sporting organisations was affected by the already established notion of the sporting calendar. A memo by de Lotbiniere distinguished between Musts, 'which we cannot afford to lose without being able to satisfy the public that we have been faced with a "fancy" fee'; Shoulds, 'which we would like to include in programmes for a reasonable fee, but the absence of which from programmes would not demand public explanation'; and Mights 'which we don't mind if we broadcast or not'[11]. It is important to note that the annual sporting calendar is not simply a construction of the BBC but is modified by its relation to outside organisations, such as sports governing bodies, and by its need to 'satisfy the public'.

Here in explicit form was the BBC's own hierarchy of sports events. The Musts were horse racing's Derby and Grand National, the Oxford and Cambridge Boat Race, cricket Test Matches, Wimbledon tennis, the soccer Cup Final and some soccer internationals, Rugby Union internationals, and major boxing fights. The Shoulds were classic horse races, cricket matches leading up to the Tests, international tennis, league football, boxing involving potential challengers for professional titles. The Mights included county cricket games, amateur cup final and snooker matches. In the development of this sporting calendar after the war, coverage on television itself increased the popularity of some sports, notably show jumping (see D. Williams 1957, 1968).

Television was at first very much the poor relation. The Coronation in 1937, the Victory Parade in 1946 and the 1948 Olympics were major OBs that did a lot to publicise the medium and probably boosted set sales, but it was the 1953 Coronation that marked the significant breakthrough (see Ross 1961: 91). The massive publicity that television received by its coverage of this event ensured that it would overtake radio as the primary medium. The links between major state occasions, major sport achievements and national identity were to be particularly marked in 1953. Hillary and Tensing climbing Everest, England's Ashes victory and Gordon Richards' Derby win prompted TV critic Peter Black to suggest that 'some benevolent force was trying to cheer us all up' (Black 1972a: 169).

The Coronation itself was very much a television event – the first of its kind in Britain. Rehearsals of the timing were geared to the needs of broadcasting, Peter Dimmock advised the Duke of Norfolk on the choice of music, 20.5 million people were estimated to have watched, and in the next 12 months the number of licensed sets rose by 50 per cent. Building upon the radio days, the BBC coverage of the 'ritual expressions of corporate national life' was to develop into a strong reinforcement of the authority of the Corporation, linking it with that part of the state that represents itself as eternal and above politics, the monarchy. The ritual nature of the BBC's calendar of national occasions further helped to give the monarchy an air of calm, comforting permanence.

Throughout the 1950s and the 1960s the BBC continued to build big audiences for major occasion broadcasting. As the competition with ITV began, the BBC was able to draw with great effect upon the authority derived from its tradition of association with major national events. The whole concept of a national event became integrally linked with the BBC coverage of it: it seemed more appropriate to be watching, say, the Cup Final on BBC. Obviously many of the major sporting events covered by the BBC already had an in-built connection to the monarchy because of the presence of royalty, and the particular attention this is given by the BBC in its Annual Report is noteworthy:

> Among the many other Royal and national occasions at which the BBC microphones and cameras were present, one that particularly stands out in the memory was the closing ceremony of the British Empire and Commonwealth Games in Cardiff, when a recorded message from Her Majesty proclaimed the Duke of Cornwall as Prince of Wales.[12]

This event linked themes of Empire, Nation, Monarchy, and Monarchy as a family, on the site of a major popular sporting ritual, extended by the BBC's broadcast to a large audience. It demonstrated the centrality of the BBC's sport coverage to notions of Britishness and national identity. In the 1964/65 Report, four great occasions were highlighted in photos, the four great occasions being the State Opening of Parliament, the State Funeral of Churchill, the Election night coverage, and Mary Rand's win in the Olympic long jump.[13] In response to competition, the BBC attempted to maintain the prestigious aura of its national event coverage, and tried to fix in the public mind the notion of 'BBC for Sport'. This was partly based on the greater scope of the BBC coverage, but the appeal to 'authority' was also present:

> Once again this year many millions of people looked to [the] BBC as the service to watch for all kinds of sporting programmes and took it for granted that the BBC would continue to cover the major events of many different sports. They knew that the BBC had a tradition of employing special skills and techniques to convey the essential mood of a sporting occasion as well as its highlights. They also appreciated the authority of BBC coverage and felt that international or national events are not covered by the BBC in isolation, but rather as the culmination of all the earlier stages of contest which have been shown earlier in the year, or in previous years.[14]

The BBC, in short, had become a primary definer of national identity, a forger of national unity. In contributing to the production of the imaginary coherence of national identity, it was articulating two elements of national culture most decisively de-politicised – sport and the monarchy. It was not merely accident or coincidence that found the BBC at the focus of this powerful ideological articulation. As early as 1949, BBC Television Controller, Norman Collins, had written on the future of the nascent medium:

> With nation-wide television, when the King leaves Buckingham Palace, the Mall will extend as far as the Royal Mile and the King will ride simultaneously through the Four Kingdoms. A Royal Wedding will be a nation's wedding. On Remembrance Day the shadow of the Cenotaph will fall across the whole country and on great rejoicings the fireworks of

Hyde Park will burst and sparkle at every fireside. The Lord Mayor of London will no longer be drawn merely through the streets of the capital but through every town and village where the spectacle of his coach and horses will bring back the magic of the fairytale. And sportsmen who play cricket on the green or follow a local football team or belong to a church tennis club will have Lords, Wembley and Wimbledon all paraded before them for their pleasure. In short this country will at last discover what goes on there. And the discovery will be well worth making.[15]

There is here a quite explicit awareness that broadcasting would produce a new form of national event: in extending major occasions of state and of sport throughout the land it would make the royal wedding a nation's wedding. In doing so a new audience would be forged; the mass of the people would be welded together in union with all the authority and pageantry of the royal family and the state. Inevitably, as the officiating archbishop at this union of state and people, the BBC itself would acquire the patina of authoritativeness. In institutional terms, therefore, the BBC was well placed to play a dominant role in the process whereby sport would be represented to the nation.

BBC AND SPORT ORGANISATIONS: THE FACILITY FEE

The dominance of the BBC in the field of broadcasting was matched by its dominance over the organisations of sport. Until the arrival of ITV in 1955, the BBC was the only purchaser of a commodity, sporting competitions, for which there were many suppliers. These suppliers, the sporting organisations, were rarely able to band together out of mutual interest. Television sport in the United Kingdom has generally been a buyer's market.

If the central place the BBC occupied in the production of images of national identity gave it a social authority, then, in the field of sport, this social authority was underpinned by the economic power the BBC was to gain in its dealings with sport during the monopoly years. This dominance was not maintained without struggle; indeed it was the threat of ITV that in turn provoked the BBC into committing more money to secure long-term contracts, thus securing its dominance.

In its negotiations with outside bodies the BBC claimed that its right to cover events was analogous to that of the press. Consequently fees were regarded as 'facility fees' – payment offered by way of compensation for inconvenience – and did not constitute a payment for broadcast rights. This principle was crucial in the development of broadcast sport. The BBC clung tenaciously to it during the introduction of television, during the period of the Second World War and the re-launch of television in 1946, and, under increasing pressure, right up till the 1950s. The imminent appearance of a competitor made the BBC realise the value of signing sports on long-term contracts. Yet, before this, the BBC had already privately conceded that it was buying rights and not merely facilities:

> In the case of facility fees the amount paid is not always an exact assessment of the value of the facilities offered. For example, in the case of the Grand National the sound broadcasting fee, while preserving the title of a facilities fee, in fact constitutes to a considerable extent a payment for the right to broadcast. The same situation may arise in the case of television OBs and it seems to me important therefore that there should be co-ordination.[16]

However, in its negotiations with outside bodies, the BBC continued to stand by its policy:

> It has never been the Corporation's policy to pay for the right to broadcast. . . . It is our firm belief, however, that the promoter should receive a fair payment for the facilities which are offered in the form of space, and as a reimbursement for any inconvenience or expense incurred on our behalf.[17]

During the immediate post-war period, the BBC attempted to settle on a fee of 25 guineas as standard. It was to become a point of contention with the athletics authorities that, as a facilities fee, the BBC held that this payment included an allowance for lost seats at camera positions, and consequently no extra compensation was paid. Right up to the 1950s, the facility fee policy was still being advocated as viable:

> I have fought most assiduously to hold down fees and stress that they are for facilities and not broadcast rights. If this position can be held during the next two or three years, we should establish a position (which sound broadcasting has long held) where a television broadcast is excellent publicity so that promoters want them and do not demand greatly inflated fees.[18]

Inside the BBC there was, however, a growing realisation of the problems this policy would encounter. In 1947 Head of Television Maurice Gorham had written to Orr-Ewing that the BBC would eventually have to pay far more for television than for sound broadcasts, 'as we are buying the event, and not merely the right to have someone describe it'.[19] It was external pressures that were to force the shift in policy, pressures stemming from the sport organisations, and in particular the Association for the Protection of Copyright in Sport, and, more crucially, from the threat of competition from ITV, which began to emerge as a distant reality from 1952 onwards.

Even before the Second World War, during the first three years of television, some sporting organisations were suspicious and wary of the new medium, particularly the Jockey Club and the British Boxing Board of Control (see Briggs 1965: 613). These suspicions were to grow after the war as television began to expand. The main worries were the effect of television on live attendances, the possibility of re-diffusion of television to paying audiences in cinemas, and the low level of fees being paid. The sport organisations did not share a unified hostility to television. Major sports were more inclined to be hostile than minor sports, which were anxious for publicity. The Football League was at this time hostile to TV as such, the MCC was worried not just about re-diffusion, but also about people watching in shop windows, while the boxing authorities eyed with envy the money boxing was earning from TV in America.

However, many of the leading associations combined to form the Association for the Protection of Copyright in Sport (APCS) in November 1944. The organisations represented included the All-England Lawn Tennis Association, the MCC, the Rugby Union, the Football League, the National Hunt Committee, the British Boxing Board of Control and the Jockey Club. It intended to gain for sport promoters a copyright analogous to that held by authors. Promoters could then deal with television and re-diffusion from a more secure base (see Briggs 1979: 871). To achieve this it was necessary to attempt to modify the Copyright Act of 1911. The early reactions of the BBC to the threat of pressure from sport organisations were combative:

> If the obstructionists cannot otherwise be brought into line they . . . should be given to understand that the BBC will support those organisations willing to co-operate with mutually advantageous broadcasts, but will exclude others from the air altogether pending a change of attitude.[20]

BBC Chairman, Haley, stated that the BBC should 'resist all high fees', particularly for racing and boxing, claim free access and facilities wherever they were given to the press and pay only nominal fees when it broadcast. He declared that 'it is doubtful if there is any general public sympathy with those who seek to force the BBC to pay high fees' (Briggs 1979: 841). The BBC attempted to counter restrictions on coverage of football, professional boxing and horse racing by turning to other sports such as speedway and amateur boxing.[21] The attitude of the Greyhound Racing Association (GRA) was to cause particular problems. The BBC would not at this time show greyhound racing, in accordance with the wartime ban, but the GRA controlled White City and Harringay, venues for many top athletics, boxing and show jumping events.

The struggle was not left to market forces, but produced state intervention. The absence of major sport from the screen was causing concern in Parliament, and the Postmaster-General (PMG) wanted more sport on television. In 1950 he established the Sports Television Advisory

Committee. An experimental period had been agreed during which representatives of leading sports organisations had agreed to negotiate with the BBC the showing of around 100 events per annum. The Committee was to advise the PMG about the direct and indirect effects of televising sport. The BBC took a keen interest in the formation of this Committee and, although initially it declined to participate, after the third meeting de Lotbiniere began attending as an observer.

This was symptomatic of a change in attitude within the BBC. It was beginning to become clear that the facilities fee principle could not be held to. Harmonious routinised relations with sport organisations were important to the BBC, as outside broadcasts provided a significant proportion of air-time. As television gradually expanded, more money was becoming available. By 1952 the possibility of commercial television was becoming more likely and the importance of good relations and long-term contracts with sport organisations became apparent. Internally the BBC was admitting to itself that it had been getting sport too cheaply.[22]

By 1954 Wimbledon was getting around £1500 for the tournament, about £125 per day. Referring to the earlier period when the fee was merely nominal, de Lotbiniere had commented, rather disingenuously, 'I have never attempted to conceal my belief that Wimbledon treated us generously. I assumed it was the deliberate policy of an amateur sport towards a public service' (Briggs 1979: 859). This form of relationship, at best tenuous, was being replaced by a more straightforward one of commercial bargaining; de Lotbiniere himself urging that more be spent on sport:

> We have got to deal with these authorities year after year and it does not pay us to strike a bargain that may subsequently appear to be very much in our favour. To my mind if you are dealing with people who have got something you want year after year, the essence of a good bargain is one that suits both sides.[23]

In a 1954 meeting with the APCS, the BBC explained that it was not interested in obtaining exclusive rights, and wished in future to settle fees 'by means of sensible and business-like negotiations with the sporting interest concerned taking full account of the conditions of the particular sport' (Briggs 1979: 879). After this meeting, according to Briggs, relations rapidly improved. It should be remembered that this was in a period of rising fees. In other words, the most important factors in the easing of BBC's relations with sport organisations may well have been the expansion of television and the imminent arrival of ITV as a potential competitor.

Chapter 3

Production practices and professional ideologies

Quite frankly, unless we can give the results *as they come in* and stay on the air until 5 o'clock to present them in tabulated form the programme is not worth doing at all. I see this as a sports news programme and I do not see how we can go off the air at the very moment *the* news of the day is happening.

(Paul Fox, during planning for *Grandstand*, 1958
(BBC Written Archives Centre 1/8/58 T14/493/1))

The institutional structure of broadcasting establishes a framework for the production practices that take place within it. The parameters of these practices are established by the details of the structure: the departmental divisions, hierarchies, chains of command and accountability, division of labour, organisational rules, systems of resource allocation, modes of decision-making, and relations with the external world outside the institution.[1]

The production practices are the form in which social production actually occurs within the institution. It is important to hold open the distinction between what formally happens (i.e. according to the structure) and what actually happens. Practices are, in part, informal ways of negotiating formal conventions and constraints. There is a further distinction to be made between the routine practices of production and the framing of these practices by certain kinds of knowledge – historically acquired competences (Hall 1972). A similar distinction can be made between practice itself and discourse about practice. Actual commentary, for instance, is distinct from the various descriptive and prescriptive guidelines for commentators (see Bourdieu 1977). As a working method of analysis, the professional competences that frame practices and discourse about practice can be distinguished by referring to them as professional ideologies. In practical terms, of course, the distinction is much less clear. This chapter examines the formation of a practice of commentary; the growth of conventions of visual coverage; and the development of magazine format programmes, and their role in the construction of a unified 'world' of sport (see Whannel 1986c).

COMMENTARY

The whole concept of a commentary is one of the bases of the process by which broadcasting mediates sport, and it was the first and central production practice of radio sport outside broadcasting. So in the process of formulating this practice many crucial principles were articulated, at first tentatively, later more surely, then inscribed in codes of practice and finally becoming part of professional common-sense. Indeed there is far more written about the formation of practices of commentary than there is about the development of visual encoding – camera positions and cutting patterns.

The first four outside broadcasts suggested by the BBC in 1925, but rejected by the press, illustrate also that from the start the conflicting aims of naturalism and construction were present. It proposed a running story of the first half of the England v. Scotland rugby match, a 'coded narrative' of the Boat Race (the key to the code along with a plan of the course having been published exclusively in early papers that day), a 'coded narrative' of the Cup Final,[2] and broadcasting of various sound impressions of Derby Day (Briggs 1961: 264).

The development of commentary itself was possible only after 1926 and the formation of the Corporation. An early commentator, Captain H.B.T. Wakelam, commenced on the new practice at a rugby match with very little to guide him. The most striking thing about his own account of his commentary practice is the stress on 'naturalness' – he attempted to be 'perfectly natural', to use 'ordinary conversational language', to 'talk in plain simple everyday phrases', and make 'natural spontaneous remarks'. His four basic rules were: be natural, be clear, be fair and be friendly. The conversational tone drew upon the dictum that in radio you should behave as if the audience is one person, and just address that person. The use in commentary boxes of a second person (a 'number two') also reinforced the conversational style (Wakelam 1938: esp. 202–3). From the start, naturalism was mobilised in an attempt to render the discourse transparent.

But two separate impulses existed in uneasy relation as these codes developed, one towards realism, the other towards entertainment. So there is on the one hand the impulse to describe the scene, show what's happening, give the audience an accurate picture, and on the other the impulse to get people involved, keep up the interest, add suspense, shape the material and highlight the action. The second impulse laid a greater stress on the actively created, constructed aspect of a commentary. Raymond Glendenning (1953: 66) referred to the commentator as a story-teller, as an artist painting a picture with words, and said, 'I regard the commentator as the equivalent of an artist – the occasion is his canvas, the action his colours, and the tongue his brushes' . John Arlott described the conflicting needs to be a television receiver, a news reporter, a painter to capture the impressions, and a poet to capture the atmosphere.[3]

The balance between these impulses and the precise way the practice is inflected depended upon the constraints and problems presented by various sports. Cricket, Alan Gibson pointed out (1976: 155), needed an adequate supply of background information and the ability to keep the commentary going without obvious padding, without making the listener feel bored. With rugby football, on the other hand, the difficulty was to keep up the pace – getting out the words swiftly and accurately enough to tell people what is going on without lagging behind the play.

Commentary makes the link between contributor and audience, and a major concern of broadcasting has been where the balance between expert and popular should lie. That is to say, should contributors be experts in a sport or expert broadcasters; and are they to address the general audience or the expert audience? Right from the start of radio broadcasting, concepts of professionalism began to develop. Broadcasting became identified as a specialised skill. Early use of outside experts on sport was found to be inadequate as 'good radio'. Stobart, Head of Talks, reported in July 1925 that he had tried to bring 'men of the moment' to the microphone to record their impressions of cricket, football, tennis and boxing, but too often their displays had been 'little short of lamentable'.[4]

Gradually, through a process of trial and error (cricket and tennis in their respective extremes of pace presented particular problems), a practice was formulated. It was during the 1930s and 1940s that informal conventions began to be systematically structured, largely under the influence of Seymour Joly de Lotbiniere, OB Head from 1935, and regarded as 'the architect' of commentary technique (Johnston 1966: 16). He wrote in the *BBC Handbook* of 1939 that 'commentary is an art and its successful practice depends on attention to a specifiable technique'.[5] To this end he instigated regular Monday morning meetings at which rigorous post-mortem discussion of the Saturday performances of commentators took place.

The conventions of good commentary included: keep up the interest with suspense; keep it simple; there is a need for explanation and interpretation; there is a need to shape material into a logical order; blend descriptive and associative material as imperceptibly as possible; it must sound spontaneous; vary the pace; let sounds (crowd noises, etc.) speak for themselves.[6] Through the 1930s and 1940s a team of trained professional commentators was assembled. These people were chosen more for their ability to broadcast than for their knowledge of sport, although many combined both, and de Lotbiniere felt that the expert on the subject was not necessarily the best person to broadcast on it (Snagge and Barsley 1972: 66).

When television was re-launched in 1946, the practices of commentary had to be reconstructed for television, although many of the principles of the radio practice were simply carried over into television. Television Outside Broadcast Manager Orr-Ewing followed de Lotbiniere's practice in instigating Monday morning post-mortems. He formulated some guidelines – emphasising the need to explain technique from time to time, and the need to give the score every five minutes at least – and commented drily, 'there is no time for any but the most memorable wisecracks' (Briggs 1979: 867).

Again there was a tension between the conflicting drives towards realism and towards entertainment. Brian Johnston (1966: 30) saw the central problem of television commentary as 'to talk or not to talk'. He reiterated 'golden rules': never speak unless you can add to the pictures; don't describe what the viewer can see; let the camera tell the story, etc. Dorian Williams (1968: 97) emphasised the need to 'convey something of the atmosphere of the occasion', and the need to 'communicate something of the excitement and interest of the spectators'.

The formation of the practice of television commentary then depended in part on balancing the need to convey excitement and build interest verbally with the need to 'let pictures speak for themselves'. The developing practice was closely monitored. Commentary in the various sports was the subject of much internal discussion. When tried as a commentator, athletics official Jack Crump couldn't be given 'any true dramatic sense', and was used instead as a contributing expert.[7] Commentators were reminded to 'let cheers tell as much of the story as they are capable of telling . . . the commentator, while matching himself to the mood and raising his voice to combat the sound level, should keep his comments to the bare minimum'.[8]

By 1952 de Lotbiniere had produced a fully systematised guide to the new practice of television commentary, running to 24 separate items and six pages long.[9] It provided the basis for the new professional technique of television commentary, and a formalised method of framing events, foregrounding individual interest and building a mode of address around points of identification for the viewer. It stressed the need to watch the monitor, to add to the picture rather than interrupting it, not to be afraid of silence, to leave the picture to tell the story. It was important to be pithy, brisk and accurate. The score should be given regularly, essentials should be repeated, suspense built and technique explained.

Interest should be promoted by associating competitors with localities, (e.g. 'the Birmingham boy'). 'You should build partisanship, but do not be partisan yourself. It should be "England's chances are brightenening", not "our chances are brightening".' An instruction to 'give things their right sequence' outlines de Lotbiniere's notion of building pyramidically to highlight the key information:

> 12 competitors
> they are: a-b-c-d-e-f-g-h-i-j-k-l
> 'a' is the one to watch. He . . . etc. . . .

Contained in this convention is the basis of selective construction and the process of a personalised singling out of the star individual so central to the current practice. Two elements can be seen in uneasy combination: the concept that the picture tells the story, and the dictum to build in suspense and partisanship. This produced a need to manage the contradiction between partisanship and the journalistic code of neutrality. A note to commentators for the England v. Italy football match of 1949 told them to 'build partisanship in the viewer' while not groaning whenever an English movement broke down, and said, in rather contradictory way, 'if we are to err at all, let us err on the side of being generous to the visitors' (Briggs 1979: 847). There is little material about this, but it indicates that issues of patriotism and nationality present certain problems that need to be negotiated.

While the BBC played a major role in articulating national identity, sport presented a particular problem of national unity. In many sports England and the three subordinate national components of the United Kingdom, Scotland, Wales and Northern Ireland, compete as separate teams. Football commentaries have several identifiable modes of address: in club matches, neutrality prevails; in England internationals against foreign sides, partisanship prevails; in England playing Wales, Scotland or Northern Ireland, there is an uneasy combination of the two; and in Scotland internationals against foreign teams, the level of surrogate partisanship – committed yet distanced – often depends on how well Scotland is doing.

The conventionalisation of the professional practice focused attention on the degree to which individual performers could internalise and operate the conventions successfully. Much attention was paid to the choice of commentator. A *Camera Report* on an early golf production commented that Henry Longhurst was knowledgeable, pleasantly conversational, had an admirable sense of humour and ability to comprehend the needs of a television commentary.[10] By contrast, a BBC *Viewer Research Report* on a floodlit football match between Tottenham Hotspur and Racing of Paris in 1953 said several viewers had complained of the commentator talking too much, and a few had objected to the unsportsmanlike bias in favour of Tottenham.[11]

There was much debate throughout the 1950s over the respective cricket commentary styles of Peter West, E.W. Swanton and Brian Johnston, while for Wimbledon, Maskell was seen as excellent, although occasionally it was suggested that he lighten his style a bit. After early coverage of table tennis, a *Viewer Research Report* reported that some viewers felt that a commentary was hardly necessary and others felt that the commentator talked too much. There was also internal criticism of the lack of expert knowledge of table tennis that the commentator displayed.[12] In defence, the producer said that the commentator knew sufficient about the game and his television commentary was fast becoming expert, adding that he did not think viewers wished to be troubled with minor technical points.[13] So another balance had to be struck – the balance between professional broadcasting ability and expertise in the subject. Peter Dimmock stressed the importance of team work between the outside broadcast producer, the commentator and the cameraman, and reiterated the golden rule, 'when in doubt, leave it out' (see Andrews and MacKay 1954: 195). He held yearly meetings to review the art, in which telerecordings were closely analysed (Wolstenholme 1958: 23).

The development of the practice of commentary, the decisions as to style and types of contributor, were all dependent on a set of assumptions and hypotheses as to the nature of the audience for sport. How commentators should talk was determined by a concept of whom they were trying to talk to, and de Lotbiniere stressed the importance of the marginal viewer, the viewer not fully committed to sport. It was indeed to become a crucial axiom within televised sport that the sports fan was likely to watch anyway, and the audience that had to be secured was that with a more marginal interest in sport. The audience should be 'addressed intimately, e.g. "Many of you may remember . . .", rather than "Viewers may remember . . ." '.[14] The 'Notes' point out that the audience 'will number millions, but they are listening as individuals, probably alone, not as a vast audience' (Talbot 1976: 180). This personalised form of direct address was to be an important element in television sport presentation. The winning and holding of broad heterogeneous audiences presented problems for the mode of address. Johnston offered a typology that gave a revealing insight into broadcasting's conception of its audience:

> The expert cricketer who is looking in resents being told what stroke the batsman has played, or does not want to hear about the tactics of the game. . . . Many viewers know next to nothing about cricket. They don't understand the tactics of the game, they may not even know the names of the places on the field. Many of them are women and like to be told little tit-bits about the players. They like to be told how old so-and-so is or have pointed out to them his little mannerism of touching his cap before the ball is bowled.
>
> (Johnston 1952: 67–8)

One distinctive feature of the assumed audience model during this period is that two oppositions – expert/novice and male/female – become condensed together. The implicit assumption becomes one of male expertise and female ignorance, as guidelines for cricket production suggest: 'During the day, particularly on a weekday, our audience must, generally speaking, be predominately of the female sex, and I feel that they would prefer more commentary than the average male viewer.'[15]

These types (the expert; the novice and potential initiate; the woman from outside the 'culture of sport') are remarkably strong in forming a structure through which professionals conceive the audience; although the actual expression or strategies chosen vary – for instance, some argue that it is the experts that want informed comment and discussion, whereas the casual viewer wants the action, and the women want personality and colour. Wolstenholme (1958: 23) made a similar division of the audience into three groups:

> The smallest group is the real soccer fan. Then comes the sports fan who is not particularly interested in soccer but will watch anything in the sporting line. The largest group of viewers is composed of people who are not sports fans but who are watching for entertainment. The commentator must see that the third and largest group gets its entertainment without upsetting any of the other two groups . . . almost an impossible task.

Clearly here there is a significant cultural distinction within sport itself. The cultures of sport in Britain have been distinctively male, rooted in masculine values and patriarchal exclusiveness. The knowledge of sport is differentially acquired by men and women. Television is identifying this, and reproducing it, not simply in its assumptions of the woman, drying the dishes, who likes to be told 'little tit-bits', but also in its very desire to inform women, which thus marks them as the subordinate onlooker, observing the culture from outside. Only Test cricket, with its blanket coverage on both media, has been able to resolve this by offering a choice between the expert discourse offered by television and radio's more popular discourse (see Johnston 1975).

The growth of television sport, and the introduction of sophisticated technology, gradually brought analysis more to the foreground. Commentaries were increasingly provided by people with first-hand experience of participation and the ability to explain to the viewer what they can both see happening.[16] The greater use of experts does not in itself of course mean that commentary style is any less popular in tone than before indeed the tendency has been for expert contributors, used regularly, to become popular television personalities, while becoming more adept at broadcasting, and their sporting expertise gradually appears less significant.

By the beginning of the 1960s the practice of commentary was already conventionalised to the degree that new initiates absorbed its tenets as part of their apprenticeship and it gradually ceased to be a matter for major aesthetic debate. Such discussion as there was now focused upon minor tinkering and the eradication of annoying mannerisms; as when it became necessary to ask all commentators to refrain from saying 'I'm afraid that's all we've got time for' at the end of their segments.[17] And it was not only the practices that, once established, became permanent and unchanging features, but also the practitioners. Steven Barnett (1990) points out that, of 14 contributors to Dimmock's book *Sports in View* (Dimmock 1964), half were still contributing to television sport in 1990.

The target audience and the strategies for winning it have also changed less than one might expect. The executive producer of ITV's World Cup Rugby coverage in 1991 said he wanted to capture a wider audience than the traditional rugby spectator, intended to give viewers 'the best seat in the house', and hoped to make the game 'easier to understand for the ordinary people'.[18]

VISUAL CONVENTIONS

There is a great deal of information about the development of the practice of commentary, but far less on the development of visual conventions. This is not necessarily because there was not much internal discussion about the problems of camera positions and cutting styles – there may well have been. However, the evidence for this in the BBC Written Archives is sparse. It may well be that some of the principles of a visual style were merely derived from the well-established conventions of realist cinema. Certainly television merely took over a lot of standard realist conventions from film-making – the 180-degree rule, the principle of complementary angles and so on, as Desmond Davis (1960: 48–9) makes clear:

> At a football match, a cricket match, a tennis tournament, the rule is: draw an imaginary line down the centre of the football field from goal to goal, down the cricket pitch from wicket to wicket, down the tennis court at right angles to the net, and keep all your cameras the same side of this line. It does not matter how close they get to the line as long as they don't actually cross it, but the moment they do actually cross it you will be in trouble and the audience will lose all sense of direction.

These conventions aimed at transparency, strengthening the claim of television to reflect events and minimising its own active construction of representations.[19] In the early days the principal conflict seems to have been between the abstract 'ideal position' and the constraints of stadium design, which did not always permit these positions. The key decision in the first instance was the positioning of the main camera, because, given the working of realist conventions, the other positions would to an extent be determined by the main one. In early football coverage the half-way line position was not the automatic first choice, as it required excess panning (Wolstenholme 1958: 21). It was only after trial and error that the half-way line became seen as the best position. Many of the visual conventions were formed before the development of modern devices like high-quality zoom lenses. Feedback about camera positions played a role in this process.[20] Quite why particular positions were regarded as satisfactory was often not spelt out; there was genuine uncertainty, and consequent interest in viewer research:

> There was some difference of opinion as to the best camera angle on a game of table tennis, but many seemed to like a side angle showing the net centre screen, with both players simultaneously. Several did not care for the concentration on one player in close-up, so that no general picture of play could be seen.[21]

Where substantial experience had already been obtained, attempts were made to formalise the conventional camera positions. So it was decided that the most satisfactory camera position for watching tennis was immediately behind and above the court.[22] A *Camera Report* on table tennis in 1948 contained a chart marking the two main preferred positions to the nearest inch.[23] In 1952, cricket producer Anthony Craxton wrote the guidelines 'Cricket Production', and, while coverage style was still an open issue, the placing of the main camera was already firmly established:

> It would be ideal to be able to place all three cameras at a uniform height of about twelve feet from ground level. This however is not possible as it is essential to have a camera in line with the wicket and this necessitates a lens height of about twenty feet. This camera should be at a sufficient height that when looking down the pitch the head of the umpire at the camera end is about a yard below the level of the popping crease at the opposite end. This means that one can get both wickets and the batsman and bowler in the tightest of close-ups.[24]

It should be noted that, once the main position is established, the secondary camera position derives from it. For cricket it was felt that the secondary, or fielding, camera should be fairly close to the main one, as 'it is very important to avoid constant changes of viewing points' (Johnston 1966: 40). The rather rigid application of realist principles meant that the main camera position left only certain limited options for the secondary position. The commitment to these rules of television grammar and the attempt to maintain a transparency effect were to be important determinants upon television sport style.

A second area of debate was to develop around the correct use of close-ups. If the function of the realist style was the maintenance of transparency, the function of the close-up was personalisation. So, just as at the verbal level, there was a tension between the impression of realism and the building in of entertainment value. Cecil McGivern, Controller of Television during the 1950s, constantly argued for a more personalised approach. Following the 1952 Wimbledon Championships, he sent a memo praising the excellent close-shot of well-known tennis coach 'Teach' Tennant, and wondered why she was not shown at the moment of her pupil's greatest triumph.[25] In 1956, when for the first time the BBC had competition from ITV, which also covered Wimbledon throughout the 1950s, McGivern watched some of the coverage with two sets side by side. He felt ITV's coverage was better, and commented that ITV gave many more close-ups and showed the face more often (see Figure 3.1).[26]

CONFIDENTIAL

Controller Programmes, Television

WIMBLEDON 1956   5th July 1956

H.O.B.Tel.

I have watched Wimbledon as much as possible with the BBC picture alongside the I.T.A. picture. This amount is only a small proportion of the total transmitted time and judgement is therefore difficult and dangerous.

I did, however, get this impression very strongly indeed, that I.T.A. gave many more close-ups than we did and that of the close-ups, I.T.A. gave the face more often than we did.   I became worried at the extent that I began to watch the I.T.A. screen more than ours.

As regards commentators, I can make only this statement. While agreeing that 'Little Mo' is no expert commentator, I found her fresh, eager voice and free-and-easy colloquial manner added an extra interest and warmth.

In fact, I am worried by I.T.A.'s coverage of Wimbledon as compared with ours.

I presume that the O.B. Department has been carefully considering our handling of Wimbledon as compared with I.T.A.s and I shall be glad if you will let me have an objective report. I hope that the overall report can negative my views obtained, as I said, from not as much viewing as I would have liked.

dcm   (Cecil McGivern)

Figure 3.1   BBC Memorandum from Controller of Television, McGivern, to Head of Television Outside Broadcasts, Dimmock, 5/7/56 (T14/1407/14). It was relatively unusual for the BBC to feel threatened by ITV's sports coverage. This memo suggests that the introduction of competition made the BBC more concerned with audience appeal, and shows that the development of the use of close-ups was in part a consequence of this.

Producer Bill Duncalf pointed out that ITV drew on greater resources of staff and equipment for Wimbledon.[27] The following year, Dimmock believed the BBC was now using 'the right amount of close-up' and felt there was little doubt that the picture quality was superior.[28] However, in 1958, the new Television Controller, Kenneth Adam, thought ITV still used more close-ups but said, 'Otherwise, our pictures were better, our commentary more authoritative but less gay'.[29]

It is notable that the sport output of this period was so closely monitored from above, that competition was taken very seriously, and that there appeared to be pressure from above for greater personalisation. A 1958 report discussed changes in operation and adjustments to the use of extra cameras, but implied that the basic conventions were satisfactory.[30] A 1950 memo on table tennis called for close-ups of the winners as they left, suggesting that the competitors 'pause for a moment so that the viewers could really take a look at them'.[31] Efforts were made to arrange the presentation and trophy table and the entrance and exit of players in positions suitable for the cameras.[32] The positioning of players for the cameras before, after and during intervals of events has indeed become a feature of television coverage of ice skating and table tennis.

The development of conventions for use of close-ups can be followed closely in cricket. In the early 1950s a third camera over extra cover was regarded as 'to some extent a luxury', to be used sparingly.[33] By 1966 this third camera had been fitted with a zoom, and was used to add 'small snippets of atmosphere among the crowd – the small boys and their score cards, the newspaper covered head, or the post-lunch sleeping member' (Johnston 1966: 40). The close-up was still seen primarily as a way of providing colourful shots on the periphery of the event. By the 1970s, the close-up was a much more integral element, providing reaction shots and giving the viewer 'a sense of the atmosphere and drama of the match' (Johnston 1975: 26). During the 1980s close-ups became a central element in cricket presentation. The development of the close-up has always been an area of conflict between the desire for visual personalisation and provision of drama and atmosphere, and the need to show clearly the scene as a whole. Raymond Baxter comments on this in a memo about the problems of covering motorised sports:

> the frequent use of wide camera angles is imperative if the relative positions of competitors are to be made clear to the viewer. But a close-up view of man and machine in action is essential to the visual excitement afforded by the event. Thus I suggest that the general rule should be to mount *two* cameras at each camera point. In this way a wide angle can be used to report the relative positions of the approaching leaders, cutting to individual close-ups as desired.[34]

The conflict between the use of close-ups and wide shots, and the way it is resolved in various situations, is the basis of style and patterns of cutting. At one end of the range of available styles is that which aims at an appearance of minimal mediation. Early on in tennis coverage, Gorham laid down a ground rule that games should as far as possible be covered on one camera, mixes during a rally being 'confusing'.[35] In 25 years of tennis coverage the BBC has not drifted far from this principle – rallies are still covered predominately by one camera. The BBC's style in this respect differs from US or French coverage.

Craxton's cricket guidelines exhibited similar caution. He warned that restlessness in cutting patterns through continuous cutting should be avoided, and that producers must not fall into 'the major trap of distracting the viewer with "off the field" close-ups at tense moments in the game when all attention is demanded on the actual play'.[36] So a principle emerged that gave producers greater freedom during breaks in action, while regarding action itself as something to be covered without obtrusive visual transitions. But there was also a counter-pressure to keep programmes interesting. Producer Phil Lewis warned of the danger of boring the viewer with too predictable a cutting pattern, and called for plenty of variety, governed by close attention to the pace and mood of the event (Johnston 1966).

The development of television in different countries reveals stylistic differences. It has been suggested that West German football coverage during the 1970s used a more 'neutral' style – longer shots, fewer close-ups – than Britain did (Buscombe 1975: 47–53). Styles of course do not remain consistent over time, but gradually modify each other. However, some foreign responses to the pictures provided to the rest of the world by a BBC/ITV consortium during the 1966 World Cup reveal some of the different values involved in stylistic choice. ARD found the sudden change of cameras in critical phases of the game disturbing, *Figaro* said 'It will no longer be possible for us to watch a televised football match other than through the eyes of English cameras', Telisitana Mexicano felt that 'too much close-up technique was used in the games, sometimes producing a miscontinuing [sic] of the game', and NRK Norway felt hampered by the prevailing close-ups.[37] It should be pointed out that the full comments from these and other sources also contained much praise for the quality and technical excellence of the coverage.

What these responses indicate is that there are choices involved in cutting style, and different broadcasting organisations have placed the balance between simple and complex styles at different points. They highlight that the combination of long and close shots chosen by British television represented only one possible mode of representation. As a mode of representation it can be seen as a way of managing the potentially conflicting needs – to offer an apparently unmediated reflection of events and to establish points of viewer identification with recognisable star personalities. The representation is a product of the need to hold on to the transparency effect whilst building in entertainment value.

MAGAZINE FORMATS

A key characteristic of television form is the magazine nature of many of its programme forms. The magazine programme, the collection of discrete items linked by a presenter, has been a standard form in many areas of television. In relation to sport, three variants of the form, all of which emerged during the 1950s, have proved remarkably resilient. These are the Saturday afternoon programme, the Saturday evening highlights and the midweek magazine. These programme forms construct, out of a diversity of different events and different items, a unity, the unity of the world of sport. Our entrance into this world is mediated by the presenter – our guide to the programme and its events.

The presenter provides the articulating point for the set of representations that the programme assembles. He (and until the late 1980s it was invariably 'he') articulates the discourse that enables the seamless suturing of a range of discursive elements into the unity of the programme form. The unity produced is the unity of the 'world' of sport, separated from the real world of social and political conflict. The mode of address employed to hail us to this world has to accomplish two conflicting points of identification. First, a range of enthusiasts for different sports have to be positioned as generalised sports fans, willing to take an interest in all sports. Second, television's need to win and hold a large heterogeneous audience means that the address must also hail and position both sports fans and the general audience. The conflict between expert and popular modes of representation has to be negotiated.

The magazine form of sport coverage has a significant pre-history in radio and in the early experimental period of television between 1936 and 1939 (see Cardiff 1980: 29–48). As a result of the development and refinement of the multi-source technique (constructing radio programmes from a number of separate sources) and the expansion of OB resources, it became possible to launch in 1934 the first 'afternoons of broadcast sport' (Briggs 1965: 119). This marked the first point at which broadcasting clearly identified Saturday afternoon with sports – a construction later enshrined in *Grandstand* and its ITV rival *World of Sport*. There were to be a number of radio variants of the magazine form (see Briggs 1979: 849, also Snagge and Barsley 1972: 78–84 and Andrews and MacKay 1954). In television too a monthly sports review, *Sporting Magazine*, appeared as early as 1937 (Ross 1961: 53). This, however, would appear to have had less influence, as it was not until four years after the 1946 re-launch of television that a magazine format appeared in the shape of *Television Sports Magazine*. This is not to say, however, that the forming of programmes out of collections of items was an unusual method in the 1940s. An early feature on golf, an outside broadcast from Moor Park on a Saturday afternoon, featured a brief history of the club, a lesson by the club professional, some views of members in play, and a demonstration by three professionals.[38]

From the early 1950s television was beginning to rise to a position of dominance over radio and Peter Dimmock emerged as the shaping influence on the development of TV sport. In 1954 the BBC launched *Sportsview*, the first BBC television programme to have its own full-time production team, the *Sportsview* Unit, which was in effect an embryonic sports department. The magazine format was successful in a variety of areas during this period – apart from *Sportsview*, *Tonight*, *Panorama*, *Monitor* and *Grandstand* all emerged in the 1950s.

Between 1954 and 1958 three of the most basic forms of sport programme – the Saturday afternoon coverage, the Saturday night highlights and the midweek magazine – were all developed. While sport broadcasting continued to expand through the 1960s and into the 1970s, the significant developments centred on technological advance and expansion in range of sports and events, rather than on innovation in programme form.

The process had begun with *Television Sports Magazine*, on the air fortnightly from various locations between 1950 and 1952. The programme was aimed at 'people already interested in sport or who might become so. The first thing therefore is to attract and hold attention'.[39] The programmes featured a wide variety of items, including demonstrations of technique, quizzes, personality profiles, actual competitions, items on jobs to do with sport, reviews of sport publications, making of sport equipment; de Lotbiniere emphasised that the material must be interesting and as universal as possible. In a publicity handout for the programme by editor Berkeley Smith, it is obvious that the programme was attempting to put together an audience combining sports fans and casual viewers; aiming to cater 'not only for the great body of knowledgeable sports enthusiasts in this country, but also for the thousands of viewers who have been introduced to sports through their television screens'.[40]

This characterisation of the target audience was a fundamental principle of television sport and its particular mode of address. Television always has to fight to assemble heterogeneous audiences, and in sport coverage the conflict between expert and popular modes always has to be handled. In a new proposal for a sport magazine programme, Kenneth Wolstenholme argued that *Television Sports Magazine* lacked topicality, and suggested a programme that would mix the past, the present, the future and the controversial.[41] But the 'controversial' was always likely to be marginalised. Alec Sutherland, in a 1951 memo, suggested an item on the struggle of professional footballers for better conditions.[42] This was rejected by de Lotbiniere because of the delicate state of negotiations over TV football.

The tendency of sport to attempt to insulate itself from social and political conflict was already marking television. Like any specialist journalists, the dependency of the BBC Outside Broadcast department upon good relations with its suppliers, the sports organisations, was inevitably going to hamper any attempts to establish a tradition of investigative reporting.

Sportsview

The programme that was to establish the Wednesday night sport slot began originally as a fortnightly programme, but its success meant an early change to weekly output. From the start the programme was intended to win a large audience – it was aimed consciously at the family audience, Paul Fox commenting that 'Mother may not be especially interested in sport, but we still want her to enjoy *Sportsview* if possible'.[43] The expert/popular distinction is frequently displaced onto a male/female one. Just as 'family audience' denotes the general audience as opposed to the 'sports fan', 'mother' represents a lack of knowledge and competence, assumed to be the domain of masculinity. There is no doubt that *Sportsview* made a major impact when it arrived, as Peter Black (1972b: 132) suggested:

> Apart from *Panorama* it is the sole survivor from the pre-ITV era of television. It reflected not just an interest in sport, but an exhilarating relish for the professional opportunities now being opened up fast by new technical facilities. Dimmock and McGivern got the management of the day to spend far more resources on a single programme than any half hour programme had had before. It was the first series programme to operate independent of a department. Within two months it was clear that something quite new and exceptional had arrived. It was no coincidence that when *Panorama* went weekly it also began to mingle outside broadcasts, film, studio techniques, and to develop a *Sportsview*-type style of presentation in which a very strong unified editorial drive and command was apparent.

The *Sportsview* style rested on immediacy, slick presentation and sporting personalities. There was an emphasis on 'the latest news', the programme was described as living 'by its topicality' and there was a stress on 'what's going to happen' (Briggs 1979: 850–2). The *BBC Annual Report* for 1954/55 boasted that almost every sporting personality of note was interviewed in the course of the year. With the approach of competition, the stakes were high. A two-hour programme – heralded as 'probably the greatest sporting night of the year' – was scheduled against the opening of ITV in October 1955, and an effort to attract more women as viewers was made, with a programme devoted entirely to women's sport (Briggs 1979: 853). The BBC was aware that ITV had tentative plans for sport programmes that might appeal to women and had plans to feature women's hockey, although there is little evidence that any significant gestures were made towards constructing a female audience for sport.[44]

Sportsview grew along with the expansion of the OB department which spent much of the 1950s pressing for greater resources. In 1955 Dimmock was pressing for an increase in the film allowance, a full-time film editor and crew, and a 25 per cent budget increase.[45] *Sportsview* was placed in an 8.30–9.00 slot on Wednesday night, which Dimmock regarded as the best of both worlds – not too late to mean overnight expenses to participants, and yet late enough to permit the inclusion of an afternoon football story. The schedule was altered later on, and continual discussion as to the best time took place. Paul Fox referred to the need to balance the start time between being late enough for film reports while early enough, in summer, for live open-air OBs, and suggested 8.30 or 8.45.[46]

It was, then, upon a combination of organisational, professional and technical advance, that *Sportsview* attempted to win a general audience and became the first fully successful magazine format programme. The fact that it had its own independent production team meant that it established many of the practices and conventions for subsequent developments in BBC sport.

Sports Special

Plans were made to launch a new Saturday evening programme with filmed highlights from three football matches, interviews, football news and items on other sports. *Sports Special*, screened from 10.00 to 10.30, presented considerable logistical problems (Wolstenholme 1958: 28–35). This process was emphasised in the programme's publicity:

> Tonight at 10.15 *Sports Special*, the first edition of a weekly series, is on the air. The BBC Sportsview unit, with the assistance of studios and film cameras, and live outside broadcasts from key centres throughout the British Isles will present up to the minute coverage of the best in today's sport. Aeroplanes, a helicopter and a fleet of cars and motorcycles are standing by to rush personalities to the studios. Tonight's programme is introduced by Peter Dimmock.[47]

Sportsview Unit editor, Paul Fox, stressed the need for slickness and punch and strict timekeeping, and emphasised the importance of the regional contributions in the competition with ITV.[48] The introduction to the first show made a point of addressing the sport follower more specifically than *Sportsview*:

> 'Good evening and welcome to the new programme. Its title is *Saturday Sports Special* and it is especially for sports enthusiasts. I do stress this,

because with the *Sportsview* programme on Wednesday night, we try to include something to interest all the family. But with this programme we aim to give you, with film reports and personality interviews, a complete picture of the day's news in sport.'[49]

The opposition between the 'sports enthusiast' and 'all the family' provides a distinction between two different ways of addressing the audience. It also suggests again the implicit 'maleness' of the concept of sports fans.

Sports Special was well received by the press, although there were great technical problems with timing and co-ordinating regional contributions. Controller of Television McGivern was also unhappy that there was far too much talk and not enough action. He called for a programme with at least 95 per cent film and telerecording of the day's sport.[50] In reply to Dimmock about this demand, Fox pointed out that even 30 per cent film was straining the resources. The programme had only six cameramen, three editors and two writers, and, even if extra staff were available, there were no extra cameras, sound cameras were at that time hard to obtain, and there was not enough cutting-room equipment.[51]

McGivern was still unhappy about the amount of action in the programme and said, 'I feel that this present *Sports Special* is wrong and will *not* achieve a majority audience. And a majority audience is from my point of view its purpose'.[52] Dimmock replied that the programme now had 20 minutes of film. To show more would require greater camera, sound, editing, transport and lab facilities. Agreements with the Football League allowed only 15 minutes of football. Cost prohibited film coverage from Scotland, so their contribution had to be live (and therefore basically news and interviews), and the programme was desperately understaffed.[53] It is, however, clear that during this period the amount of action in the programme was increased, and the pressure made the programme aware of the need to win a broad audience.

Three features of the programme are worthy of note. The emphasis on slickness points to the growing importance of technical professionalism and to the practice of achieving transparency, a seamless representation in which audience awareness of technical intervention is minimised. The emphasis on pace, immediacy and action shows the commitment to the production of excitement as a prime entertainment value. In some ways the contradiction between realist style and entertainment value is here resolved under the sign of 'slickness, pace, and immediacy'. The initial target audience, the sports fan, in itself to a degree a television construct, has to be modified in the light of pressure to win also the 'majority' audience.

Grandstand

As sport coverage expanded during the 1950s the BBC had regular outside broadcasts on Saturday afternoons, sometimes from two or three separate locations. It made increasing sense for these OBs to be grouped together under a programme heading.[54] Using a studio presenter to link the various OBs would make it possible to handle fluctuations in timing or problems of weather. It would also be possible to include a constant flow of up-to-date news. Bryan Cowgill's original 1958 proposal for a three-hour plus programme, with one major and two minor OBs, established the form the programme eventually adopted.[55] Racing was expected to have prominence as the one major sport regularly available during the October–December period earmarked for the experiment. Cowgill stressed the project was an opportunity to present multiple OBs in 'a much more attractive package than has been achieved before'. The studio and technical facilities needed – teleprinters, extra telephones and operators, telecine for 16mm and 35mm, and omnibus talkback between the studio control room and the various OB points – were to be important to the success of the programme.

After a meeting of OB members in April 1958, and further discussion, Cowgill produced a more detailed proposal, which went into greater details about problems of timing and the need for new technical facilities, notably access to an Ampex video recorder, the first video recorder and only recently commercially available.[56] He stressed the importance of team-work and said it would be desirable to have the same camera crew for at least six weeks, particularly at the start of the programme's run.[57] There were many problems during the development of the programme, the major one being the proposed schedule, finishing at 5.00pm, which meant cutting *Children's Hour* back to 45 minutes. This was strongly resisted, and the BBC hierarchy insisted that *Grandstand* finish at 4.45, despite strong protest from Paul Fox, who insisted that as a sports news programme it had to stay on the air until 5 o'clock to present a proper results service.[58]

It was only after the programme had been on the air for several months that Fox's argument carried the day.[59] In autumn 1959 *Grandstand* was extended until 5.00pm, and Fox and Dimmock then began lobbying to cut *Children's Hour* down to 40 minutes, so that the BBC's sports news, *Today's Sport*, could start at 5.40pm, thereby beating ITV.[60] Other battles took place over the installation of teleprinters, the financial allocation to the programme and the need for new technical facilities, particularly an Ampex video recorder and a Lawley fast film developer. It was less than three weeks before the programme went on the air that Fox got Dimmock to agree to the title *Grandstand*, in preference to Dimmock's own suggestion, *Out and About!*[61] The launching of the programme made great play of the immediacy with which the results and news would be brought to the screen, and the human and technical system was described in detail:

Around Peter Dimmock, who will introduce the programme for the first few weeks, there'll be gathered all the machinery that goes with high-speed sports reporting. Batteries of tape machines, a giant sized scoreboard, the sub-editors' table – they'll all be on view in the studio so that not a moment is lost in passing the latest sports news on to viewers at home.[62]

Indeed the programme has always made a point of including the apparatus of fast news in the picture, so sub-editors can be seen in the background, presenters have news handed to them while on the air, and of course the football results were eventually to be displayed as they arrived on the teleprinter. A great stress was placed by Fox and Cowgill on the need for technical slickness, particularly in the constant handovers between studio and outside that were a feature of the programme's style.[63] The introduction of the programme, with a menu elaborated with brief appetite-whetting visits to the OB sites, established in 1958, still survives in similar form 30 years on. The *Grandstand* team pressed vigorously to develop the programme and raise its profile. In 1960, Fox was lobbying the *Radio Times* for better billing and also a front cover for *Sports Review of the Year*.[64] In 1961 the basic format featured three or four main OB slots – a 30 minute Fight of the Week, 70 minutes of racing, 40 minutes of rugby league or union, and another 80 minutes on diverse sports. Ronnie Noble pressed for an overspend of £2800 to improve this last slot.[65] In this period *Grandstand* cost approximately £2000 per hour, compared with a TV studio programme average of £3000 per hour.[66] While rights fees had risen since the introduction of competition from ITV, they were still relatively low. Major rugby matches cost £2500, cricket Test Matches £1600 per day, top show jumping events £1200 per day, and athletics £2000 or less, while Wimbledon was a bargain at less than £600 per day.[67]

From the start the programme aimed to hold together the needs of fans for different sports by switching between events fairly frequently. When motor sport commentator Raymond Baxter demanded longer slots for his sport, Fox referred to the need to provide a mixture for everyone's taste; to hold both the mad horse-racing fan and the motoring fanatic.[68] Once the programme format was established the BBC had a success. It remains in some ways the most complex regular programme – being four and a half hours of predominately live television using multiple outside sources. Originally operating with a specially earmarked crew, it gradually became a matter for routinised professionalism, a programme 'which any studio crew could be expected to handle' (Ross 1961: 204).

For all that, the programme placed great demands on the professionalism of the crew, particularly producer and presenter, and Cowgill stressed the crucial importance of organisation and teamwork (see Coleman 1960: 163–9). Similarly presenter Frank Bough stressed the importance of preparation and future planning – the homework, the meticulous preparation and the problems of timing. He talked of the need to produce information rapidly and faultlessly, the need for producer, editor and presenter to 'get used to each other's professional habits', and the difficulties of working with a talkback system through which the presenters hear the combined voices of everyone in the control room, the VT engineers, vision and sound engineers, and production assistants checking timings (Bough 1980: 64).

Indeed it may well be a mark of the thorough and complete professionalism needed to operate a programme like *Grandstand* that both Cowgill and Fox subsequently rose to managing director level with Thames and Yorkshire respectively, Fox eventually returning to the BBC in the late 1980s. *Grandstand* firmly established the concept of Saturday afternoon for sport. Like *Sportsview*, *Grandstand* refined the whole process of articulating diverse elements into a unity by establishing a strong overall programme identity, linked to a personality presenter, giving the assemblage a strong coherence. A technically ambitious programme, it required a routinised professionalism in which technical slickness was paramount and immediacy foregrounded as a point of identification within the mode of address. So in four short years, between 1954 and 1958, the BBC established the basic shape of regular sport broadcasting.

Chapter 4

BBC v. ITV competition

Since the BBC have long been the prime network for sports, Sir Lew [Grade] would happily leave the games to the BBC and offer a movie on ITV. 'We've never really resolved it,' admitted one network controller. 'Our plans for Saturday have never come off, which is one reason the BBC does so well at weekends.'

(Green 1972: 108)

If it's live and exclusive it must be ITV Sport.

(ITV advertising slogan, 1991)

By the end of the 1950s the BBC dominated sports coverage, whose practices and conventions were consequently largely those of the BBC. Major sport events had become national events, and the BBC benefited from the authority and prestige of association with major state, royal and sporting occasions. It had established close relations with many major sports, based around long-term contracts, and this, coupled with the built-in handicaps ITV suffered as a result of the regional system, gave the BBC a powerful position in sports coverage.

The BBC attitude towards the appearance of a competitor has been characterised as complacent. The Outside Broadcast department, however, is generally regarded as an exception to this. Despite the rapidly rising fees being demanded by sport organisations, which, seeing the approach of ITV, realised they were in a stronger position, the BBC endeavoured to secure a number of long-term contracts with sports, seeking exclusive deals of between three and five years.[1] Before ITV was on the air, for example, the BBC had secured a three-year exclusive deal with the Amateur Swimming Association.[2] Its success in this area was to make it difficult for the new commercial companies to make progress in sport coverage. BBC sport programmes and outside broadcasts of national events were the only ones that never lost huge audiences to the opposition (Black 1972b: 130).

This was certainly recognised as a problem within ITV. Bill Ward, who was with the BBC from 1936 till 1955 when he joined ATV as Head of Light Entertainment, believed Dimmock was the only man at the BBC who thought it would succeed, and 'he did make our life difficult in the sporting area'.[3] Dimmock also employed key staff on a contractual basis, with large increases in pay to discourage them from going to ITV.

BBC's consolidation was aided by state intervention. Concern that television organisations might acquire exclusive contracts for major occasions had led the government to reserve the right to make non-exclusive rules by statutory order.[4] Towards the end of 1955, the BBC had just announced TV rights for Test Matches and Ascot, when Postmaster-General Dr Charles Hill reminded BBC and ITV of the clause in the Television Act of 1954 which disfavoured exclusive broadcasting of events of national interest. BBC and ITV had tentatively agreed that the Grand National, the Derby and the Cup Final were national events, but both sides sought further guidance.[5] Some papers found it extraordinary that a government that believed in free competition should find it necessary to intervene.[6]

Talks were held between BBC and ITV to try and agree on listed events.[7] The BBC wanted just the FA Cup Final, the Grand National and the Derby to be listed, while ITV wanted also the Scottish Cup Final, Wimbledon, the Boat Race, Ascot and, bizarrely, but doubtless with its Welsh and Scottish regional commitments in mind, the Eisteddfod and the Highland Games.[8] The preferred Post Office list included the Derby, the Grand National, the FA Cup Final, Wimbledon, Test Matches and the Boat Race.[9]

Meanwhile, in Parliament, Hill's attention was drawn to an ITV attempt to get exclusive TV rights to the 1956 Olympics. Hill was opposed to coercion by the state on the issue and wanted a voluntary agreement.[10] Lobbying the Pilkington Committee, the Epsom Grand Stand Association, backed by the Lawn Tennis Association (LTA), the All-England Lawn Tennis Club (AELTC), the Oxford and Cambridge Boat Clubs, and Tophams Ltd (owners of the Grand National course), wanted Section 7 of the Television Act repealed, but Pilkington declined to advocate this (Pilkington 1962).

Ten events were eventually adjudged to be 'national events' in which neither side was able to obtain exclusive rights. The events included the Cup Final, the Boat Race, Wimbledon tennis, Test Match cricket, the Grand National and the Derby (Sendall 1983: 51–2). The prevention of exclusivity was to be of immense benefit to the BBC. It was very difficult for ITV to cover Wimbledon, the Test Matches or the Boat Race more completely than the BBC already did, and in each case it ultimately rejected the opportunity; although it not only covered Wimbledon during the 1950s, but was believed by top BBC staff to be doing it better.

PLANS AND PROBLEMS

In establishing the commercial system, the Independent Television Authority (ITA) decided on a federal structure, dividing the country up into regions, each of which was to be allocated as a monopoly franchise to a different company. To further complicate matters, the first three regions – London, Midlands and the North – were divided into weekday and weekend segments. These were allocated in various combinations in an attempt to create relatively equal-sized population areas. Associated Rediffusion had London weekdays, ATV had London weekends and Midlands weekdays, ABC had the weekend in the Midlands and the North, and Granada had weekdays in the North (see Black 1972b, Paulu 1961, Thomas 1977, Garnham 1978).

Because of this, the early plans of ITV were diffuse. Four different companies, with separate bases and orientations, each had their own ideas of how to provide the service. It was only after the first few years that the stabilising mechanism of the network system had begun to impose a greater co-ordination and hence homogeneity upon the programme output.

None of the first four companies seems to have had sport as a very high priority.[11] Just as each franchise was different in region and combination of days, so the first four companies were different in character. Granada stemmed from the Bernstein chain of cinemas and, without partners, retained a central family control. Associated Rediffusion (AR), by contrast, brought together Associated Newspapers (later to drop out – possibly one of the poorer financial decisions of the century) and financial solidity in the shape of British Electric Traction. Associated Broadcasting Company (ABC) grew out of the Associated British Picture Corporation, and Associated Television (ATV) had the combined huge theatrical power of Val Parnell, Prince Littler and the Grade Organisation. In the BBC the Oxbridge influence had been central to the BBC view of sport. There was also a not insignificant RAF presence in the post-war OB dept. These particular cultural formations had much less influence upon the four ITV companies, with their roots in film and show business.

ATV's base in entrepreneurial show business made it ill suited to relate to the amateur paternalism characteristic of British sport organisation, as suggested by the story that Lew Grade, overhearing an ATV staffer phoning the Amateur Boxing Association and the Amateur Athletic Association, sternly told him that ATV wanted no dealings with amateurs, only professionals.[12] Associated Rediffusion's approach, based upon straightforward populist commercial principles such as 'give the people what they want', was no closer to the dominant traditional values of the sport administrators:

Let's face it once and for all. The public likes girls, wrestling, bright musicals, quiz shows, and real-life drama. We gave them the Hallé Orchestra, Foreign Press Club, floodlit football, and visits to the local fire station. Well, we've learned. From now on, what the public wants, it's going to get.

(Roland Gillett of AR, in Black 1972b: 21)

The General Manager, Captain Brownrigg, an ex-director of staff at the Admiralty, announced that he would run AR 'like a ship', referred to memos as 'signals' and his office as 'the bridge' (Mitchell 1981: 200–4) and took pride in his lack of any detailed knowledge of the entertainment business (see Shulman 1973: 21). The hard-nosed financial tone of AR's management gave AR no great advantage in dealing with sport institutions, whose amateur ethos was nowhere plainer than in their handling of money. BBC's Oxbridge foundation provided a not insignificant advantage in sustaining good relations with the world of sport.

Granada and AR had no access to weekend slots, and while AR attempted a sport magazine, *Cavalcade*, Granada never made sport a priority. The weekend companies ATV and ABC were more active. ATV valued the world of entertainment more highly, with sport occupying a relatively low place, while ABC from the start saw the importance of OBs to its two-day output (see Thomas 1977: 157). These two companies together spearheaded the attempts to outbid the BBC during the 1950s.

In the battle to obtain rights, however, ITV was too often in the position of mopping up fairly marginal sports and events such as water polo and amateur wrestling.[13] It was able to compete more vigorously over racing. The BBC was paying £20,000 per year for all racing at Kempton Park (around 78 races a year). This was the largest fee ever paid for a series of OBs, working out at around £300 per race.[14] But ITV won exclusive weekday coverage of racing at Sandown Park, Hurst Park, Lingfield and Windsor, as well as Cheltenham National Hunt meetings and Alexandra Palace evening meetings – at a cost estimated at £100,000 per year. It also acquired motor sport at Brands Hatch and Donington.

In 1959 the BBC was able to renew its exclusive contract with British athletics for another five years.[15] ABC made big efforts to break into weekend sport, planning 5-a-side soccer on Sundays featuring famous ex-footballers. It also tried to recruit Peter West and/or Kenneth Wolstenholme and Eamonn Andrews.[16] The BBC planned a combative two-pronged response. It would try to get the League and FA to intervene but it would also schedule old matches – former internationals and Cup Finals – Fox commenting, 'I only hope we have the courage to do this, if it comes to a showdown'.[17]

Fox was also very keen that the BBC should do wrestling, but Dimmock, aware of the Governors' disapproval, turned the request down.[18] In reply Fox argued that ITV's wrestling was threatening *Grandstand*'s audiences.[19]

After close monitoring of the competition, Ronnie Noble produced figures to reinforce Fox's case. The BBC Audience Research Department compared audience figures for *Grandstand* and ITV's wrestling during autumn 1962. *Grandstand*'s audience fluctuated between 3 million and 4.5 million. ITV's wrestling steadily built an audience growing from 3 million to top 5 million by the end of October. But Dimmock and the Governors remained adamant that professional wrestling was not a suitable sport for BBC.[20]

Several factors mitigated against strong ITV competition over sport. First, the BBC was consolidated in the field. Over many years it had developed expertise, equipment, contacts and contracts. It had much of the available production talent under contract, and, thanks to Dimmock, most major sports under long-term exclusive contracts.

Second, the regional structure prevented ITV from benefiting from economies of scale. No single company was large enough, or had a big enough audience, for it to be worth investing substantial capital in OB facilities, and no single company could muster large bids for exclusive contracts. ABC, as a weekend company, had most incentive, and did make a determined, but unsuccessful, bid to get the rights to televise League football in the 1950s. Each company had its own set of priorities. Competition with the BBC required co-operation between the companies, which was hard to establish, with the network system itself only gradually taking shape in an ad hoc manner. Had ITA opted for franchises based on programme type, rather than region, a commercial contractor could have been in a considerably stronger position to challenge the BBC. Similarly, had the companies opted to establish, along with Independent Television News (ITN), a nationally based, jointly owned sport company, ITV sport would have been in a stronger position.[21]

Third, sport was not in the mid 1950s an obvious audience winner. Only show jumping and tennis were seen as reaching both sexes effectively, and ITV did indeed compete with the BBC in covering Wimbledon during the late 1950s. Television had not yet discovered the huge audiences for World Cups and Olympic Games that were constructed in the 1970s. The regional structure continued to present problems even after the development of substantial co-operation over sport. No one could agree on a weekend programme, and while London Weekend had ambitious cultural projects, ATV, led by Sir Lew Grade, was keen to schedule films rather than sport to compete with *Grandstand* (Green 1972: 108). Referring to the early days, Bernard Sendall (1982: 324) called ITV sport 'sparse, random and sometimes amateurish'.

So in institutional terms, the BBC, by the nature of its structure and the position of authority it occupied by virtue of its close association with the major occasions of state and monarchy, was in a good position to establish dominance in sports coverage. Consequently, the process by which production practices were formulated and became routinised and conventionalised was also dominated by the BBC.

REORGANISATION AND EXPANSION: FROM ABC TO LWT

In the 1960s the ITA insisted that ITV should provide good sports coverage as part of its public service remit. So, ironically, the state now seemed to be acting to secure the competition it had previously helped to limit. The ITA was unhappy about the situation during the early 1960s; it pressed for greater competition over sport and continually expressed concern about professional wrestling, regarded as unrespectable in sporting terms.[22] It became increasingly concerned at the failure to compete with *Grandstand*, and eventually ABC came forward with plans for a new approach which led to the launching, in association with ATV, of *World of Sport* in autumn 1964 (Sendall 1983: 238).

The first major breakthrough for ITV was the decision in 1966/67 to establish a central sports unit, which would be responsible for the acquisition of transmission rights and planning of sports programmes on behalf of the network.[23] In August 1967 a Director of Sport was appointed and transmission rights for the Football League Cup, cricket's Gillette Cup and Brands Hatch motor racing were acquired. The ITA commented that 'in general there were encouraging signs of a new impetus in the presentation of sport on ITV'.[24]

The basic priorities for Independent Television Sport, as the central unit became known, were to secure rights to more of the major national sporting events and to improve the production and presentation of sport by building up a strong team of producers and commentators and acquiring more sophisticated equipment. Acquiring rights caused problems; with the BBC strongly entrenched 'there was little doubt that the task of attracting a majority of the sporting audience to Independent Television would be a long one'.[25] In 1965/66, ATV and ABC contracted with the Football League to televise football highlights on a Sunday, but the ITA was still pressing for improvements in sport coverage.[26]

Eamon Andrews was lured away from the BBC by an offer of £39,000 per year, which included £500 per *World of Sport*, a move which John Bromley felt helped give the programme credibility.[27] ITV still felt that the quality of the programme was inconsistent. Various attempts were made to re-jig *World of Sport*, but by 1967/68 the ITA still felt that the overall standard of the events was not consistently high, in either importance or general popularity, although they covered a wide range of tastes and interests in the sporting field.[28]

The programme was revamped after the franchise reallocation of 1967/68. The new company London Weekend Television (LWT) from now on assumed the initiative, taking over *World of Sport*. Eamonn Andrews chose to stay at ABC, and Richard Davies emerged as his successor. In a remarkable bit of personality reconstruction, LWT changed his name to Dickie, he grew a moustache and sideboards 'and suddenly it all gelled and we had our personality presenter'.[29]

LWT felt that *Grandstand*'s structure was outmoded; far from satisfying the viewer, it was causing annoyance and frustration – it meant watching for three or four hours to catch maybe half an hour of the one sport the viewer wanted to watch.[30] In fact the fragmented approach of BBC's *Grandstand* did not work for ITV, partly because of the lesser appeal of some of its sports, and partly because of the advertising breaks. It is clear that the programme form of BBC's *Grandstand* itself acted as a constraint on ITV. Unable to copy it, it had to define itself against it. *World of Sport* was now arranged in five sections: On the Ball, Racing, International Sports Special, Professional Wrestling, and the results sequence.

LWT also introduced in 1968/69 a more elaborate football highlights programme, *The Big Match*, on Sunday afternoons. In 1968 director Bob Gardam left Anglia to do football for LWT. Gardam had been responsible for the first regular video highlights of football in 1962, had introduced the low-angle camera, persuading Wembley to dig a special pit to enhance the effect, and was felt to have great journalistic talent – Bromley later cited his placing of a camera on Sunderland manager Bob Stokoe at the end of the 1973 Cup Final against Leeds, thus obtaining the memorable image of Stokoe running half the length of the pitch to embrace his goalie. Brian Moore, regarded by many as the best football commentator, was also signed up, LWT spent £60,000 on slow-motion machines, and LWT Head of Sport Jimmy Hill became the first television football analyst. But the strictures of the network system were still a major handicap. In 1968 ITV had outbid the BBC for cricket's 1968 Gillette Cup Final, the first big event Hill and Bromley bought. They scheduled till 6.45 but the match overran and they had to go off the air three overs from the end, triggering public outrage and apoplexy at the MCC, which cancelled its option for a second year. Cricket has yet to return to ITV.[31]

Only LWT was fully committed to sport and in 1969 ITA rejected a proposal to schedule an hour of non-sport entertainment between the racing and wrestling on Saturdays, insisting that *World of Sport* must remain unbroken and *On the Ball* must be retained (Potter 1990: 178). In 1971 the ITA said that LWT's sport was the best in the business and the envy of the BBC (Potter 1990: 279). Sport still needed to be defended against the dictates of the market. The ITA felt that a reasonable amount of good sport coverage was an essential part of a properly balanced public service. In 1977 the ITA felt improvements noted in 1971 had been sustained and built upon and noted that *World of Sport* had overhauled *Grandstand*, winning a 53 per cent audience share in 1976 and 55 per cent in 1977 (Potter 1990: 280–2).

ALTERNATION AND DUPLICATION

Despite development and expansion, then, competing with the BBC in sport coverage still presented difficulties for ITV. The BBC was still prepared to outbid ITV to obtain exclusive contracts, and it tended to be preferred by sport organisations, in part because of the flexibility that two channels gave them. BBC's coverage had achieved a high level of technical and professional sophistication. It was difficult for ITV to do the same thing better. It never attempted to do it in any dramatically different manner as a way of winning an audience. (It is worth noting the contrast between this and the greater self-confidence it began to develop in the late 1970s and early 1980s.) And it had the handicap of the advertising breaks. This means that, at times of simultaneous coverage of major events like the Cup Final, a significant proportion of ITV's audience turn to BBC at the first ad break and don't turn back again (see Figure 4.1).

During the 1970s, the growth of coverage of major international events meant that often BBC and ITV were showing sport, sometimes on all three channels, and on occasion both were relaying identical pictures, to the anger of many viewers. The issue of non-exclusivity had been the most difficult aspect of the 1954 Television Bill, with around ten drafts being rejected before the notion of encouraging voluntary agreement, backed up by reserve powers held by the PMG, emerged (Sendall 1982: 52). ITV tried providing an alternative to BBC sport, put pressure on the BBC for an alternation agreement, and attempted a more aggressively competitive structure. But with no agreement amongst the independent companies on how to handle sport, these strategies lacked conviction. ITV tried unsuccessfully to get exclusive rights to the 1970 World Cup and, when no agreement could be reached on alternation, ITV covered the Munich Olympics mainly on external news bulletins (Potter 1990: 288–9).

In the build-up to the 1974 World Cup, the Independent Broadcasting Authority (IBA), in an attempt to avoid simultaneous broadcasts of the same match, tried to negotiate a 'pattern of complementary transmissions'. The BBC rejected this approach and the IBA commented that it couldn't 'reasonably be expected, in its own interests, or in the interests of the viewing public, to adopt any other attitude than that of fair shares for both services'.[32] In 1974 the BBC had advanced a six-point case against alternation. First, it argued, alternation would deprive half a million viewers unable to receive ITV. Second, over a long period audiences had shown a preference for BBC sport. Third, of the six national events included in the PMG's agreement on non-exclusivity, ITV had never shown the Grand National or the Boat Race, had covered a Test Match only once, and in 1969 had withdrawn from Wimbledon coverage as a result of poor audience figures. Fourth, the BBC had made a considerable investment in the coverage of various sports such as athletics in which it provided more

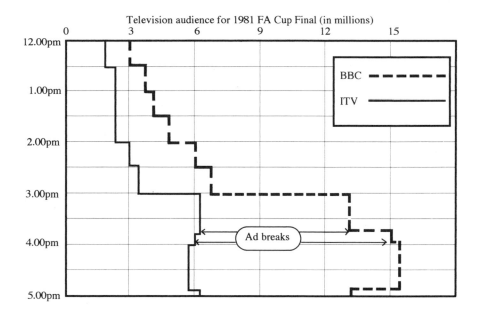

Figure 4.1 BBC Audience Research graph showing Cup Final audience, 1981. Note that during the two half-time advertising breaks, indicated by arrows, a significant number of people appear to turn from ITV to BBC. In other words, some of the people who chose to watch ITV appear to have changed channels at half time and never returned to the channel of their original choice. (BBC Broadcasting Research Unit, 'Daily Viewing Chart', *Daily Survey of Listening and Viewing*, 1981)

year-round coverage than ITV would be prepared to do. Fifth, alternation would have an adverse effect on the morale of its staff. Sixth, since 'ITV was set up to compete with the BBC it would be strange if the BBC as the national and senior broadcasting organisation were in effect to withdraw from that competition in such an important area'.[33]

In 1975 the IBA and the Independent Television companies offered to forgo their right to cover the Cup Final in return for a BBC withdrawal from the England v. Scotland coverage, with a reversed arrangement the following year. The BBC rejected this but offered an alternation deal on the European Cup, which was eventually adopted.[34] Two years later the IBA tried to negotiate some form of alternation for the 1976 Olympics from Montreal. After prolonged negotiations this again was rejected by the BBC, but this time the Independent Television companies decided not to cover the Olympics, but to provide instead alternative general programming.[35]

In effect the BBC simply argued from a position of strength that it had the contracts and the dominant share of the audience so why should it forgo its position. It can be clearly seen how the 'non-exclusive ruling', intended to protect BBC from competition, had in fact greatly strengthened its position. This, combined with the introduction of BBC2, made ITV's attempts to compete with cricket or Wimbledon tennis coverage all but pointless.

The question of alternation and duplication was the main issue of sport broadcasting for the Annan Report (1977). Annan found the BBC's argument persuasive but ultimately rejected it, saying that broadcasting organisations were required to compete for the sake of, not at the expense of, the public interest, and that the competition was therefore a regulated one.[36] Annan felt it would be reasonable for the BBC to recognise ITV's wish to carry some major national sporting events without the audience having to pay the price of duplication. Consequently they made the following recommendation:

> The broadcasting authorities should not jointly televise the same event with the same pictures but should agree to share their coverage of such events. They should also reduce other instances when they cover the same event at the same time to the barest minimum, and, after holding discussions on this matter should make a public announcement of the agreement reached.
>
> (Annan 1977: 346)

However, the BBC remained reluctant to, as it saw it, let ITV win by negotiation the audience it could not win by competition. In 1978 the IBA raised the issue again, suggesting a coin-tossing to determine who should cover the next Olympics and who the World Cup. This was rejected out of hand by the BBC.[37] ITV eventually withdrew from coverage of the 1984 Olympics after a deadlocked dispute over staffing with ACTT, which diminished the chance of a future major alternation deal, and ITV began to evolve the strategy of opting out of some major event coverage, whilst securing others exclusively.

ITV's COUNTER-ATTACK

State action, in the relatively autonomous shape of the ITA, failed to secure an evenly balanced competition. During the 1970s it was no longer the ITA, but some of the companies, fuelled by a growing economic advantage over the BBC, that began pushing for more aggressive competition for sport coverage. If the IBA was the force behind ITV's bids for alternation, LWT and Thames, in the second half of the 1970s, spearheaded a move to compete more aggressively with the BBC. Like previous attempts, this had only limited success and was handicapped by tensions within Independent Television as to the best and most economic ways to win an audience. During the 1970s the changing economic conditions of broadcasting tended to favour Independent Television. In a period of rising inflation, governments committed to holding down public expenditure and an emerging recession, both organisations were under a degree of economic pressure.

The BBC felt this pressure to a greater extent. Right up till the start of the 1970s it had been economically sustained by expansion of the system. Because the number of licence holders was increasing in the 1950s and early 1960s, its revenue rose even without a licence increase. By the time saturation was reached, colour was on the way and a whole new source of revenue began to flow. But during the 1970s this increase was not enough to protect the Corporation against the rapidly rising costs of inflation and it became necessary to press for more frequent increases in the licence fee. Governments of the period were reluctant to agree to licence increases of the scale needed.

Independent Television was also hit by inflation and its costs also rose steadily. But its main source of revenue, advertising, had a greater resilience. Advertising revenue levels ensured that income kept pace with inflation. ITV's position relative to the BBC improved, the network had more money to spend on production, salaries in ITV rose faster, it could attract staff more easily, and it could bid more for coverage of events.

To some people within ITV the time seemed ripe for a counter-attack on the sporting front. Bryan Cowgill, who had risen from being the first *Grandstand* producer in 1958 to BBC Head of Sport by 1964, Head of Outside Broadcasts by 1973, and Controller of BBC1 in 1974, moved to become Managing Director of Thames in 1978. Cowgill's predecessor at Thames, Jeremy Isaacs, had been no great fan of sport, and ITV had not tried to produce a competitor to *Sportsnight* since *Cavalcade* in the 1950s. Cowgill was intent on launching a midweek sport magazine and almost his first action on moving to Thames was to appoint Sam Leitch as Head of Sport. Leitch had edited *Sportsnight* and *Match of the Day* and became BBC Head of Sport when Cowgill became BBC1 Controller.

Their plans for a midweek sport magazine met with opposition from within the ITV system. There was a feeling that a sport magazine could not win an audience as early as 9 o'clock in the evening as effectively as other types of programme. This meant resorting to a 10.30pm slot. Other Independent Television companies were reluctant to take the programme even then, except when it featured football. A bitter blow for Cowgill must

Evening News

NIGHT SPECIAL

LONDON: FRIDAY, NOVEMBER 17, 1978   8p

Court threat over £5m ITV soccer deal

BBC: WE'LL PUT THE BOOT IN

Miss World gives prize to mother

THE new Miss World, Silvana Suarez from Argentina, was full of smiles today as she started her year's reign which could earn her £20,000. And as she breakfasted on strawberries and champagne, 19-year-old Silvana announced that she will give her £5,000 prize money to her mother. "My parents are poor," she said. "So I will give my mother the money to spend on what she likes." See story and picture on Page Three.

Your best Weekend News starts on Page 19

CLIFF MORGAN, BBC's head of outside broadcasts, today attacked ITV's £5 million deal to screen League football exclusively and warned: "It looks like war."

He said: "If they want to play games and have a battle then we will have to draw up a campaign for a battle. And that's no good for anybody.

"I don't believe this matter is all over. As far as we're concerned it has just begun. This is round one."

The BBC, he said, would have to pull its sleeves up and "put the boot in."

Mr. Morgan said he was angry because ITV had broken a gentlemen's agreement that they would negotiate jointly over football coverage.

Cloak and dagger

If the deal goes through Match of the Day will finish at the end of this season.

BBC will not be able to screen any League or League Cup games. But they will still be able to show FA Cup, European and international matches.

BBC chiefs were meeting today to decide if they could take legal action against ITV for breaking the agreement on joint negotiations.

Under the LWT's offer the 92 Football League clubs will share £5 million spread over three seasons.

This compares with £420,000 a season under the present agreement.

ITV will start a new Saturday soccer show with Brian Moore from the start of next season.

Alec Weeks, BBC's executive producer of football, who started Match of the Day 14 years ago, warned that they would fight the deal all the way.

He accused ITV of playing dirty.

"We have sat around tables with them

CLIFF MORGAN
"Just round one."

Alan Hardaker, left, and John Bromley, London Weekend controller of sport, after they signed.

EVENING NEWS REPORTER

and talked of joint agreements and keeping money down.

"Now we have all this cloak and dagger business and ITV have pulled a fast one."

Weeks said: "When we put football on the screen side by side with them, 80 per cent of viewers watch BBC.

"Why? Because we're better at presenting football, at camera work, commentary — everything.

"To hell with any agreements. The Football League said in 1966 that soccer had to be shared."

Managing Director of BBC Television, Alasdair Milne said: "I was astounded because we have had a joint negotiating body for many years who deal with the League games and the arrangements thereof. The last I heard was that that joint body was happily negotiating.

Mr. Milne said there had been a great deal of cheque book buying of sporting contracts recently.

He said the reported deal for League

Football was six times the going rate.

"I would not have paid that kind of money to buy even if it had been open to me."

As ITV chiefs celebrated, John Bromley, LWT controller of sport, said the deal was "signed, sealed and delivered."

He said: "We do not regard ourselves as cheats. It is a bona fide deal genuinely negotiated.

"We have been often to the BBC and asked to talk about alternating and we have been shown the door. Now the BBC is squealing."

Slightly worried

"There was agreement to some extent with the BBC on the question of joint negotiation.

"But we were getting slightly worried when we realised that the football clubs were going to ban soccer on TV.

"I haven't had many calls from the BBC in the last 15 years saying it was going to do a deal. Why should we ring them?"

The deal was clinched after Michael Grade, LWT's director of programmes, approached Labour MP Jack Dunnett, chair-

Contd. on Page Two

TELEVISION 28-30   In Town 7   Stars 12   Letters 13   Short Story 33   City 46, 47   ENTERTAINMENT 32-35

Figure 4.2a

DAILY EXPRESS

THE VOICE OF BRITAIN

No. 24,380   Saturday November 18 1978   *Cloudy*   TV Pages 19-26   8p   ★★★

...ow they'll fight for cricket, racing, the lot...

TV WAR!

WINNERS The London Weekend team yesterday: Mike Grade (left), with Brian Moore and John Bromley

LOSERS BBC men Alec Weeks (left) and Cliff Morgan last night: "If it's war they want it's war they'll get"

THE rival teams are poised for action—ITV waving cheque-books, B.B.C. wearing red faces—but this is not sport . . . it's WAR.

For after scooping League football for its Saturday screens ITV is after exclusive rights for the rest of Soccer and racing, cricket and tennis as well.

While B.B.C. chiefs were fuming about losing "Match of the Day" their rivals were considering how to snatch all sport's once-shared prestige events.

Such as the F.A. Cup, the Derby and Grand National, Wimbledon, and Test matches — the magnets for millions of viewers.

On the Soccer scene Thames TV, with its eye on midweek, is ready to make a massive counter-bid to any attempt by B.B.C. to grab the F.A. contract — now shared and expiring next May —covering international and F.A. Cup matches.

OFFERS

F.A. secretary Ted Croker said: " Almost certainly we shall be inviting offers for all matches, with the likelihood of accepting the highest bid."

The Home Office has power to prevent the granting of exclusive rights for " national events " if one channel objects.

So ITV might insist on a share of the F.A. Cup Final—and then outbid B.B.C. for an

Sanity rules as Leyland reject strike: Page 2

ITV set for new coup as BBC fumes over deal

By David Miller and John Jones

exclusive contract on Cup rounds and internationals.

The current contract is for under £500,000 a season for all matches.

John Bromley, of London Weekend, who helped negotiate the League deal for £5 million, said : " We still have some money in the kitty."

In the wider field, Brian Cowgill, ex-B.B.C. and now ITV sports boss, said : " It is the only answer to B.B.C.'s continued intransigence in refusing reasonable ITV requests to alternate on the Olympic Games and World Cup."

While B.B.C. Director-General Ian Trethowan was claiming he needed " a decent increase in the licence fee to restore the balance with ITV, his sports executives were fuming.

" If it's war they want, it's

war they'll get," pledged Cliff Morgan, head of outside broadcasts.

" And my lads are in just the mood to do it," said Alec Weeks, the corporation's Mr Football.

Ex-Welsh Rugby International Morgan complained of the coup which will kill " Match of the Day " : " This wasn't defeat, it was deceit."

Then he said : " But we will fight back—and we've got just the buggers here to do it I'll tell you."

The B.B.C. team — and indeed most of ITV and the Football League—were kept completely in the dark about the astonishing coup set up by London Weekend's Mike Grade.

Anchor-man Brian Moore

HOW WE WON: SEE PAGE 8

sparked the idea that League clubs might play his game.

Grade made his first moves through Labour M.P. Jack Dunnett, Notts County chairman and League negotiator. A brandy at the House of Commons paved the way.

Detailed negotiations were held at the M.P.'s London flat in secret.

Then League officials and club chiefs meeting at Wembley approved the deal without knowing who was involved.

It was sealed by Mr Grade with a letter and a £1 note to legalise it.

PROTEST

Jimmy Hill, key man of B.B.C.'s " Match of the Day," coming home from a trip to Cyprus, said : "The League took advantage of a back-alley approach, but I don't blame ITV for making it."

He attacked the League's " lack of integrity " and bad example and said : " They have broken a gentleman's agreement."

Cliff Morgan also asked: " Was it fair business practice ? "

But Alec Weeks declared : " We are not downhearted— we are not beaten yet."

In that never-ending war, three B.B.C. Saturday programmes—Michael Crawford's " Some Mothers Do 'Ave 'Em," the vet's " All Creatures Great and Small," and Larry Grayson's " Generation Game "— top the week's national ratings. London Weekend's best was Friday's now-ended " Mixed Blessing " at No. 13.

TODAY: Weather Page 2 • Holidays Page 15 • Letters Page 28 • Startime Page 30 • Gardening Page 32 • Finance Pages 34, 36, 37 • Sport from Page 38

Figure 4.2b

have been the lack of support from Yorkshire, headed by his old *Grandstand* colleague Paul Fox. The proportion of sport on ITV remained fairly static, providing around 10 per cent of the total output (Potter 1990: 277).

Consequently *Midweek Sports Special* was unable to become a regular weekly magazine, appearing only when there was football or a major event to feature. The lack of a regular slot in the schedule handicapped the programme's attempts to build an audience. Cowgill's attempts to strengthen his sport department suffered a tragic and bizarre blow at the start of the 1980 Olympic year, when Sam Leitch and his deputy Paul Lang died within a week of each other. The main achievements of this offensive were the development of stronger links with gymnastics and the revamping of *Thames Sport*, shifted to Thursday night after Thames lost Friday night to LWT at the start of 1982.

THE 1980s: FROM SUMO TO SATELLITE

The introduction of Channel 4 in 1982 ushered in a new era for British television sport, stimulating growth in independent production, building an audience for American football, cycling and sumo, and fostering a fresh approach to the conventions of production (see Digance 1986 and Whannel 1988b). ITV Sport changed direction dramatically during the 1980s. *World of Sport* was dropped after 20 years, ex Sports Head John Bromley later commenting that the decision sapped the morale of the sports department.[38] Wrestling was dropped, and all racing was switched to Channel 4. The *Off the Ball* presenters, ex-footballers Ian St John and Jimmy Greaves, underwent a process of demotic sanctification, emerging as *Saint and Greavsie*. The two channels began to diverge in style. For the 1988 Seoul Olympics, in which live events were in the middle of the British night, the BBC used a large austere studio set, which rather dwarfed a lonely and chilly looking Steve Ryder. ITV and Channel 4 went for an informal and at times overcrowded living room, with so much emphasis given to the chat that the Games sometimes seemed marginal. One night the tennis final thundered on unseen for some minutes, while the panel regailed us with momentous items such as Harvey Smith's low opinion of the bacon butties.

Contracts were acquired for the exclusive rights to British athletics (1985), the Football League (1988) and the 1991 Rugby World Cup. These events, along with major boxing title fights, formed the core of ITV's sport by the end of the 1980s. In the wake of poor audience ratings for its coverage of the Seoul Olympics in 1988, ITV announced it would not be covering the Barcelona Games in 1992. Under a new 'live and exclusive' rubric, if ITV couldn't have an event all to itself (Football World Cup apart), it intended to remain aloof.

The break-up of the old cosy BBC/ITV sharing of football, prompted partly by deregulation and the rise of satellite television, was of great advantage to the football authorities, which were now able to encourage more competitive bidding. With parts of its competitions going to ITV (Football League), BBC and British Satellite Broadcasting (FA Cup and internationals), and Sky (Zenith Data Systems Trophy and Leyland Daf Cup), football was getting around £20m annually in TV fees.[39]

Satellite television arrived at the end of the 1980s, offering three channels dedicated to sport. Deregulation of broadcasting led to a scrapping of the listed events clause, triggering fears that an audience-hungry satellite channel would be able to outbid the terrestrial stations for major events.[40] These fears gained substance in 1989 when the vast bulk of the German TV audience were deprived of the sight of Wimbledon triumphs by Graf and Becker, the German rights going to a satellite and cable combine (see Boyle and Blain 1991: 2).

But in 1990 the BBC retained the rights to Wimbledon for three years, after vigorous competition, being forced to offer £9m, as against the £5m it paid for the previous five years.[41] However, the main opposition was not satellite, but ITV, which was prepared to outbid the BBC but could not satisfy Wimbledon, which chose to remain loyal to the BBC.[42] Otherwise the BBC began to lose ground. It secured a new six-year snooker contract in 1989, but failed to regain athletics, lost the Rugby World Cup and much football to ITV, and some cricket to satellite. Its current contract for major British golf events has seven years to run, until 1997, by which time the renewal of its Charter may dramatically change its financial conditions. ITV paid £3.5m for the Rugby World Cup and plans to show 26 matches live, spending another £4m on production.[43]

The satellite channels began acquiring the rights to some major sporting events, such as cricket's B & H Cup and the Bruno–Tyson fight, but a crisis was looming. Major financial problems led to a merger between the two satellite organisations, Sky and BSB; although, with Sky clearly the dominant partner, the deal became known in BSB circles as the merge-over. Sport channel Eurosport fell foul of the European Commission, which ruled that its cosy arrangement with its major supplier the European Broadcasting Union (EBU) was unfair to its competitors, and, with no buyers for Murdoch's share of Eurosport, the channel seemed doomed. The main impact of satellite so far has been a greatly increased demand for cheap programming, for more packaged sport, more cheap imports, more repeated items, and more synthetic events. ITV, too, has greatly increased its use of cheap imports – mostly of American material such as College Football and truck racing. It is still too early accurately to assess the impact of satellite TV on television sport. BSkyB has acquired exclusive rights to the next cricket World Cup in 1992, but the B & H Cup is returning to the BBC, and the Test and County Cricket Board (TCCB) turned down

BSkyB's offer for English Test Matches, apparently feeling that sponsors would prefer access to the BBC's larger audiences.

Fears of major events disappearing onto satellite channels in droves may be exaggerated. In the USA there are few major events on satellite – although some are on cable. Sponsors are likely to be hostile to cable and satellite for some time to come, since neither is yet capable of reaching the huge audiences commanded by terrestrial network television. There were just under 125,000 homes with satellite dishes by mid 1989.[44] However, as broadcasting is restructured during the 1990s, the potential revenue power of pay-per-channel and pay-per-view distribution systems could be a powerful force for change.

PROFESSIONAL IDEOLOGIES

Despite all these changes, the dominant production practices have remained surprisingly static. The professional ideology is still strongly marked by its formative phase. A key element of the professional ideology of broadcasting is, precisely, professionalism, and nowhere more so than in the Sport and Outside Broadcast departments. Descriptions of *Grandstand*, *World of Sport*, *Sportsnight* and the like invariably stress the total professionalism, dedication and teamwork involved. Indeed in these days, with little live television, these programmes are considerably more complex and demanding than most television.

This professional self-confidence is reinforced by a great belief in the superior quality of British television generally and its sport coverage in particular. BBC and ITV sport teams may be in all-out competition, but nothing unites them as much as an indulgent chuckle over the supposed inadequacies of, say, Italian football coverage.

There are three principal sets of practices in television – those related to journalism, to entertainment and to drama. The journalistic practices of news, current affairs and documentary are rooted in a reflective ideology. That is, they assert the conventions of impartiality, neutrality, balance and objectivity as guiding principles. It is on this base that their claim to authoritativeness rests. Entertainment practices, on the other hand, are rooted primarily in the principles of 'good television'; that is, in the provision of programmes to a high professional and technical standard, offering lively, exciting spectacle with personalities and stars, and appealing to a broad heterogeneous audience. The values are those of showbusiness, and it is predominately by the standards of showbusiness that success or failure is measured. Dramatic practices are built upon the conventions of the theatre and story telling. Despite great differences in the degree of cultural prestige, mainstream drama from Shakespeare to situation comedy depends in part upon audience involvement in a narrative.

If these three practices are plotted in the form of a triangle it is possible to suggest a dispersal of television's forms and genres within the triangle according to the respective importance of journalistic, dramatic and entertainment values (see Figure 4.3). While entertainment is in a broad sense a characteristic of most television, I am using it here to denote something a bit more specific – the conventions attached to that aspect of television most specifically associated with showbusiness; the production of those programme forms that television refers to as light entertainment.

Figure 4.3 Schematic diagram of practices and programme forms of popular television

Television sport can be seen as sited at the intersection of these three practices and is therefore placed at the centre of the triangle. It constitutes an interesting fusion of these three sets of conventions. While television sport has its own distinct set of production practices, the professional ideologies framing this practice are structured by the three more general practices of journalism, drama and entertainment. The ideological field produced by the intersection of these three practices has in turn had its reciprocal effects upon the practice of television sport production. This passage by Dimmock exemplifies this intersection:

> The job of the television Outside Broadcast department . . . is to bring to viewers' screens as many as possible of the interesting public and sporting events at the very moment they are taking place. It is this spontaneity which makes a television outside broadcast more exciting than either a studio item or film . . . the sense of immediacy and intense realism of an outside broadcast cannot fail to grip viewers who, although perhaps many hundreds of miles from the event itself, may find themselves clutching the side of their armchairs with almost as much excitement as if they were actually present.[45]

This early description of the OB department shows many of the elements of the ideology: the immediacy and spontaneity of 'at the very moment', the 'intense realism', and the identification of the audience, 'clutching the side of their armchairs'. Journalistic practices make their impact upon this ideology through television sport's relation to the real. Like news and current affairs, its principal relation is to a referent out in the real world. Journalism and reportage are an important element of sports coverage, and the practice of sport representation has its own set of news values. Out of this stems the emphasis upon immediacy, spontaneity and unpredictability. Indeed 'liveness', even in this age of video, remains an important element of the rhetoric of appeal offered by television sport. But the reportage aspect also ties sport coverage to the conventions of neutrality, impartiality, balance and objectivity. Sport is in this sense merely a special, ghettoised form of news.

But while sports events exist independently of television's own practices and are events in the real world, they are events of a very particular kind. They are systems of closure, coherent and autonomous sets of rule-governed activity, bounded in both space and time. It is in this sense that we could speak of sport events being structured. It can be said that these structures are narrative structures in that they pose an initial enigma – 'Who will win?' – which will be resolved by the end of the event. The principal divergence from fictional narrative is that in sport the result is not known at the start of the text and cannot simply be determined by the conventions.

The development of its own star system is the point at which television sport makes contact with entertainment practices. First, the high value placed on the professionalism necessary to produce a 'good show', a lively, exciting spectacle, is common to both. In the case of sport's major occasions, colour pictures, the presence of international competitors and teams, the beaming of pictures around the world by satellite, give the spectacle a truly global dimension.

Second, the increasing cross-penetration of the sport and showbusiness star system is a product of the convergence of the two practices. Sport stars show up on chat shows, showbusiness stars appear on Cup Final Day and all meet up on the new breed of game show. Like showbusiness, sport appears as a world of its own, segregated from the real social–political world. As such it has a strong tendency to the self-referential. Third, television sport utilises entertainment practices in that it is addressing and attempting to win and hold a broad popular audience, and must therefore be 'popular' and produce pleasure in the context of the world of television entertainment.

TECHNOLOGICAL DEVELOPMENT

Outside broadcast achievements from the start depended in part upon the development of expertise and equipment in the outside broadcast section of the engineering department. The BBC structure from 1925 to the present has kept engineering separate from programming. This had its effects on sport broadcasting. While technology was central to the development of sport broadcasting, the separation of technical and programming aspects gave technical advance an abstract scientific–progressivist character, somewhat separate from any aesthetic, social or political considerations.

It is in the light of professional ideologies that sense can be made of the relation between sport broadcasting and technology. The demands of sport coverage did act as a spur to particular kinds of technical development (e.g. action replay and slow motion, satellite communication, etc.) and major sporting events have been used as showcases for new technological innovation (e.g. the introduction of colour).

Raymond Williams (1974) has stressed the need to restore notions of 'intention' to the study of cultural practices and technologies. In this sense three strands can be seen in the introduction of new technologies in sport broadcasting. The speed and immediacy with which the event reaches the screen has been enhanced. The realism of the coverage has been heightened. Producers have acquired greater control over the material, greater ability to reconstruct it.

The origins of outside broadcasting lay in attempts to expand the range of radio and television by moving outside the studio. At first, range was limited by the inadequacy of wireless relays between OB vans and the main transmitter, and land lines had to be laid on. In 1936, the Television Advisory Committee (TAC) authorised the installation of a TV cable which ran from Alexandra Palace–Broadcasting House–Park Lane–Piccadilly–Shaftesbury Avenue–Buckingham Palace–Victoria Station. This was later extended to West Kensington, for Olympia and Earls Court. So the anticipated importance of the royal family, the theatre and arrivals at Victoria Station was structured into the possibilities of the first OBs. However, there proved to be problems with the size, cost and inflexibility of this cable and experiments were made to make the use of ordinary telephone cable possible.[46] Improvement in wireless relays began to expand the range of outside broadcasts, although, at first, areas without a line of vision to Alexandra Palace were excluded. Eventually improvements in wireless techniques and the spread of transmitters meant that, with the aid of land lines, pictures could be transmitted almost anywhere in Britain.

The next stage came with the development of the Eurovision network of permanent land lines linking much of western Europe, developed in the early 1950s (Ross 1961: 128–39). But the major breakthrough for sport coverage was the growth in satellites, which eventually led to the possibility of beaming live pictures around the world from any of the five continents.[47] Immediacy is now technically universal; given the financial will, any event can be flashed around the world.

The second strand of development grew out of the desire for greater realism, more 'true-to-lifeness'. An early breakthrough was the introduction in 1948 of the new CPS Emitron cameras, which gave a much better picture, free of smearing, and a useful degree of depth of field and focus, which was particularly valuable for OBs (Ross 1961: 75–6). In the same year, a new parabolic reflector microphone, used for reinforcing and giving better definition to sound effects, was introduced (Briggs 1979: 869). New camera suspensions were developed to reduce vibration effects on moving cameras mounted in vehicles.[48]

Early discussion of the problems of lens use on OBs pointed the way to the development of the zoom lens.[49] New mobile cameras were developed in the 1950s.[50] The BBC's roving-eye camera made it possible to track alongside horse races. The new lightweight electronic cameras of the 1960s enabled hand-held operation and led to experimentation with a whole range of 'intimate' realism such as shots of teams in the dressing room tunnels. Of course the major technical innovation in this strand was the introduction of colour in the late 1960s. Wimbledon and other major events were used to promote colour, and they still form a large part of the rhetoric of ads for television sets. An advert for Sony in the late 1980s featured John Cleese as a viewer reaching into the screen to pluck a highly realistic snooker ball from the table.

The end of the 1960s was a watershed for technical innovation as far as sport is concerned. By 1970 major advances in achieving speed and immediacy and in creating a greater 'realism' had been made. These were the developments most closely linked to the journalistic aspects of the professional ideology. From the mid 1960s emphasis swung to developments

that gave a greater ability to construct and to manipulate the basic elements – in particular the increased sophistication of video devices. These
developments were more closely associated with the impulses towards
entertainment and the dramatic within professional practice.

Earlier progress had been spasmodic. The multi-source technique of
programmes like *Sportsview* and *Grandstand*, now taken for granted, was
at the time innovatory.[51] The development of telerecording in the early
1950s, closely associated with the OB department, made recorded highlight programmes possible for the first time.[52] Video recording only
became available at the end of the 1950s. Even then editing was both
primitive and expensive (in terms of machine time). The major developments began in the mid 1960s with the development of action replay,
closely followed by slow motion replays.[53] These devices in themselves
transformed the formal structure of sport coverage, boosting the visual
appeal of preview and post-mortem panel discussions as well as the coverage of the event. The 1970s saw a rapid increase in the use of electronic
devices to control the image. The development of caption generators
linked to computers increased the speed with which information could be
flashed onto the screen but also increased the range of this information.
Quantel devices gave a much greater facility for split and multiple screen
techniques.

Developments in digital electronics allowed an even greater degree of
restructuring. A new video amplifier used by NBC for Wimbledon coverage makes it possible to select tighter framing on an already recorded shot.
NBC was getting its pictures from the BBC, and had an additional four
cameras of its own, but with the digital device it could select tighter
framing where required, giving its coverage more 'pizzazz' (to borrow a
technical term from US television). An NBC producer commented that
this enabled them to 'play around, get rid' of the bad stuff and make the
good a little better'.[54] It is noteworthy that the BBC is often quite cautious
with new technology. The chalkboard, a device for illustrating points by
drawing on a still image, has been technically feasible, and common in the
USA, since the late 1960s, but only recently, and rarely, is it seen on
British television. The BBC spent some time and money during the 1980s
on a device called teletrack, which by selectively sampling images, can
show the path of a ball in, say, tennis, football or snooker; but the device
has rarely been used. Anyone who has spooled through a video on fast
wind knows that this can reveal patterns of play in football or boxing, but I
have never seen this technique used.

The technology involved in the major world events has made television
sport global, but is also giving each national television network a greater
ability to restructure the material for its own needs, thus avoiding the
problems caused for the entertainment impulse by the 'neutral' style of
'originated' pictures from major events. For instance, among equipment

supplied by Thomson CSF for the Moscow Olympics was a switching grid with 159 incoming signals and 288 outgoing video and sound channels. Using a selection of these output signals, each producer was able to construct his own programme. Thomson also supplied 100 colour cameras, 275 monitors, 39 16mm cameras, 21 character generators and 40 mobile microwave relays. Ampex was to supply $7 million worth of video tape recorders, and slow motion machines (40 altogether) and tape.[55]

So far I have talked of the influence of the three practices, journalism, drama and entertainment, as if they gave rise to a simple homogeneous professional ideology. This of course is not the case. Tensions and contradictions can be seen within the production practices of television sport. These tensions can be seen as a result of the conflicts between different inflections of the professional ideology – to journalistic, dramatic or entertainment poles. Decisions have to be made, for example before football highlights, whether or not to announce the final score. Journalistic practice emphasises immediacy, conveying the news as soon as possible, and would be inclined to give the score. Dramatic practices emphasise the importance of narrative and the need of the audience not to know the result until the end.

The values of immediacy within journalism could be seen as encouraging live transmission, but this may conflict with the needs of entertainment. The use of video to produce edited highlights complete with split screens, replays and captions may enhance entertainment, but mark a move away from purer, more journalistic forms of realism. Dramatic practices might favour showing the whole of an event like snooker, whereas entertainment practices might suggest a more mixed package with interviews, previews and post-mortems, and joke items as well as highlights from the match. The respective influences of these practices upon the professional ideologies of television sport can be seen to change historically, and can also be seen to structure different broadcasting organisations' programmes in different ways (see Cantelon and Gruneau 1988, and Gruneau 1989).

Chapter 5

Made for television: sponsorship and the rise of the sports agent

In the 1960s an unholy alliance was developing. Sport was helping to make television and television was helping to make sport.

(Mark McCormack 1984: 165)

What rowing needs even more than the drawing power of TV coverage, is a personality. We've not got a Georgie Best and that's part of the trouble when you seek sponsors. Nothing sells like success and had we won even a bronze medal at last year's Olympics it would have been a lot easier now.

(Michael Stamford, Amateur Rowing Association, 1973)

In the last 20 years television and sponsorship have had a transforming effect on British sport. This transformation cannot be clearly understood without briefly examining the process of formation of the institutions of British sport. These institutions, at the end of the 1950s, were still recognisable products of the last quarter of the nineteenth century, the period in which many national governing bodies were established.

During the first half of the nineteenth century, while rural recreations continued to decline and urban leisure for the working class was severely restricted by the lack of time and space, the social basis for bourgeois hegemony in the sporting field was laid (see Malcolmson 1973, Cunningham 1980, J.E. Hargreaves 1986). From the 1840s the public schools began to place an increasing emphasis upon sport, producing a generation of muscular Christians who went on to spread the cult of athleticism into the universities of Oxford and Cambridge, and into the community through the network of Church activities (see Mangan 1981).

The rapid growth in rail transport from the 1840s meant that for the first time nationally codified rules became essential. This in turn required the establishment of governing bodies, and it was the men of the Victorian bourgeoisie whose social authority was such that they were able to dominate these bodies. It is no accident that the amateur/professional division was to be such a prominent feature of these governing bodies, because it was intended precisely to restrict and marginalise the presence of the working class (see Whannel 1983a).

This becomes clear when one compares the governing bodies established in the last quarter of the nineteenth century with those established earlier. Between 1875 and 1900 the Amateur Athletic Association (AAA), the Amateur Swimming Association (ASA), the All-England Lawn Tennis Club (AELTC) and the Rugby Football Union (RFU) all outlawed the professional, while the Football Association, unlike the RFU, had shrewdly chosen to compromise, allowing limited professionalism in the Football League and thus preventing a breakaway and remaining in overall control. In each case, though, these attempts to draw a sharp line between amateur and professional were at root a form of Victorian class distinction.

By contrast the governing bodies of racing (the Jockey Club), cricket (the MCC) and golf (the Royal and Ancient) were formed in the eighteenth century, in the context of aristocratic patronage. This class was more secure of its place and did not have the concern of the Victorian bourgeoisie to mark its place in the social hierarchy by excluding the lower orders. In these eighteenth-century governing bodies there were not the same rigid distinctions between amateur and professional; professionalism was accommodated, but kept in its place. It should be noted, though, that these sports too were transformed during the last quarter of the nineteenth century.

The governance of English sports was firmly in the hands of the male bourgeoisie, who were to continue to exercise their hegemony over sport for the first half of the twentieth century too. But the seeds of the contradiction between this traditional amateur paternal benevolence and the entrepreneurial entertainment-oriented form of sport organisation were already being planted. Large-scale professionalised spectator sport began to develop. New national competitions like the Football League and cricket's County Championship emerged (see Brookes 1978, Mason 1980, Walvin 1972). New stadia were built, promoters began to flourish, and the popular interest in sport was fuelled by the growth of the national popular press.

The last 20 years have seen a similar period of transformation which amounts to a re-making of British sport. The growth of television and sponsorship has constituted an economic force that has in turn generated a cultural transformation in an uneven and contradictory process that has affected different sports in different ways. The contradiction between the amateur and the entrepreneurial has been heightened dramatically as outside entrepreneurial forces have challenged the hegemony of the traditional authorities.

CRISES IN THE 1950s AND CHANGES IN THE 1960s

British sport after the Second World War and into the 1950s was particularly vulnerable to the pressures leading to a redefinition and transformation. Most sports, dominated by traditionalist, amateur paternalist voluntary administration, were slow to see or exploit commercial potential and in many cases had a marked resistance to the world of commerce. They were also slow to respond to the effects of an expanding leisure market in creating greater competition, which was to have a depressant effect on many sports.

Athletics and cricket began to suffer serious declines in crowds during this period, as did football. In 1955 ten days of athletics drew 290,000 to the White City, but by 1961 this was down to 160,000, and this was only the start of a decline that took crowds at some meetings down to the hundreds (Abrahams 1961a,b). The 1959 AAA Championship was watched by one of the smallest crowds for years and the AAA had a £6000 deficit. The next two years saw a slight improvement but in 1962 the crowds were the lowest since the war and there was little improvement for the next four years. By 1967 the Annual Report saw bankruptcy as a very real threat. In 1969 the Saturday attendance of 8000 at the AAA Championships was the lowest since before the First World War (Lovesey 1979).

Cricket too was suffering. The total gate at the County Championship games slumped from 2,126,000 in 1949 to 750,000 in 1965. A 1956 Political and Economic Planning (PEP) report into the cricket industry said cricket could not survive on its gate revenue alone. Many counties were heading for bankruptcy and secretaries were finding it harder than ever to attract enough money from private benefactors. The traditional structure of the game was close to collapse (Brookes 1978: 155). Football, because of its large following, had generally had greater financial security than many sports, but its crowds too were falling. Annual Football League gates dropped from a post-war boom peak of 41.2 million in 1948–9 to 28.6 million in 1960–1.

It is true that the return of servicemen after the war, and re-opening of public entertainments like football contributed to unusually high crowds in the 1940s. But during the 1950s, sport and other traditional communal forms of entertainment such as the cinema, the dance hall and the pub all declined in popularity. They were increasingly challenged by new family and domestic-centred leisure activities based on the car, the television, the record player and home improvement.

The old amateur/professional distinction was beginning to break down under the weight of its own contradictions. An impoverished institutional administrative structure was committed to a distributive role, fostering a broad base for sport, but lacking the resources to support it. While British spectator sport was losing appeal, top-level sport on television was highly popular, sport was becoming more international and top-level sports stars, even if amateur, could expect significant earnings, above or below the counter.

Many sports underwent significant changes as the elite level of sport began to be restructured by economic forces. The danger of top tennis players and athletes being tempted into professional sport and of top footballers being tempted to go abroad led to a reworking of the old amateur–professional divisions. Cricket abolished the old distinction between gentlemen (amateurs) and players (professionals) in 1962. Tennis abandoned its amateur-only rules to go open in 1967. Athletics remained amateur but the pressures that led to the changes in amateur status rules in 1981 and 1982 were already beginning to develop. Football abolished the maximum wage in 1960. Meanwhile television sport was on the threshold of a period of development and expansion, and sponsorship, up till the 1960s a relatively small-scale phenomenon, was entering a period of rapid expansion.

In a whole series of sports the power and authority of traditional sport organisations was to be challenged and threatened by entrepreneurial interests. The traditional organisations were characterised by under-capitalisation, voluntary management and an amateur paternal–benevolent ideology. The new entrepreneurs operated with market-place economic principles and the ideology of showbusiness and the rapidly growing leisure industry. The possibilities opened up by television, sponsorship and a world-wide star system formed the basis of the emergent power of the new entrepreneurs. They were able to win the allegiance of top stars by offering them the opportunity to maximise earnings that the traditional authorities could not provide.

The contradiction between traditional authority and new entrepreneurship developed in different forms in different sports. Some, like Rugby Union, fought a rearguard action against commercialisation for much of the 1960s and 1970s. Some, like golf, became dominated by the new entrepreneurial forces. In many others, such as athletics, tennis, football and cricket, there was a prolonged period of negotiation, contestation and manoeuvre, resulting in a series of unstable equilibria between tradition and modernity.

THE SPONSORSHIP EXPLOSION

Although sport sponsorship goes back at least to 1861, when Spiers and Pond underwrote the cost of a cricket tour, if not to the Ancient Greeks, it was not a phenomenon of any great significance until the mid 1960s. In 1957 the only sponsored event on television was the Whitbread Gold Cup (Wilson 1988: 157). Two factors were of particular importance in the emergence of sport sponsorship as a major force: the development of television sport in the 1950s and 1960s; and the banning of cigarette advertising on television in 1965.

In 1950 there were just 340,000 televisions – 2 per cent of British households. By 1954 there were over 3 million. The launch of ITV in 1955 gave a further boost and by 1960 82 per cent of the population had access to television (Paulu 1961). The launch of BBC2 in 1964 led to an increase in the amount (although not the percentage) of sport on TV, gave the BBC the means to increase the range of sports and provided space for Sunday cricket and extended coverage of cricket, tennis and golf (Bough 1980: 118–35).

Just as the growth of jet travel in the 1960s was making sport more international, so the spread of communication satellites gave television live access to international events around the world. Telstar, launched in 1962, bridged the Atlantic, in 1964 the Tokyo Olympics were broadcast live to 39 countries, and the 1968 Olympics were the first to be seen in colour in Britain. Technological advances in video editing, slow motion action replay, and high-quality colour gave a great boost to the spectacle of existing televised sports and led to the successful promotion of new ones – most notably snooker.

Meanwhile, in 1965, the government had banned the advertising of cigarettes on television. While not all sponsorship was from cigarette firms, it was firms like Rothmans, John Player and Benson and Hedges that led the way. Sport sponsorship in Britain grew from less than £1m in 1966 to £2.5m in 1970, and this was only the beginning. By 1976 it was £16m, by 1980 around £46m, and by 1983 it was thought to be topping £100m (Howell 1983: 9–10) (see Figure 5.1). In 1989 sponsorship was estimated at £200–275m, but there is no easy way of assessing support spending, which can amount to as much again. Tony Moore of the Institute of Sport Sponsorship affirms that sponsorship is television-driven to a large degree.[1] The British figure represents around 10 per cent of the world total although, in the era of the globalisation of culture, separation of these figures along national lines is increasingly fraught with methodological problems.

Early sponsorships were somewhat arbitrary and established on the whim of top executives, while advertising departments were unenthusiastic. For example, Gallaher promoted golf because one of the directors liked the sport. It put up British golf's first tented village and its first grandstands and later became the first golf sponsor to pay a four-figure sum (Wilson 1988: 159). Only gradually did they become part of a comprehensive promotional strategy.

In the early 1970s one-third of all sponsorship came from tobacco companies, and by 1986 five of the top six events (measured by amount of TV hours) were tobacco sponsored. Despite a voluntary code of conduct, in which the tobacco industry undertook not to spend more in real terms

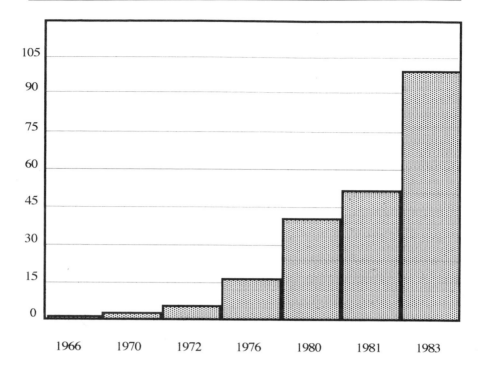

Figure 5.1 Estimates of sport sponsorship in the United Kingdom 1966–83 (showing money paid by companies to sponsor British sport in £ millions).

than it had in 1976, 16 per cent of all TV sport was still tobacco sponsored. Since this date restrictions have been tightened and British television will now not allow any new tobacco-sponsored events (Wilson 1988: 163–71, and see also Chapman 1986, Taylor 1986).

As sponsorship proved its worth as a device for marketing and for establishing a corporate image, tobacco and alcohol sponsors were joined in increasing numbers by financial institutions, in particular Cornhill with their highly successful sponsorship of Test cricket. Sponsorship is sometimes portrayed as a new form of patronage, which to a certain extent it is. But it is also firmly driven by entrepreneurial interest. A 1977 survey by the Cranfield School of Management found that 'There is very little evidence to support the view that sponsorship is an altruistic activity'.[2] Sponsorship was being adopted for pragmatic and commercial reasons and the main three criteria were: the ability of a sport to attract media coverage; a link between the sponsor and sponsored regarding the product, the product image or the corporate image; and the demographic profile of participants or spectators of the activity. The report pointed out that 'media coverage may not be of the over-riding significance which it is believed to be. If all coverage by TV, radio and press were to be stopped only 12% of respondents indicate that they would definitely not continue to sponsor'.[3] Although the respondents may indeed have claimed this, there was extensive evidence to point to the vital importance of television coverage in attracting sponsors.

In 1970 a Benson and Hedges memo had established criteria for sponsorships. They intended to sponsor only major activities, with national coverage on television and in other media guaranteed. Title sponsorship was essential, there should be no sharing of sponsorship with others, and the audience profile should be right (Wilson 1988: 160–1). Sales figures are a notoriously unreliable guide to the success of a sponsorship, and audience awareness research can tell a more significant tale. In 1981, when Cornhill's banners at Test Match cricket appeared 7459 times on television, the awareness level (the number of people who mentioned Cornhill when asked to name all the insurance firms they could remember) shot up to 17 per cent compared with 2 per cent in 1977.[4]

Of the top ten sponsored sports in 1982, all were amongst the top eleven most televised sports the previous year.[5] Rugby Union, with its continued resistance to sponsorship, was the only heavily televised sport not to appear in the list of ten most sponsored sports. Over 70 per cent of the time devoted to sport on television in 1981 went to just six sports – horse racing, football, cricket, tennis, snooker and golf. These six, with motor sport, made up the top seven most sponsored sports. That television coverage was attracting sponsorship could hardly have been clearer.

Sport in Britain has always depended on a balance of state, commercial and voluntary support (see Collins and Jones 1990). But from the mid 1960s, the commercial sector has become of dramatically greater significance (Gratton and Taylor 1986, 1987). The process has been highlighted by the relative decline in the role of the state in the 1980s (see Collins 1990). As most public finance of sport is dispensed at local level, the influence of the national state has been primarily strategic rather than economic (see Evans 1974, Coghlan 1990, Macfarlane 1986 and Howell 1990).

The rise of entrepreneurship produced problems for both BBC and ITV, as sponsors were basically obtaining television advertising by the back door. The BBC waged a long battle against 'heart of the action' advertising (trade names on athletes), which became increasingly hypocritical as it made concessions to powerful sports like football, whilst continuing to take a firmer line with more minor sports. The ITA attempted to invoke three criteria for assessing sponsored events, asking:

1 Would the event have taken place anyway?
2 Did it already command wide public interest?
3 Did it include an unacceptable level of publicity?

Jeremy Potter (1989: 109) says that in many cases none of these questions could be answered with an unequivocal yes or no, and at times the rulings of the broadcasting authorities appeared self-contradictory.

SUPERSTARS AND FRINGE BENEFITS

From the mid 1960s entrepreneurship became increasingly central to sport, and the forms it took constituted a challenge to the entrenched power of the traditional authorities. There are three main forms in which this entrepreneurship grew: first, the emergence of agents acting for star individuals; second, the emergence of agents acting for, and dealing with, governing bodies; and third, the emergence of maverick individuals whose actions constituted a direct challenge to the authority of the governing bodies. None of this would have happened in so dramatic a form without television.

One major effect of the growth of televised sport has been the heightened visibility of star performers and the consequent boost to their access to fringe benefits. England footballer Kevin Keegan was reported to have earned well over £250,000 in 1978, only half of which came directly from football. The rest came from media fees, endorsements and promotion deals. He had, at various times, contracts with Nabisco, Lyons Maid, Mitre Footballs, Arthur Barker publishers, British Export Fashions, Patrick UK (boots), Fabergé (Brut), Harry Fenton suits, BBC, LWT and Heinz Beans. He had three companies – Kevin Keegan Investments, Kevin Keegan Enterprises and Kevin Keegan Sports and Leisure – registered in the Isle of Man where the tax was 21 per cent.[6]

In the late 1970s Bjorn Borg's promotional contracts brought him $50,000 a year to wear Tuborg headbands, $25,000 to wear a shoulder patch for Scandinavian Airlines, $200,000 for wearing Fila clothes, $50,000 for wearing Tretorn shoes, $20,000 for using VS gut, $100,000 for his US racket and about $100,000 for a different European racket (Kramer 1979: 271). By the 1980s these earnings were easily available even to those in supposedly amateur sports. In 1980, US marathon runner Bill Rodgers made between $200,000 and $250,000 selling his own brand of shoes and clothes, speaking, writing, giving clinics and from three Bill Rodgers Running Center shops in Boston.[7]

Sebastian Coe has had deals with C&A, Nike, ICI, Blue Arrow and Diadora. He was the first British athlete to do a TV ad while still competing (Horlicks) and the first fee he ever received off the track was for a speech to the senior management of Hambros (Wilson 1988: 62). The Diadora contract was worth £110,000 per year, while Blue Arrow used to pay him £150,000 a year for 15 days. Daley Thompson's contracts with Epson, Fabergé, Adidas and Lucozade could have been worth even more than Coe's. Cram, the only other British athlete in this league, was getting

£12,000 per race at one stage, plus £50,000 from Kellogg's and £50,000 from Nike (Aris 1990: 111–13).

In 1986 tennis stars Ivan Lendl and Martina Navratilova each made over £1m, and top American baseball and basketball stars were also in the £1m a year category, soon to be joined by golfers and American footballers. The really big money was in the major television sports in North America – deprived of this outlet, footballer Diego Maradona had to scrape by on a mere half million, whilst cricketer Ian Botham at the peak of his fame was down at the poverty line with a paltry £30,000 directly from county cricket, although this probably was more than doubled by Test earnings, sponsorship and other deals. Steve Davis was by far the best rewarded British sport star with somewhat over £300,000, but now Nigel Mansell has been able to benefit from his prominence in the heavily sponsored global television sport of Grand Prix motor racing to leap into the millionaire class.

By the 1980s top sport stars expected to make the majority of their money from ancillary sources. Of the $1.5m Nick Faldo made in 1988, only $350,000 came from prize money, another $400,000 was in appearance fees, and the rest came from sponsorship, advertising and promotional work (Aris 1990: 39). Only one-tenth of Boris Becker's multi-million dollar tennis income comes directly from playing (Wilson 1988: 55). Not surprisingly, playing competitive sport doesn't necessarily remain the overriding first priority in all circumstances. Bjorn Borg gradually dropped out when he found there was more money for less sweat on the exhibition circuit. Ian Botham was allowed to miss the first half of the 1991–2 New Zealand winter tour in order to do A Question of Sport and a Christmas pantomime.

THE RISE OF THE SPORTS AGENT

Along with the increased prominence of television sport, emergence of international stars and growth of sponsorship came the growing power of a new role, the sports agent, a middle man who handled economic relations between individual sport stars, sport organisations, promoters, sponsors, advertisers and television companies. Such agents have become a major and powerful new feature of world sport. As they often seem able to obtain commission from more than one of the parties to an agreement, it is sometimes hard to see in whose interest they are acting.

In the 1950s Jack Kramer's professional tennis circuit was increasingly successful in luring top tennis stars away from the amateur game. In the 1960s Mark McCormack laid the foundations of a massive sporting empire by representing the business interests of three top golfers. In the 1970s West Nally brought a new level of capitalist rationalisation in its handling of sponsorship promotion and advertising contracts for international governing bodies like the Federation of International Football Associations (FIFA) and the International Amateur Athletic Federation (IAAF). Like

Kramer before him, Kerry Packer challenged the authority of a governing body, in this case cricket, by launching an alternative Test series. (Packer, however, had no interest in running cricket, but merely wanted to clinch the television rights. He did.)

In the 1980s Adidas boss Horst Dassler entered the game with his ISL (International Sport and Leisure). Its powerful position is best expressed by a throwaway line favoured by its executives: 'We're a small company. Really, we only have three clients: the Olympic Games, the World Cup and the World Athletics Championships.' The 1980s have seen the increasing success of challenges from outside sport organisation, entrepreneurs like Peter Ueberroth and Barry Hearn not simply coming to dominate, respectively, the 1984 Olympic Games and snooker, but becoming fêted as commercial heroes as well. The process is best charted by tracing the growth of the Mark McCormack empire.

Stephen Aris rightly asserts that McCormack, more than anyone, shaped modern sportsbiz and says that 'It was he who first realised that within the golden triangle of sport sponsorship and television lay vast wealth just waiting to be tapped' (Aris 1990: 9) . McCormack first came to prominence as the agent of the three golfers who dominated the game during the 1960s, Arnold Palmer, Gary Player and Jack Nicklaus. He signed Palmer in 1960, his second client was Gary Player, and the third Jack Nicklaus, signed when still an amateur. These three dominated the next two decades of golf. By 1969 they had won 20 of the major championships. From 1960 the American Masters was won successively by Palmer, Player, Palmer, Nicklaus, Palmer, Nicklaus, Nicklaus. In 1959 Palmer was earning $59,000 but in just two years McCormack increased this to more than $500,000 (Aris 1990: 18). Starting with these three was a lucky break and the foundation of McCormack's empire and his umbrella company, the International Management Group (IMG). By 1966, McCormack judged, 'we were organised, we had the right people in place and we knew where we were going. I thought we had better diversify' (McCormack 1984: 163). He went on to represent, among others, Jackie Stewart, Chris Evert, Jean-Claude Killy, Billy Jean King, Michael Parkinson, Peter Alliss, Muhammad Ali, Angela Rippon and, in perhaps the ultimate triumph for diversification, the Pope. He is rumoured to take an average of 25 per cent, sometimes more, in commission.

McCormack became a pioneer in the field of made-for-TV events and set up a subsidiary, TWI (Trans World International). McCormack had already sold a show, *The Big Three Play Britain*, featuring Palmer, Nicklaus and Player, to the BBC. TWI followed this with *International Golf*, which ran for years. TWI was to develop the made-for-TV event with increasing sophistication. It set up the Legends men and women's tennis tours, the world championship of women's golf, the Pepsi Grand Slam and the World Triathlon Championship.

After acquiring a dominant position in golf by the early 1970s, IMG rapidly expanded its operation into tennis. According to Jack Kramer, apart from Connors and Evert, virtually all the top talent in tennis was controlled by Donald Dell or Mark McCormack (Kramer 1979: 273). By the mid 1980s IMG management consulting and marketing was operating out of 15 offices around the world. It controlled 12 companies whose work ranged from creating and implementing sports events for over 100 corporations to operating fashion modelling agencies out of New York and London. In 1983 gross revenues exceeded $200m (McCormack 1984: 161).

McCormack now claimed that TWI was the world's leading independent producer of sports programming and the world's largest representative of television rights to international sporting events. It produced or co-produced nearly 200 hours of sports programming each year, including the Superstars and Battle of the Network Stars for ABC, numerous skiing, track and field events for CBS, the World Professional Figure Skating championships and the Chevrolet World Championship of Women's Golf for NBC. It represented international television rights for Wimbledon, the US Tennis Open, the National Football League, the National Basketball Association and most of the major golf championships. Another IMG subsidiary, Merchandising Consultants International (MCI), advised major corporations on sponsorship and marketing deals. It had more than 100 corporations on its roster. McCormack is quite clear about the importance of star personalities and says that, if he were forced to repeat IMG's initial success today, he would have to wait for the right combination of factors: an emerging new participant sport, with seeming whirlwind growth potential, and 'a superstar who embodied the essence of that sport' (McCormack 1984: 237). McCormack is aware of his power to influence the direction that sport takes but claims that he doesn't interfere:

> In a sport such as tennis where we represent many of its corporate sponsors, all merchandising and TV rights to Wimbledon, the television rights to the US Open, fifteen of the top twenty men and women players and run numerous events and series of events, I have no doubt, if we wanted to, we could make an impact on the way the sport is structured and the way it is governed. This would be very short sighted.
>
> (McCormack 1984: 172)

In the context of such accumulated power it is hard to take McCormack's claim of non-involvement with the policy of sport organisations seriously. In fact McCormack's organisations have acquired a significant power to define the cultural nature of sports such as tennis and golf. One effect of this growth in importance of entrepreneurship was that sport organisations increasingly came to identify sponsorship as crucial to survival. It was believed that television coverage was essential to attract the more lucrative sponsorship deals, so sports increasingly emphasised the need for coverage. Television's own practices, then, became particularly important. Sports were more eager than ever to ensure that they could provide what the television professionals wanted.

SPORT MADE FOR TELEVISION

By the early 1960s it was already clear that the power of television was sufficient to get sports to organise their programmes to suit the needs of the broadcasters. Athletics events were timed to slot into *Grandstand*'s schedule and horse races were routinely timed with television in mind.[8] The practice was not universal, however. Sports authorities often resented television's demands, which could cause friction on the ground.[9] However, during the 1960s the power of television actually began to produce noticeable and at times dramatic changes in the presentation, organisation, finance, competitive structure and even sometimes the rules of major sport. A similar process was under way in the USA, as Parente (1977) has described.

By the 1970s, television professionals had become increasingly prepared to spell out to the world of sport what it was they wanted.[10] Speaking to the Central Council for Physical Recreation (CCPR) in 1975, LWT Head of Sport John Bromley cited four basic conditions for good television sport: the sport must have simple rules and be easily understood; it must be visual; it must be possible to televise without involving too much extra work and expense, i.e. it must be practical to televise it; and the event must be capable of drawing a reasonable crowd at the venue.[11] The following year, ITV's Tony Preston and Tony McCarthy, addressing a CCPR seminar, listed five criteria for a good television sport:

1 It should be played where people can see what is happening, i.e. the event does not range over large areas so as to make the filming of the action difficult.
2 People must be able to understand what is going on, so the sport must have simple rules.
3 The sport must fit into a reasonable time scale.
4 People must be interested in the sport and be prepared to go along and watch the game. It was not a good idea to film an event being watched by only a few people as this created a bad impression.
5 An element of skill should be present in the game as this created good television.[12]

As well as having a clear idea about what it wanted from sport, television also, by and large, got it cheap. The occasional headlines about multi-million pound deals created a false impression. The high fees paid for two or three major sports had to be set against the large number of hours devoted annually to television sport. It is hard to put an exact cost-per-hour on television sport – it could be somewhere between £40,000 and £60,000. The companies have always been quite secretive about detailed figures, and all have their own ways of dividing their accounts into direct and indirect costs. Figures from the Broadcast Research Unit in 1983 suggested £60,000 per hour for ITV and only £20,000 for the BBC, which has the advantage of being able to defray rights costs and production expenses over a greater quantity of hours (Clarke 1987). Channel 4's cost per hour in 1986/87 was just over £16,000, a figure kept low by the use of cheap purchased material (Whannel 1988b). This makes sport, along with game shows and some studio-based current affairs, the cheapest form of television. By comparison, series drama can cost well over £250,000 per hour. These figures need to be treated with some caution, as Barnett argues (1990). Within the average there are considerable extremes, according to type of programme, type of sport, slot in the schedule and projected audience. However, in general sport does provide a cheap form of television, and television, whilst paying huge amounts for some major events, has always got much of its sport very cheaply.

Indeed, while athletics and football could push for big fees, most minor sports were forced to compete with each other for the attentions of television, which, in a buyer's market, could afford to play them off against each other. At the 1976 CCPR Conference, Alan Hart, Head of BBC Sport, took a tough line over fees: 'An event which might cost £200 to buy and another £4,000 to televise for a good but hardly world shattering 15 minutes was expensive by any standards'.[13] In fact television at £16,000 an hour was fairly cheap, even in the 1970s, and the amount actually paid to the sport was pitifully low. One theme of this conference was the merit of two or three minority sports combining in one venue over 48 hours in order to fit the needs of television. The financial value of series like *Top Table* and *Jack High* (bowls) to television was that enough material for seven programmes could be recorded in 48 hours. Each of these series cost only twice as much as a single 30 minute slot of the same sport on *Grandstand*. The lure of sponsorship was often enough to encourage minor sports to accept low fees from television.

TRANSFORMATION IN SPORT

The importance of television coverage resulted in a whole series of transformations as sports tried to ensure that their events were presented in forms suitable for television. One-day cricket was perhaps the most dramatic example. As a response to the financial crisis developing in the 1950s, the MCC was making cautious moves towards sponsorship and investigating the possibility of a one-day knockout cup. The following year a Midlands experiment, inspired by Leicestershire and televised by ATV, proved one-day limited overs competition to be practical. Meanwhile

American company Gillette, faced with competition from the new Wilkinson Sword blade, was looking for a truly English activity to help its image. By 1963 cautious overtures had led to Gillette providing a trophy and £6500 for the Gillette Cup – a small beginning for a cricket revolution.

Meanwhile the interests of television, professional cricketers and tobacco companies were about to combine in a dramatic fashion. Bryan Cowgill of the BBC wanted a regular cricket series, but one that could be televised start to finish and that would attract a new cricketing audience by offering a beginning, a middle and an end, but above all a definite result. He wanted a format that 'would encourage the players to be aggressive in their approach, where the hitting of sixes would bring rewards, where the scoring of the series' fastest fifty and the taking of wickets by bowlers rather than merely containing the run rate would put money in their pockets' (Bough 1980: 19). Rothmans, anxious to retain a television visibility after the cigarette advertising ban, agreed to sponsor a series of televised Sunday cricket featuring the Rothman International Cavaliers. The experiment was so successful, both in providing cheap Sunday afternoon programming for BBC2 and in pulling in crowds to cricket, that, after a 1967 match staggered the MCC by attracting 15,000 to Lords, the counties stepped in and set up their own Sunday League, sponsored by John Player. By 1972 West Nally had set up a third one-day competition sponsored by Benson and Hedges (see Ross 1972, 1981, Laker 1977, Bose 1983, B. Willis 1981). It is worth noting that in cricket a fair proportion of revenue is still used, in distributive fashion, to sustain an otherwise economically weak base – most of the £10m annual sponsorship and TV income being used to support the county game (Aris 1990: x).

The BBC, and Bryan Cowgill, also took a leading role in the introduction of open tennis. By the 1960s both Wimbledon and the BBC were becoming unhappy at the constant disappearance of top players into the professional circuits. Cowgill suggested an eight-man trial professional event to be staged at Wimbledon in August 1967. The BBC provided $35,000 for the singles, and Wimbledon contributed $10,000 for the doubles. Once Herman David and Wimbledon became converted to the cause of open tennis, the rest of the tennis world rapidly followed suit and by 1968 tennis became open to professionals (Kramer 1979: 259).

Football had a degree of resistance to the forces transforming British sport since the 1960s. Its substantial revenue from spectators, and status as the major national sport, gave it a greater negotiating power with television. The Football League resisted live football until 1983 and placed restrictions preventing any recorded football material being televised on Saturday afternoons. During the 1970s, however, rising costs, escalating transfer fees and wage bills and declining gates put pressure on the game, while the growing potential of sponsorship became irresistible.

The Football League finally agreed to live football in 1983, in exchange for which television allowed shirt advertisements – thus greatly increasing the sponsorship potential of major clubs. This turned out to be the first step towards the current situation, with the Football League locked into a conflict between the interests of the elite clubs, demanding a breakaway Premier League which would give them a higher share of television and sponsorship revenue, and the lower division clubs, fighting a rearguard action to retain the Football League's distributive function, maintaining full-time football throughout the country (see Redhead 1986, Wagg 1984, Walvin 1986).

Clearly there are many sports whose popularity is largely due to television exposure. Television made show jumping a popular sport in the 1950s and 1960s, and did the same for snooker and darts in the 1970s and 1980s. Increasingly sports are prepared to devise made-for-TV events or contemplate changes in the rules, timing, presentation or form of events.

When Channel 4 chose to feature basketball, the sport was full of enthusiasm. The staging was noticeably aimed at the camera – with individual introductions and microphones to catch the coaches' briefings. But things soon turned sour. Over-enthusiasm by clubs led to overspending on imported American stars, causing a cash crisis when overnight success refused to come.[14] Sponsors had unrealistic expectations of the publicity value to be obtained and quarrelled with Channel 4, which refused to allow them to attach their own name to the team name. Some owners mimicked football club chairmen in using teams to project their own egos. Meanwhile, after a promising start, audiences fell away, and the clubs began to bicker over the format and organisation of the game. David Last, founder of leading club Crystal Palace, said, 'The amateurs who run the game didn't decide whether it was a TV entertainment, a spectator sport or a participant game'.[15]

Many of the proliferating snooker tournaments featured shorter matches than most professionals regarded as a fair test of skill. There were also allegations that the angle of entry to pockets had been altered to increase the chance of high breaks, to please the television audience. The Kellogg's round-the-city cycling on Channel 4 introduced a whole new mode of racing to Britain as a way of meeting television's requirements (see Digance 1986). Ice skating decided to remove the rarely televised compulsory figures from the skating programme.[16] Advocates of the change felt it would allow more time for free-skating and streamline the whole package for TV.[17] A breakaway attempt to form World Championship Squash, with revolutionary rule changes and a multicoloured transparent-sided court, was largely inspired by hopes of TV exposure.[18] The introduction of new rules and a see-through court did result in some television coverage, but it is still not a good TV sport – it is too fast. Traditional archery competitions involve a competitor shooting 144 arrows, but in 1990, 'in order to attract a family audience and make it more suitable for television', the Grand National Archery Society planned to introduce new competitions involving shoot-offs of only 15 arrows.[19] Billiards devised a new format for Channel 4 involving the best of three short games, but never looked like dislodging snooker in the hearts of the audience.[20]

Of course change is not necessarily a bad thing. To attract television, some bowls tournaments shifted from the traditional 21-up to the best of three 7-ups.[21] An altered scoring system is capable of enhancing the drama, whilst retaining the essence of the sport. Basketball could potentially be improved by adopting some version of games and sets, to give individual scoring attempts greater significance. But the significance here is that it was television, not the live audience, that was now the major factor in determining how a sport should best be presented.

The television professionals have been quite prepared to spell out the kind of changes they would like to see particular sports make. One sport with a large popular following but persistent problems with television coverage is badminton. People within the game resent the lack of coverage,[22] but BBC commentator Barry Davies has argued that it does not easily fit the conventions of television, being a game with no natural pauses. 'The game's subtleties and disguise cry out for the use of slow motion but when could it be used?' Davies lamented, whilst praising an experiment in different scoring methods during the Prudential mixed doubles (matches consisted of the best of five games, decided by nine points, with a clear break between games). He claimed that this increased the drama and excitement without falsifying the sport, and described some of the technical problems of camera placement and the need for careful use of close-ups, 'a necessary part of the building of personalities on which any sport depends'.[23] The traditional rules required continuous play, but a new experiment allowed 90 seconds between games to allow cameras to catch players in close-up, making it easier to forge an audience identification with the stars.[24]

During the 1970s, rowing too had begun to realise the importance of stars. The Amateur Rowing Association made several attempts to obtain more television coverage between 1965 and 1970, but meetings with John Snagge and Alan Hart (then of *Sportsview*) brought no real change.[25] The rowing authorities were concerned over the AB social class image acquired by the exposure of Henley and the Boat Race to the exclusion of most other competitive rowing[26] and were worried at their lack of star personalities and Olympic medal success, which might attract sponsors.[27] By the mid 1970s they had quite clearly identified television as a pathway to sponsorship and felt that further international success, particularly in the Olympics, would give them 'a far stronger platform with which to seek sponsorship'.[28]

It is believed important that potential stars be both charismatic and British. In the 1970s, when Barry Briggs was the top star, speedway was reaching audiences of 10 million and earning £30,000 per year from ITV. It is now in a slump with virtually no television coverage, and Briggs comments, 'The Danes' domination of the sport has made it boring. What we desperately need is a British success. Only then might television be interested'.[29]

Sponsors, too, were keen to promote change if it would lead to television coverage. Water polo had had only five events televised in 20 years, when it obtained its first sponsor, Aquafresh, for a tournament played under amended rules. Further changes were discussed 'to improve water polo's image, the rules should also be easily understood by the fans or potential fans, who will come in increased numbers to watch fast, exciting and well presented water polo'. The changes included a decreased playing area, to create the impression of a faster game, and additional balls and ball boys to save time and allow the game to flow more freely.[30] One is tempted to add that removing the water might be worth trying too.

The table tennis authorities, together with their Coca-Cola sponsors, commissioned a report in 1970, which offered extensive advice on how the game could improve its image. It suggested a professional Master of Ceremonies who would warm up audiences, and fanfares to introduce teams, who should time their entrances and exits, and line up facing each other while anthems were played. It called for players 'to be encouraged to show by their bearing much greater poise and sense of occasion', and called for development of the personality approach. It advocated a commentator with thorough knowledge of the sport, but advised that he should 'sell the match as hard as he can'. It called for non-playing captains to be seated in positions where 'better pictures are obtained of them when they are giving instructions to their players between games'.[31]

The English Table Tennis Association went actively touting for new sponsors, offering the English Open, shown on *Grandstand*, for £2500 and the English Closed, covered by *World of Sport*, for £1500, or, as a job lot, the two for £4000.[32] After extensive efforts in the build-up to the 1977 World Championships, held in Britain, the ETTA eventually obtained a series of sponsorship deals with Norwich Union.[33] With a chance of a British victory with Desmond Douglas, the World Championships gained around 40 hours' coverage on BBC, but failed to win an audience. Their one big star, Desmond Douglas, departed for Germany, and by the mid 1980s the sport was down to around two hours' television exposure per year. In 1985 the sport once again tried to re-launch itself as a TV sport, planning blue tables, scarlet nets and clothing in a variety of stripes and hoops, and hoping to benefit from the return of Desmond Douglas from the Bundesliga.[34] Sadly it had little success and it is now the view of both ETTA general secretary Albert Shipley and Douglas himself that the pace is too quick to suit television, Douglas commenting, 'if the game is to survive we desperately need more television coverage'.[35]

As the whole operation is conceived in terms of television and sponsorship, the withdrawal of television or even a cut in hours can be disastrous. A reduction in television coverage meant no sponsor could be found for the Bob Hope British Classic and the whole tournament was scrapped.[36] In 1987 the BBC responded to falling audience figures by cutting back on show jumping and as a result events began to encounter difficulties in holding on to existing sponsors and attracting new ones.[37]

New factors are currently making the future for minor sports uncertain. Broadcasting deregulation has opened the door to the sponsorship of programmes, which could mean that some money that would have gone to sport organisations may now go straight to broadcasters.[38] The new competitive environment of broadcasting will squeeze production costs, and sports may be increasingly driven to produce programme packages in collaboration with sponsors, offering them free to broadcasters in order to obtain the exposure for the sponsor. It is one of the most striking features of the period of transformation of British sport since 1965 that so many people in sport have come to see television and sponsorship as essential to survival.[39]

While sport has always been a form of entertainment, certainly since the growth of spectator sport in the nineteenth century, it has always been a very particular form of entertainment. Based on uncertainty both of outcome and of quality of performance, it therefore does not offer the same guarantee of quality as a theatrical or variety performance. It can be argued that traditionally spectators have accepted that some matches will be good and some dull. One of the characteristics of any form of capitalist entrepreneurship and rationalised production is the attempt to reduce the uncertainty of the commodity. The increased penetration of sport by capital and the resultant infusion of spectacular, internationalised and glamorised forms of entertainment can be seen as an attempt to reduce the uncertainty of the sporting commodity, at least as far as its entertainment value is concerned. Hence television's tendency to try and ensure that, even if the event is dull, by judicious highlights, action replays, interviews, etc. the programme itself can be entertaining.

Part II

Sport on television

Chapter 6

Analysing television sport: transformations of space and time

'You've got a fucking zoom, so use it.'
(Well-known commentator, to his producer)

'We join the race with two laps to go . . .'
(Typical presenter's introduction to a 10,000m race)

By 1980, one phase in the development of British television was complete and another was about to begin. The introduction of colour, video editing, slow motion, action replay and communication satellites in the 1960s had been complemented by the development of light-weight mobile cameras, chroma-key, quantel and other micro-electronic image manipulation in the 1970s. By 1980 the ability to manipulate and relay high-quality images was well established. In the 1980s the major changes concerned consumption as well as production. Domestic video grew rapidly, Channel 4 was introduced in 1982, and by the end of the decade satellite and cable channels were beginning to make significant (or at least detectable) inroads into the television audience.

The first wave of the transformation of sport had already worked its effects – even athletics was about to bring professionalism into the open. The globalisation of sport, the transformation of the major events into commercially lucrative and heavily sponsored spectacles, while under way, was still on the threshold of its decade of spectacular growth. Consequently, 1980 constitutes a good point at which to begin examining the nature of television sport from the perspective of content and text analysis. I conducted a detailed content analysis of British television sport in 1980 and repeated the exercise in 1989/90, and commenced a programme of extensive text analysis at the start of the 1980s. I re-examined television sport in the late 1980s to find that, while quantities and scheduling had changed, the forms and underlying ideological themes remained fundamentally the same throughout the decade.

CONTENT ANALYSIS: 1980 AND 1990

In 1980 there were over 1800 hours of television sport. There were far more sport programmes on BBC than ITV, with most on BBC2. Saturday, Sunday and Wednesday were peak days for sport, with 36 per cent of total sport hours on Saturday; 71 per cent of sport hours were in the afternoon. There was a marked summer peak, only partly due to the Olympic Games. June and July were peak months on all channels, containing 30 per cent of total hours for the year. While the majority of programmes were shorter than 1 hour, almost 40 per cent of sport hours were in programmes, such as *Grandstand*, longer than 4 hours. The six major sports – cricket, football, snooker, tennis, golf and racing – provided around 70 per cent of sport air-time. It was striking that ITV had inferior coverage of major sports, with virtually no cricket, snooker or tennis. Gymnastics was the only major sport with more coverage on ITV.

In 1989/90 there were 710 more hours, mostly on BBC2 and Channel 4. There were 643 more sport programmes, partly due to the introduction of Channel 4, which had almost 400 programmes, and, while there were fewer programmes on BBC and on BBC2, there were more on ITV, largely due to the expansion of night-time television. The most striking increases were in the number of programmes between 1 and 2 hours long, and in night-time programming. There was a drop in the BBC's share of programme numbers, largely due to Channel 4. The proportion of programmes longer than 4 hours on BBC increased, mainly because of the demise of *World of Sport*. The 60–120 minutes category grew at the expense of other categories, increasing by 602 hours. In 1989/90 the vast majority of ITV and Channel 4 programmes were 2 hours or less and ITV had no programmes longer than 4 hours. The BBC's share of air-time in programmes over 4 hours in length was up by 34 per cent (see Figure 6.1).

In 1989/90 the weekly profile had flattened, with a notable growth of sport on Sunday and Monday. Sunday had 225 more hours, mainly due to the introduction of Channel 4 and an increase on ITV, even though the weekend share of total hours dropped by 7 per cent, largely as a result of the demise of *World of Sport* and the growth of sport on weekdays. Similarly, the monthly profile was much flatter – the months November– April were now getting a larger share. ITV actually had fewer sport programmes in the summer, when BBC dominated. There were 118 more hours in April, 94 of them on BBC, mostly devoted to snooker.

Peak-time sport hours dropped by 38 but there were increases in the morning (by 150), afternoon (72), late evening (179) and night-time (346). The massive increase in night-time sport programmes was largely due to the introduction of all-night television in some ITV areas, and around 45 per cent of ITV sport is now screened between midnight and 6.00am. Of the additional 346 more hours during the night, 248 of them were on ITV.

There was a 3.6 per cent increase in morning sport, mostly on Channel 4. The proportion of sport programmes on in the afternoon, evening and late evening categories dropped, by 6–8 per cent. ITV featured 240 fewer hours in the afternoon, a drop of over 50 per cent for this category, partly as a result of transferring racing to Channel 4, although, on both ITV and BBC, afternoon sport has also been squeezed out by a growing competition for the daytime audience.

Without a more detailed monitoring of programme content, it was impossible to be precise about which programmes featured some women's sport. However, I did make an estimate, which included all programmes which might have contained some women's sport, even if only 5 minutes in a 4 hour programme. On this basis, in 1980 70 per cent of sport programmes probably featured no women's sport. There appeared to be even fewer programmes featuring any women's sport in 1989/90, and, as a percentage of the total, programmes containing some women's sport appeared to drop massively, from 30 per cent to 18.9 per cent, partly due to the growth in coverage of some male-only sports such as snooker and American football and reduced coverage of some mixed sports, such as gymnastics, show jumping and swimming. In 1989/90, 81 per cent of programmes probably contained no women's sport. The growth in programmes since 1980 has been most marked in male-only sports.[1]

American football and snooker alone accounted for one-third of the increase in hours. In 1989/90 the top six sports were racing, cricket, snooker, football, American football and golf, followed by tennis, athletics, motor sport and bowls. American football replaced tennis in the big six, largely as a result of night-time broadcasts. A larger percentage of programmes have been devoted to American football, athletics, baseball, bowls, cycling, motor racing, skating, ski-ing, snooker, sumo and yachting, at the expense of badminton, cricket, darts, football, golf, table tennis, show jumping, tennis and Rugby Union.

Despite the demise of *World of Sport*, there were 75 more magazine programmes, 40 on BBC2 and 35 on Channel 4, largely due to the introduction of BBC2's *Sport on Friday* and Channel 4's *Transworld Sport*. In programme numbers ITV appeared to be doing better in major sports: more football, American football, motor sport, athletics and cycling. But a lot of this was cheap and/or purchased programming scheduled in late-night slots; and the programme number total was inflated by short programmes such as the 15 minute *Results Service*, by splitting the athletics up over two channels, and by greater repeats of sports like cycling and Australian Rules football.

However, despite the growth in night-time sport, the emergence of snooker and American football, the spreading of sport more evenly across the week and throughout the year, and the reorganisation of football coverage, there has also been a substantial degree of continuity. Cricket,

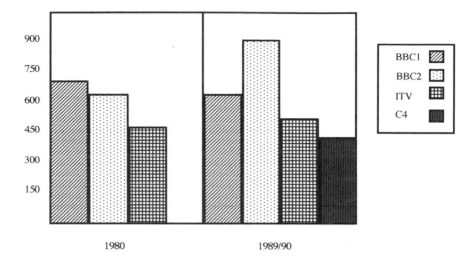

Figure 6.1a   Hours of sport on televison

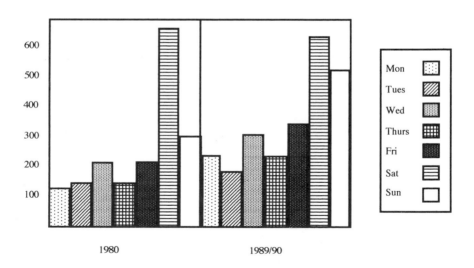

Figure 6.1b   Sport hours by day of week

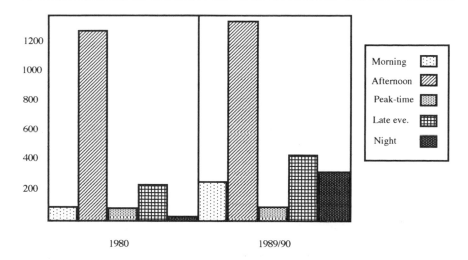

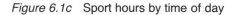

1980   1989/90

The day was broken down into five bands as follows: morning (6.00-11.59am), afternoon (12.00-6.59pm), peak-time (7.00-9.54pm), late evening (9.55-11.59pm), and night-time (midnight-5.59am). The peak-time bands ends at 9.54pm because it seemed more logical for *Sportsnight*, which often starts at 9.55pm, to fall into the late evening band.

Figure 6.1c   Sport hours by time of day

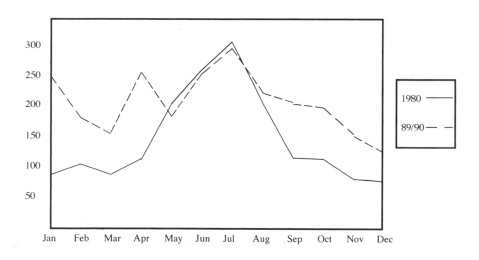

Figure 6.1d   Sport hours by month

football, snooker, tennis, golf and racing continue to provide the bulk of TV sport, *Grandstand* and *Sportsnight* remain as key fixed regular spots in the schedule, and the BBC continues to provide the greater proportion of sport hours.

MODES OF REPRESENTATION

However, the issue is not merely what is on or when it is scheduled, but also how it is represented. If television output is characterised by a series of polarities – factual/fictional, serious/popular, political/apolitical – two main clusters emerge, which correspond to two distinct traditions of practice, around which television is structured. First, the area of news/current affairs/documentary is predominately factual, serious and political, and corresponds to the practices of journalism and reportage. Second, the broad mass of peak-viewing programming is predominately fictional, popular and apolitical, and corresponds to the practice of entertainment.

Clearly these clusters are in a sense ideal-types; the practices of journalism and entertainment within television exist in a complex interpenetration. This can be seen in a variety of forms in such programmes as *Six O'Clock Live*, *That's Life*, *Jim'll Fix It*, *Crimewatch* and *This is Your Life*. Indeed, the growing tendency to present current affairs and documentary material in entertaining forms has acquired the label 'infotainment'. However, television still employs distinctive discursive modes which signify the distinction between journalism (however entertaining) and entertainment (however informative).

At first appearance, television sport might seem to be clearly within the first cluster. Its heavy dependence upon actuality independent of the institutions of television, and the large proportion of its screen time given to relatively untransformed relaying of this actuality, suggest roots firmly within reportage. But in the structure of its programmes, its modes of representation and modes of addressing its audiences, in its place in relation to scheduling and in the type of audiences it attempts to win and hold, it is also shaped by the conventions of entertainment. The presence within television sport of this contradictory interface between the practices of journalism and entertainment constitutes a key principle of the analysis that follows.

In addition, however, at the end of the discussion of television practices, I identified a third practice, that of drama. If we distinguish within the entertainment pole two slightly different elements – on the one hand drama/fiction/narrative and on the other showbusiness/variety and light entertainment – we derive a triangle, within which television's typical forms and genres can be located (see Figure 4.2). Within this triangle, sport occupies a relatively central position, pulled at different moments close to each of the three corners of the triangle.

The second aspect that I want to highlight is the unusual place sport occupies in relation to the schedules and the ratings. A predominant characteristic of the world of schedules and ratings is regularity (see Pilsworth 1980: 237–9, Paterson 1980: 79–86, 1990: 30–41). Week in, week out, the same programme types occupy the same slots, both in the weekly broadcast schedule and in the ratings. Virtually all regular sport programmes are outside of peak viewing time and rarely get into the top 20 ratings.

Nevertheless, at various times in the year, major events completely disrupt the schedules, displacing even such fixed slots as the news. By the same token, major sport events have an almost unique ability to win and hold very large audiences outside of peak viewing time, and sometimes into the early hours of the morning. It is these tip-of-the-iceberg sporting events that give TV sport its particular prestige – broadcasting's highlights of the year invariably include the major sporting events.

Realism

How is sporting actuality rendered into televised sport? Buscombe (1975) and Peters (1976) argued, along similar lines, that television sport claimed to be merely presenting reality, while in fact it was constructing a version of it, viewed from the position of an imaginary 'ideal' spectator.[2] But it must of course be remembered that there is no single realism, only various historical realisms. There are many different forms, styles and aesthetic conventions for representing the real. The combination of direct and indirect address in television sport, the use of visual devices like slow motion and action replay and the use of graphics cannot simply be seen as a variant of the realist conventions of narrative fiction. To dissect the complex combination of title montages, presentation, contributors, clips, action replays and actuality, it is more useful to think in terms of conflicting tensions between attempts to achieve transparency and desire to build in entertainment values.

The assertion that the reality effect prevents an audience perceiving television sport as a mediated construction also needs to be questioned. The knowledge and understanding we have of audiences is still limited but it could be argued that audiences for television sport, who are likely to have direct situated experience of sport events, are more likely to be aware of mediations. Certainly the culture that surrounds football appears to have a high awareness of the selective nature of highlights. Notions of a bad game looking good on television, desire to see something on action replay, speculation about what Jimmy Hill will say about a particular incident, are all commonplace. It cannot be assumed that the audience for TV sport are unaware of the mediated nature of the product.

Principles of transformation

I want to suggest five principles for analysing the visual level of television sport.

1 Sport event/TV event

The relation between sport event and television portrayal needs to be seen as one of transformation. That television sport is a constructed product is evident, but this process of construction is not free and unfettered by the real. As Tom Rall acknowledges (Buscombe 1975: 36), Bettetini's argument that television is in a relation of 'descriptive subjection' to the events it is portraying must be taken seriously. This does not mean that a sport determines the form of its representation, but rather that it sets certain limits to the possibilities of different representations. It is important to hold on to both ends of this relation: the constraints set by the nature of the sport, and the determining effects of television's own codes of representation and technological ability to recompose its images. The relation is best conceived as one of transformation.

2 Realism and entertainment

The operation of realist conventions and the desire to build in entertainment values are potentially, though not necessarily, contradictory impulses. The analysis of television sport as a form of realism does not in itself provide an adequate or stable base from which to build. It is, I would argue, more productive to hypothesise two potentially conflicting principles. The commitment to realist conventions grows in part out of film aesthetics, but also out of journalistic concepts, of showing events as they happened, of outside broadcast as a form of live relay. But, as a form of entertainment, television sport is also always seeking ways of guaranteeing the presence of its entertainment values. Many of its principles of assemblage derive from this need, from the use of close-ups to the introduction of split-screen inserts.

The realist aesthetic organises visual images according to a set of conventions aimed at producing transparency – the apparent portrayal of the world as it is, offering the spectator privileged access to an unproblematic, impartial and truthful view. Entertainment values organise visual images according to the need to highlight pleasure points – action, stars, drama – attempting to construct an entertaining assemblage capable of winning and holding an audience. This is not to say that realism does not contribute to pleasure, or that entertainment cannot be realistic. However, it is a useful mode of analysis to treat the two as distinct, and potentially contradictory. In all television sport the traces of both principles can be detected. The exact relation depends upon which sport is involved, and crucially upon the anchoring effect of the verbal level, which constantly produces particular inflections through which the visual level will be read.

3 Maximum action/minimum space

Attempts are made to obtain an ideal 'maximum action in minimum space' and consequently the amount of visual work necessarily varies widely from sport to sport. The phrase, used by Harry Carpenter to describe the value of boxing to television, was quoted by Charles Barr, who went on to argue that football, unlike boxing, does not easily fit this criterion, but British television's football coverage, in comparison with that in West Germany, goes further in attempting to make it fit.[3] In other words, more visual work is done, in this case by selection of mid shots and close-ups and by pace of cutting, in order to create the effect of maximum action in minimum space. This provides a useful hypothesis for examining modes of transformation. If the transformation is aimed at achieving this maximum action/minimum space effect, then the less the sport itself fits this principle, the more visual and verbal work television has to perform in the process of transformation. A way can therefore be provided of comparing the coverage of, for example, show jumping and golf.

4 Transformation of time

Just as space is manipulated or organised by camera placement and cutting patterns, so time is manipulated by the processes of assembling edited highlights, by the addition of action replays and by the slowing and freeze-framing of such replays. Birrell and Loy (1979: 5–18) single out five types of visual effect accomplished by television that are not available to the live audience at the event:

(a) changing the size of the image and permitting a greater range of vision (wide-angle lens, split screen, etc.);
(b) concentrating time-diffuse events into a more manageable time span (edited highlights);
(c) manipulating time to dramatise action (instant replay, slow motion, stop action, etc.);
(d) focusing on one isolated action (isolated camera, instant replay);
(e) providing more statistical information.

With a few adaptions, this offers a way of analysing transformation in space and time. 'Transformation' is to be preferred to Birrell and Loy's 'manipulation' as a term – manipulation implies conscious intention, whereas transformation leaves this question open. Point (a) should take account of camera placement and types of shot. Points (b) and (c) should cover transformation of both space and time. A distinction needs to be made between shot selection at time of recording and subsequent post-event editing.

5 Presences and absences

Visual framing produces absences as well as presences. There are a number of different aspects to take into account, from the tendency to focus on winners, allowing losers to magically disappear, through to the tendency to focus on the event to the exclusion of any social or historical context.[4]

To recap: the move from sport event to television event is a process of transformation with two organising principles – realism and entertainment – potentially in conflict. The more an event fits the criterion of maximum action in the minimum space and time, the less verbal and visual work needs to be performed by television.

VISUAL TRANSFORMATION

I want to outline six types of visual transformation. In all cases 'prime camera' or 'prime position' refers to the camera position that is used most often for a general view of the action. For the most part the other shots exist in a subordinate relation to this prime position.

In general this shot could be said to correspond to the position of an ideal spectator, with a perfect view. There will often be two cameras in this position, permitting cuts between long shot (LS) and medium shot (MS) from the same angle.

1 Simple

Sports like skating, gymnastics and show jumping take place indoors in relatively small arenas. They feature for the most part one competitor or one pair, rather than head-to-head competition. The action itself can be covered largely from LS/MS from the prime position. Close-ups (CUs) are generally reserved for the moments before and after action.

2 Cutaways

Sports like boxing and tennis have almost as simple a basis. They can be distinguished by the slightly more elaborate use of cutting. Boxing during the rounds depends predominantly upon a periodic cut from LS to MS in the prime position but also uses a lower-angle camera at a more oblique angle to the ring. Tennis depends upon the prime LS during rallies but, because breaks in the action are a more frequent and organic part of the game, the cross-cutting between close-ups of players, officials and crowd between points assumes greater importance as part of the overall rhythm.

3 Cutting patterns

In football, Rugby Union, Rugby League, cricket and snooker, the prime camera retains its dominance but the use of other cameras is more integral. There is a general tendency to move from LS to MS and then into CU at the moment that action breaks down, which can be detected in football and in both versions of rugby. In snooker, the prime camera gives the overall shot of the table and low-angled cameras to either side can reveal more accurately the configuration of balls around the bottom pockets. Their angle also enables them to match CUs of the players and see along the line of a shot. Cricket depends upon a combination of panning and cutting to follow the ball and fielders, and action replays are important in revealing what happened, but the main feature of the action (the batsman receiving the ball) is almost invariably covered from the prime position.

4 Spatial mobility

With sports in this category the primacy of the main camera begins to break down a little. In athletics, while there is still a dominant prime position overlooking the finishing line, from which the rest of the track can also be seen, this view is modified by others – low down and near the 400m start, looking along the back-straight towards the runners (first seen in the Moscow Olympics in 1980 and subsequently copied), or from small mobile trucks, travelling alongside the runners. This is further broken up by the existence of field events for which different apparent angles appear, and material is frequently fed into live broadcasts in recorded and pre-edited form. Similarly racing, spread over a greater terrain, with its use of cameras at the starting line, roving cameras, and also the pre-action locations in the paddock, depends upon greater shifts from the prime position.

5 Spatial fragmentation

The geographical layout of golf and motor racing extends this spatial fragmentation further, and it becomes harder to speak of a prime position except in respect of the final moments. Golf has resorted to elaborate strategies – use of many more cameras, 40-to-1 zoom lenses, camera towers, mobile cameras, split screens, and several commentators – to try and render an acceptable transformation. Motor racing tends to be covered almost entirely by panned long shots, with cameras placed on the outside of bends and at the end of straights, broken only by MS of crashed cars and pit activity. Despite the dispersal of cameras it still seems quite possible to accept both a visual view that offers a highly mobile ideal spectator position and a verbal commentary that is obviously emanating from a fixed position.

While some argue that watching television cannot replace the exhilaration of attending live events, Morris and Nydahl (1985) suggest that in the 1980s television producers could design sports spectacles laced with visual surprises that present a range of dramatic experiences which the live event cannot. With their ability to offer a series of rapidly changing perspectives, television has invented, in effect, an original form of drama. In particular, slow motion replay offers entirely new events outside of real time and space. Slow motion replay not only alters our perceptions of the action it reviews, but also establishes our expectations.

Sport on the screen is an entirely different experience compared with sport in the stadium but television has produced changed expectations and new frustrations – the desire to see instant replay, irritation if it is not available, the awareness that one's view in cricket is pretty inadequate, etc. Barnett (1990) argues that there are both gains and losses in this process. Viewers may lose out on the uniquely atmospheric moments of sporting drama, but their perspective is enhanced in other ways which can make live spectating a humdrum experience. It is undoubtedly true, as Barnett suggests, that stadia are increasingly prepared to adopt the role of a surrogate TV producer, introducing huge TV screens with close-ups, slow motion replays and advertisements.

The case of cricket: different strokes for different folks

The significant factor at work in all these transformations is the relation between the nature of the event itself, the need and requirements of television and the way television sees the event. Different institutional structures for television production, with different professional practices and attempting to construct different audiences, will attempt different modes of transformation. In particular, Goldlust (1987) suggests, there appear to be significant differences between the two leading styles of sports television represented on the one hand by the American commercial networks and on the other by British television, especially the BBC. He attempts to distinguish between the entertainment values of US TV and the journalistic values of the BBC, although I would argue that entertainment and journalistic values are present in both, albeit in different proportions. He suggests that Australian Channel Nine is similar to the US style, whereas Channel Ten is somewhere between US and UK, and, illustrating the general feeling among some Australian media producers that the BBC is far too austere, he quotes an Australian sports producer saying 'we try not to show the golfers walking up the fairway'.

This point was graphically illustrated during the upheavals in cricket caused by the intervention of Kerry Packer, giving the opportunity to compare different televisual transformations of cricket (see Bonney 1980, Blofeld 1978, and McFarline 1977 for accounts of Packer and cricket). The BBC, the Australian Broadcasting Commission (ABC) and Packer's Channel Nine all retained the dominance of a prime position behind the wicket, looking along the pitch. BBC's coverage was characterised by a slowish pace of cutting, the dominant use of LS and MS from the prime position, with cutaways during fielding and close-ups while the ball was returned to the bowler. The commentary could fairly be described as sparse. It should be noted that, in the case of the BBC coverage, impulses towards entertainment are here displaced onto the alternative verbal discourse provided by BBC radio – and many viewers opt for the radio commentary, turning down the TV sound. ABC's coverage had a faster cutting pace, more slow motion and action replay, a camera at right angles to the line between the two sets of stumps, and a camera at an acute angle to the wicket, a more active commentary and use of superimposed captions.

Packer's Channel Nine made frequent use of action replay and slow motion from more than one angle, so sometimes there were multiple replays. It used a camera at the opposite end of the wicket, permitting head-on shots of batsmen at either end and cross-cutting between batsman and bowler, both facing camera. This emphasised the 'gladiatorial' confrontation between batsman and bowler, a theme often echoed in Packer's promotional material. The cut between batsman and bowler broke the 180 degree rule, and the positioning of viewers was sometimes directed by the use of captions such as 'Pavilion End camera'. These shots were framed more tightly than would be usual on BBC. One effect of the cutting pattern was that bowler and batsman appeared a lot more than fielders in CU and gaps between deliveries were often filled with replays. During the 1980s BBC's style moved a little closer to the Australian models – introducing the opposite-end camera, and making greater use of action replay and superimposed statistics. Yet differences were still clear. In 1983 John Fiske analysed Australian cricket coverage, finding an average of 46–49 shots per over, at around 6 seconds per shot. Duplicating his method for the first England v. West Indies Test in 1991, I calculated British television to be using an average of 32 shots per over, with an average shot length of over 8 seconds. The representational style also varies with the type of cricket being portrayed. Fiske suggests that the difference between five-day Tests and one-day limited overs cricket is analogous to the distinction between the middlebrow novel and popular fiction (Fiske 1983).

So we have a range of transformations of the same sport, structured around different combinations of the balance between realism and enter-tainment – a contrast between the purism of the BBC and the populism of Channel Nine. The point is not that one is a correct reflection of the game, and the other a distortion. Rather, each gives an impression of the game, constructs it in a different form, just as spectators with particular cultural attitudes sitting in various sections will, in a very real sense, see a different game (see Halstorf and Cantril 1954).

Zooming in: personalisation

Obviously patterns of cutting have a degree of descriptive subjection to the event. It is hard to imagine a representation of a tennis match that does not include shots of the two players and the movements of the ball between them. This establishes broad limitations, and the range of further choices is further limited by the conventions of realism adhered to. Within this, the precise nature of the visual coverage is then further mediated by two principles: how television people see the sport – what is important about it, and what is marginal – and what constitutes good television.

There are various aspects to concepts of good television sport – absorb-ing narratives, exciting action and the presence of characters and stars being particularly important. At the visual level, action and character are central. This sets up a problem in that close-ups which are rooted in the expressive codes of the human face can either not be obtained during action, because of speed of movement, or can be obtained only at the expense of seeing the action. This gives a characteristic structure to the cutting pattern of much sport coverage whereby breaks in the action are utilised for close-ups. During action there is a comparable impulse to frame more closely, making specific incidents of action fill the screen more effectively. A move from establishing long shot to medium shot is another characteristic pattern during action sequences.

The tendency to move in, to frame tighter during action, is least evident in individual sports like skating, or one against one (or two against two) like tennis, where the long-shot frame is already as close as is compatible with retaining a relatively complete view of the action. It is in team games like football or rugby that the tendency becomes a pattern whereby commencements of play are conventionally seen in long shot, followed by moves to medium shot as soon as the play is restricted to a smaller area.

This pattern is particularly evident in Rugby League, which has a more episodic form than football as a sport. The first move to medium shot is made when areas of play become restricted, the move from here to close-up is made at the moment of tackle when a move breaks down. The pattern then recommences with a cut-back to long shot as the heel-back takes place. In sports like cricket and athletics the move-in tendency contributes to the hierarchisation of competitors. Tighter framing and cuts to medium shots single out the leading runners in athletics, the batsman and bowler in cricket.

The tendency to move in closer during breaks in play constantly highlights the characters involved in the narrative. Much of the success of snooker and darts on television could be attributed to the ease with which cameras can frame close-ups with powerful resonances (concentration, tension, calmness, elation, etc.). This process is aided by the relative immobility of the participants, the higher-quality lighting possible in indoor sports and the very short duration of specific action in darts and snooker.

Gymnastics, swimming, skating and field event athletics make similar use of the close-up in concentrating upon faces as the event is about to start. Breaks during play in football are characteristically filled by brief montages of close-ups showing the protagonists involved in the just completed action, and by action replays and slow motion replays. The percentage of close shots appears to have risen dramatically. In the 1966 World Cup Final close-ups amounted to around 13 per cent of all shots. In four major matches I analysed over the last four years, close-ups provided 20–30 per cent of the total. The average shot length in 1966 was 20 seconds, while in the 1990 World Cup semi-final between England and West Germany it was 10 seconds, and, staggeringly, in the 1990 FA Cup Final replay (BBC), it was around 6 seconds.[5] Patterns of cutting work upon the involvement and identification of the spectator. In particular the emphasis and highlighting of peak moments of action by replay lays stress on the narrative aspect of sport, while the use of close-ups builds identification with characters.

Transforming time

The extent of this structuring becomes greater in the production of edited highlights, where the mode of transformation reveals another move, from sport as autonomous event, holding television in a relation of descriptive subjection, towards sport as a televised event, when television itself has greater autonomy in the construction of its own preferred forms of narrative, characterisation, drama and entertainment.

Again, variants in the mode of transformation can be shown, according to problems set by particular sports and the conflicts between realist conventions and entertainment values. In some sports such as football and rugby, it is possible in edited highlights to retain a narrative continuity in the form of realist transparency. That is to say, the selection and rejection of material during editing is concealed – cuts in football are often made at goal kicks, for example – and so the edited version retains something of the continuous form of the live version.

This becomes harder in sports demarcated in a more systematic numerical manner. Cricket, tennis and snooker are all sports where every significant action alters the score or the formal position (e.g. the number of balls left in an over). Cuts cannot therefore be made with the same transparency – there is a need for some form of verbal relay to act as an explanation. Generally this involves either a return to the presenter, the use of a voice-over or some form of superimposed caption. This helps preserve narrative continuity but produces problems in maintaining realist transparency.

The reconstruction work in the production of edited highlights can, however, ease problems for the maintenance of entertainment values; for instance, gaps between moments of action or particular events, e.g. in golf, athletics or swimming, can be eliminated, thus constructing a more continuous series of actions. This technique is sometimes used during live athletics when gaps are filled by recordings of earlier events. It also allows the reconstruction of narratives that could not be clearly presented in the live coverage. The additional focusing on key competitors that becomes possible allows another presentation, particularly in golf, show jumping and skating, of the events as a contest between leading contenders.

The formal reconstruction of edited highlights reveals those points at which the two elements, character and narrative, are drawn most neatly together. The highly fetishised peak moments of action (see Peters 1976: 13) – the moments of victory, knock-outs, boundaries being hit, wickets taken, goals or tries scored, fences cleared, balls potted, matches won – are made to stand out in sharp relief. More emphasis on these moments pulls them out from the overall context. Framing and camera position provide a first-level emphasis; editing, based upon the premise of eliminating the ordinary and retaining the exceptional, adds a second. The peak moments of action are further emphasised by the use of action replay and slow motion replay. Post-mortems discuss the action, but as centred upon these peak moments, illustrated with further repeats. The best moments then find their way into title sequences and the greatest become further inscribed into sport history via retrospective celebrations of great moments in programmes like BBC's *Sports Review of the Year*.

Television's handling of space and time began to change dramatically during the 1980s. Influenced by Cheerleader's coverage of American football and some other sports on Channel 4 from 1982, short montages of action, often with up-tempo music, began to occupy a more prominent role, especially in *Grandstand*. Sport coverage appeared to take on some of the characteristics of what some call postmodern culture – disjointed juxtapositions, a focus on surface appearances, and a tendency for form to subsume content. After many years with a virtually unchanged form, *Sports Review of the Year* underwent a dramatic transformation in 1990, organising its material chronologically, month by month, instead of anthologically, sport by sport. As a result the programme jumped restlessly and endlessly between sports. There were 128 items in 100 minutes, an average length of 47.8 seconds. There were 19 items longer than 1 minute, but only three longer than 3.55. Of these, one, motor racing, featured two interviews, one was the Commonwealth Games, featuring several sports, and the other European athletics, featuring several events. This isn't just the 3 minute culture, it's the 47 second culture.

Yet television sport remains remarkably traditional, and *Sports Review of the Year* still looks like the annual school prize day. What lifts it above the tedium of the school hall is the treasure house of golden memories it can offer. It is in these peak moments of action that character and narrative come together with great significance. These moments of action represent key points in the narrative. At the visual level they also represent a peak moment of achievement for an individual who becomes abstracted from the context of his/her team and from the context of the event itself as successive repeats abstract the moment from the action as a whole. As such they also represent the moment when the spectators' involvement in the narrative is potentially joined most effectively to their identification with a character. It is at these moments, which make up the pantheon of sporting memories most firmly inscribed into sport history and link achievement firmly to the individual, that the individualist character of television's representation of sport is most clearly foregrounded.

Chapter 7

Assemblage and framing

'Let me tell you what we've got for you this afternoon . . .'
(BBC presenter)

'Stay with us, you won't miss a second of the action . . .'
(ITV presenter)

A key characteristic of television is the assemblage aspect of its production – the process whereby programmes assemble sets of diverse audio-visual elements in various combinations. Understanding the principles of these combinations helps clarify the way programmes organise their representations of the sporting world. Stuart Hall suggested (1975: 95–6) that television is a hybrid medium and appears to be a relatively untransformed reproduction of presentational forms typical of other arts and entertainment. He argues that a very high proportion of television is conceived in the naturalistic mode; that channel functions appear to predominate over medium ones; that studio situations characteristically mix the modes of transmission; that sport programmes like *Grandstand*, which combine live, studio and filmed inserts, are television originals, with nothing quite like them in any other medium. Consequently, he urges that attention must be paid to that feat of 'collective socio-technical co-ordination and control', the assembly process. Even in today's postmodern times, when the accelerated pace of cutting and juxtaposition seems to some to have produced a 'three-minute culture', this holds up well as a skeletal account of television as a medium.

Examining the ways these elements are combined in television sport – the ways in which television structures, handles, its 'raw' materials – demonstrates the privileged place occupied by presentation and the space constructed in the text for the setting up and framing of sport. Actuality is rarely channelled to us in unpackaged form, but comes complete with opening and closing titles, and 'topping and tailing' by a presenter at the very least.[1] In as much as television sport has a typical form, it could be said to be that of the magazine programme.

The magazine format involves the construction of a programme from a number of discrete items linked together by the role of presentation. The construction within the text of a series of places for presentation links means that every item in the programme is framed. Part of the work accomplished in these spaces is that of giving the programme coherence, imposing a unity upon diversity.

The assemblage orders the material and establishes hierarchical relations between the elements, marking their respective importance. Hierarchies of sport are marked not just by length of coverage but by their place within the assemblage. The magazine assemblage facilitates smooth handling of the conflict between the uncertainties of sport and the need to deliver entertainment value. Even where the sporting event is a disappointment, the programme can still succeed in being an entertaining package. The studio material consequently has a tendency to expand. In the extended coverage given to major events there is a proliferation of preview and post-mortem material.

The majority of sport coverage adopts some variant of magazine form. *Grandstand*, *Sunday Grandstand*, *Sport on Friday*, *World of Sport*, *Sportsnight*, *Midweek Sports Special*, and indeed the now deceased *World of Sport*, all consist of diverse studio and actuality elements concerning various sports linked by presentation. Even single-sport programmes like *Match of the Day* and *The Big Match* conform to this pattern. Coverage of events such as Wimbledon or the World Snooker Championship uses presenters who at the very least top and tail the programme. Similarly, many series – *Pot Black*, *Floodlit Rugby League* – while being predominately edited actuality, began and ended with a presenter, separate from the general commentary.

GRANDSTAND AND *WORLD OF SPORT*

These two programmes dominated television sport for two decades, and occupied an interesting and unusual place within the weekly flow of television.[2] At four and a half hours, they were by far the longest regular programmes on television. They were of similar length and occupied similar places in the schedule. They both utilised a magazine format and both drew upon sport as their subject matter and source material. The key role of the presenter was similar in the two, and they both began (at least between September and May) with a football preview and ended with a results sequence (see Whannel 1991).

Yet they also had significant differences. The BBC structure was more elaborate and flexible, varying from week to week. ITV had a fixed regular structure, and the programme was divided into sections, discrete blocks, with none of the alternation between items that characterised *Grandstand*. They were further distinguished by separate logos, and separate presenters – e.g. the appearance in shot of ITV's racing commentators, Brough Scott and John Oaksey. By comparison, the BBC tended to have more sports per programme, jumped back and forth between them, varied the pattern of its assemblage, had, apart from *Football Focus* and the results sequence, no fixed regular spots, was more liable to extend its length for major events, and was more likely to link its presentation from the site of major events rather than from the studio.

BBC's actuality was predominantly live, although video was increasingly used to handle gaps in live action, or clashes between live moments in two events. ITV used more pre-recorded items – much of the International Sports Special section was filled with pre-purchased items, and the wrestling was recorded and edited. In *World of Sport*, partly through contractual problems in competition with the BBC, there was a greater use of foreign material and consequent emphasis on the exotic.

Similarities were also striking, especially the presence/absence of football. Neither programme could, owing to contractual restrictions, feature regular live football. However, the cultural centrality of football, its importance in the sport media's set of news values and, not least, the cultural and economic importance of the Pools ensured its constant presence. (Television's service to the gambling industry with its football and racing coverage ought surely to qualify it for a share of the betting levy.) Both programmes, between August and the following May, were framed, and permeated throughout, with football. Beginning with the previews at about 12.30 and ending with the results sequences, both programmes were punctuated throughout with latest scores and other football news. Football was heavily present even in its absence. Television's construction of the 'world' of sport is often most revealed at those moments when direct continuous actuality is denied to it.

PRESENTERS AND MODES OF ADDRESS

The magazine format on television includes a variety of items calculated at least in part to appeal to diverse sectors of the audience. These items, however, are presented within the format of a 'show' and are introduced, linked, by a presenter. The presentation serves to impose unity upon diversity – to create homogeneity out of a set of heterogeneous items. It gives the programme an identity. The continuity of presentation serves as a guide through the material, administering the breaks and smoothing the transitions from item to item (see Hall 1975: 104–5).

The magazine format gives the programme a flexibility in dealing with the uncertainties of sport. If a boxing match ends in the early rounds, action replays, interviews and post-mortem discussions can fill up the rest of the programme without appearing as a drastic overturning of conventional structure. A *Match of the Day* in 1978 was confronted with a rare double crisis for its 'goals, stars and action' values.[3] There was extensive bad weather, many games were off and the BBC was able to show only one game instead of two, and furthermore this game – Stoke City v. Leicester City – was goal-less. The resultant assemblage showed the programme not only coping with this crisis but exulting in its ability to cram in even more goals than normal. Thanks to opening and closing montages, Goal of the Month and a review of championship contenders, complete with clips, there was a total of 33 goals in the programme. Similarly *The Big Match*, stuck with a boring 0–0 draw, inserted a repeat of the goals from the 5–5 draw between Bristol Rovers and Charlton Athletic the previous week.[4] Such programmes have a striking ability to play around with their 'raw' materials to ensure the consistency of their entertainment values.

The importance of this is considerably heightened on major occasions where a mass audience may be expected, especially when, as on Cup Final Day, both channels were until recently in competition. As a result both used to start coverage in mid morning. Two other consequences can also be seen: first of all, the attempts to heighten the immediacy, the closeness, the sense of 'being there', by capturing the players live at almost every moment possible from breakfast onwards; second, the attempt to add to the heterogeneity of the appeal via the inclusion of other programme forms, such as the quiz show, in football guise (e.g. football as a subject matter, contestants representing the two teams) and stars from non-sporting contexts, particularly those who also have a football connection such as Eric Morecambe or Elton John (see Colley and Davies 1982, and Masterman 1980; the Open University course on Popular Culture (U203) also featured two television programmes about the televising of the Cup Final).

The presenter is an important figure within British broadcasting generally. As Krishan Kumar has pointed out (1977: 239), it is these men, the 'anchormen' or 'linkmen' of the regular programmes, who map out for the public the points of identification with broadcasting, and they have become increasingly prominent in the broadcasting organisations' strategy. The importance to the programme identity of the presenter is apparent in the close links between the two. In many ways the identity of the programme is built around the presenter. Hence it was *World of Sport* **with** Dickie Davies and *Match of the Day* **with** Jimmy Hill. This link was perfectly demonstrated when for a while BBC's midweek sport magazine was called *Sportsnight with Coleman*.

Margaret Morse (1985) argues that television is a strongly discursive medium – much of which employs direct address. Narrators as hosts, presenters, news and sportscasters look directly out of the screen at the viewer position at one time or another, establishing a position for the audience as narratee. She suggests that part of the pleasure of viewing is bound up with this relationship with the presenters.

If the role of presentation establishes a relationship with the audience, and also provides the core structure of the magazine assemblage, the *work* of that presentation provides three important things. First, it serves to clarify, to organise, to make coherent, the collection of material in the shape of programmes. Second, it provides a particular mode of address by which contact is made between programme and audience. Third, it sets up, cues in and provides a way into the material offered.

The contradiction between the construction of unity around the 'world of sport' and the 'sport fan' and the quite specific and separate appeal of different sports – gymnastics and moto-cross for example – means transitions between these items have to be handled, the passage of the viewer from one to another must be smooth. The problem is heightened for ITV by commercial breaks, particularly when sport is on both channels (hence the endless reminders: 'Don't go away', 'We'll be back in a moment', 'You won't miss a thing', 'We'll be back after the break'). But perhaps the most important aspect of this presentational work is the particular way it makes contact with, speaks to and serves to position the audience, offering it a way into the programme. The characteristic mode of address involves a particular complex use of 'shifters' (see Barthes 1967: 22–3, Brunsdon and Morley 1978: 58–70). Crucial to this is the various ways in which presenters use 'we' and 'our':

We: the television production team

In these examples, the 'we' means the presenter and the production team:

> 'Well, we've got the result of today's big race, now';
> 'We've heard that Nottingham Forest are now leading two goals to nil';
> 'We'll have the other results as they are coming in';
> 'Our cameras are at Doncaster';
> 'Our main event today features darts';
> 'We are devoting both of our Sports Specials to this spectacular';
> 'Our ITV Seven selection';
> 'We are covering a unique occasion';
> 'We resume our coverage'.[5]

The emphasis is very much on the team – the 'we' and 'our' – with the presenter merely the front-person. It is rarely 'I've got the racing results', or 'They've got the racing results'.

You: the audience

Counterposed against this 'we' is a 'you' – the audience – whose presence is marked right from the start of things: 'Our very warm welcome to you.' So the audience is set up as distinct from, but in a relationship with, the 'we' of the television team – a relationship that is continually referenced and reinforced throughout the presentation.

We/you: the donor/recipient relationship

The basis of this relationship is one of donor and recipient, of broadcaster as Santa Claus. The language of presentation continually casts the production team as providers of a gift which is being given, or has been given, or will be given, to the audience:

> 'We've got a very busy programme for you this afternoon';
> 'We've got the half-time scores for you';
> 'We've got four races from there for you';
> 'Your commentators are Harry Rigby and Richard Duckenfield';
> 'As you know we always like to bring you great goals and odd incidents';
> 'We have an extra item for you';
> 'We're planning to show you all the best';
> 'We'll keep fully in touch'.[6]

So the production team are the ever-active providers, able to lay on, as promised, a constant stream of gifts which they 'know you'll enjoy', and the audience are positioned as the passive, but presumably grateful, recipients. The rhetoric here has echoes of that employed by Butlin's Redcoats when addressing campers. But the presenter's position is more complex:

We: the presenter as viewer

The presenter is marked first of all as of the production team, but also uses another 'we'; which seems to place him/her with the audience, as a fellow recipient:

> 'We'll be joining Bob in just a moment';
> 'We'll be in good time for our first race';
> 'We've already seen some of the heats in the RAC championship';
> 'We're going to see one or two of the highlights now';
> 'The score as we join is six points all'.[7]

In this usage 'we're going to see', the presenter seems to join the audience as just another sports fan – with the clear implication that just as the home audience get comfortable to watch their sets, so the presenter is doing the same thing in the studio. In a sense, the presenter becomes a personification of the audience as a whole – just as pleased to be a recipient as the rest of us should be – we enjoy along with the presenter.

We/our: shared experience

This permits the presenter to comfortably reference 'our' shared experience as viewers and sports fans, marking our anticipation of enjoyment to come:

'I'm sure we're in for a real treat this afternoon';
'I'm sure that you, like me, are beginning to get that tingle of excitement';
'Before we settle down to enjoy an afternoon and evening of athletics . . .';
'We may very well see the first British leap over 19 feet today'.[8]

This ease with which shared experience may be referenced in turn gives an entrance into the domestic routines of audiences, who are ever being invited to rush home from work, settle down or stay up late. Indeed broadcasters construct schedules that both reflect and, arguably, help to construct family routines (see Paterson 1980, Pilsworth 1980). Jonathan Martin, BBC Head of Sport, explained his 1984 Olympic calculations to the *Radio Times*:

> 'The 800 metres, for example, is on at ten to two in the morning, our time. And my kids will be in bed then, and so, normally, would I be. My wife is always busy in the morning, so when could she watch? I had to come up with answers for a typical family: a way of projecting the games to serve the needs of a typical family.'[9]

Presenters typically build in reference to our personal routines:

> 'If you've been out all day and you're just sitting down to your tea, rest assured you can now relax and see them all with us . . .'[10]

It is this shift in the sense of 'we' that presenters are continually operating over, and it is what enables them to speak for us in a form of populist ventriloquism.[11]

Our: patriotism

And of course in sport a key characteristic of this assumed 'shared experience' is the unproblematic national unity that is patriotism. British competitors and teams are without dispute 'ours' and presenters have no difficulty in 'speaking for us all' when they talk of 'our' current champions or ask what 'our' chances are or praise 'our' magnificent success. This should be qualified by reference to tensions within the United Kingdom and its separate national regions – an English success is not 'ours' to Scots, who also are likely to notice the way successful Scottish or Welsh teams become 'British' in the media . . . until they fail (see Geraghty, Simpson and Whannel 1986: 28–35).

The mobilisation of patriotism is not simply a matter of identity. In framing the event, in summing it up and in providing closure, presenters are also offering a position to inhabit, a particular inflection of patriotism. Signing off after the England v. West Germany World Cup semi-final in 1990, Desmond Lynam said: 'There it is, England are out, but they played with pride tonight; and if you're going to have a drink at the end of the evening, perhaps you should do it with pride and not aggression tonight. It's been a good night for English football, we've all enjoyed it, I certainly hope you have. Bit disappointing but there it is. I'll see you Saturday.'[12] So, in the nicest possible way, we've been told how we should feel, how we should behave and where we should be on Saturday.

The rhetoric of presentation

The central point is that sport presentation is characterised by its dual relationship, expressed in the sense of 'we', to the production team and to the audience. The presenter is able to appear both as a representative of the donors and as a personification of the recipients, and in the end serves to weld the two together into a unity. Desmond Lynam's closing words at the end of the closing ceremony of the Seoul Olympics were, 'Well, I hope we've made these Olympics for you; you've made them for us, by watching them with us'.[13] The dual role, on both sides of the donor/recipient relationship, allows the language of presentation to utilise a whole set of rhetorical conversational devices, all of which help to bind the viewer to the 'world of sport'.

Invitational

'Let's now join our commentator';
'Let us return to the ITV Seven';
'Let me bring you up to date';
'Well now, let's have a look at the medal table so far'.

Questioning

'I think he's getting younger looking, don't you? Of course he is';
'Right, time, I think, for a spot more action, don't you?'
'Interesting sport that, isn't it?'
'Right, time for a spot of racing, now, I think, don't you?'
'Right, what do you know about crown green bowls? Well in case it's very little, let me tell you . . .';
'Can I just confirm the one game off?'
'It really is breathtaking, isn't it?'

Imperative

> 'Make a note of ten minutes to four for show jumping';
> 'Well, don't go away if you're a racing fan';
> 'Don't forget we're going back to the swimming pool live';
> 'Stay with ITV if you can';
> 'Get yourself a drink and then settle down and join me in a couple of minutes'.[14]

The conversational tone constructs the presenter as a genial sports fan with slightly greater knowledge, and therefore able to explain things, and a privileged awareness of the treats to come and their exact timing. But the presentation is the pivot not simply between us and the production team, but also between us and the events, and us and the expert commentators. Presentation has a very real power to define, to frame and to set up the representation of sport that television offers.

FRAMES OF REFERENCE

Part of the work of presentation is the process of addressing the audience, winning and holding its attention. There is also the process whereby events are continually located within maps of meaning (see Brunsdon and Morley 1978: 43–59). In other words, we are being given a way of looking at a particular event.

Television sport has a dual relationship to the practices of journalism and entertainment. Journalism involves selecting, ordering and hierarchising – locating events within frames of reference, maps of social reality (see Cohen and Young 1973). The same process of selection and hierarchisation can be seen at work in TV sport, which has its own set of news values, marking the respective importance of British over foreign, male over female, track events over field events, and so on.

But TV sport is also part of popular television, functioning under the sign of entertainment, and therefore also has to frame its own representations in the context of the values that constitute 'good television'. Given that it is saying 'this is entertainment', it therefore has to make clear the pleasure points it offers and establish points of identification with the audience around them (see A. Lovell 1975). The process of framing television sport places it in terms of the cultural attractions of particular kinds of entertainment.

Entertainment

Star individuals are singled out in close-up in titles, in build-ups and during actuality. The appearance of stars as experts and the concomitant tendency for experts to become celebrities, as well as the frequent utilisation of stars from other areas of the world of showbusiness, and the development of pro-celebrity events and other quasi-sports, all reinforce this particular frame.

Action

This is a primary attraction on offer. Sport, it is constantly suggested, is all about action – exciting, unpredictable events. Programmes stress the amount and quality of action they contain, particularly in the characteristic montage titles.

Immediacy

There is a stress on the liveness, the immediacy of sport – 'all the action as it happens'. A prominent part of Saturday afternoon sport is the constant reiteration of 'the latest news', 'the latest scores', 'all the news as it comes in'. On the visual level, this is highlighted by the newsroom-style sets, with workers behind desks in the background, and by the use of the video-printer. The separate sections within TV news for sport mark the extent to which sport is constantly bracketed off as a world of its own with its own hierarchy of news values (see Hall in Ingham 1978: 15–36).

Like news reporting, sports journalism operates conventions of impartiality upon which its claim to authoritativeness is founded. Geoffrey Nowell-Smith (1978), discussing the 1978 World Cup, commented on the way that image and commentary colluded to produce a position which was both neutral and authoritative and which derived its authority, in part at least, from the commentators' claim to preserve the neutrality immanent in the image.

Drama

The structure of competition provides the basis of narrative, which in the telling or re-telling can be rendered dramatic, and the stress on action, unpredictability and immediacy gives this narrative an indeterminate quality. The eventual resolution of dramatic fiction can frequently be 'read' in advance through an understanding of the conventions of drama, but the question 'who will win' a sporting contest cannot be predicted, and is genuinely uncertain. This uncertainty is a major point of appeal, giving rise to the convention of not revealing the outcome of recorded highlights in advance, sometimes accomplished on the news by displaying football results in vision only, having given viewers the chance to avert their eyes. Sport journalism generally is fond of theatrical metaphor – 'Twickenham is the stage for today's events'. Jimmy Hill has described football as 'theatre without a script', but Hill and his colleagues do much to rectify the omission by their construction of sport in the form of narratives with characters, stars and stereotypes.

The research of Comiskey *et al.* (1977) assumes media producers to be professional gatekeepers, with the role of the commentator being to dramatise the event, create suspense, sustain tension and enable the viewers to feel that they have participated in an important and fiercely contested event, the fate of which was determined only in the climactic closing seconds of play. Comparing two segments of ice hockey and showing them to people who later filled in a questionnaire, they found that the commentary stressing the roughness of play made the normal play appear rough, while the commentary that did not emphasise roughness made rugged play appear less rugged. They argue that there can be little doubt that commentary can substantially alter perception of play.

The commentary stressing roughness of play also proved to increase the entertainment value of the sport event. They concluded that not only does dramatic commentary affect perception of play, but it is apparently a factor in the enjoyment of televised sports as well. In related research the same team analysed six professional football games in 1976, assessing the proportion of commentary devoted to description, drama and humour. They found that a sizeable portion (27 per cent) of commentary was devoted to dramatic embellishment. Commentators' dramaturgy was rather stylised, with a great deal of reliance on a relatively small number of dramatic motifs (Bryant *et al.* 1977; see also Bryant 1989).

Major event

The select group of national and global events that occupy such a prominent place in the television year are pushed into the forefront of public life, presented as consensual national rituals involving everyone in an imaginary coherence. There is, of course, an intriguing circularity at work here – 'It must be important, look how it has disrupted the normal television schedule.'

Exotic/novelty

A way of framing the introduction to a British audience of culturally unfamiliar sports – such as surfing, Australian Rules football, etc. – is to stress the exotic character. Play is made of the strangeness of the sport or its participants, often presented as 'those quaint foreigners' – Fijian rugby players, Korean footballers or Japanese volleyball players. A distinct development should be noted here. Whereas unfamiliar foreign sports were characteristically presented within this frame of reference until the 1980s, Channel 4 has been responsible for breaking the mould. By taking sports like American football, Australian Rules, sumo and baseball seriously, on their own terms, and by taking time to explain something of the rules, tactics, subtleties and cultural backgrounds, it has succeeded in building audiences for them. In part, of course, this merely echoes and reproduces the continuing globalisation of culture partly in terms of US cultural imperialism; but it does at least dislodge the smug patronising superiority of the old Empire mentality of the English.

Aesthetic

There are two characteristic uses of this frame. First, it is used in relation to sports seen as drawing upon supposed 'feminine' attributes of grace, style, elegance, poise; as distinct from masculine competitiveness, toughness and physical strength. The aesthetic frame is therefore commonly applied to gymnastics and skating – sports where the conventional privileging of male competitors over female is somewhat disrupted, if not totally reversed.

Second, the aesthetic frame is sometimes utilised for sports that lack a strong British interest at the highest level and cannot be set up in terms of a partisan identification. The pole vault has been a good example of this, as again is gymnastics, once introduced by Harry Carpenter with the words, 'I think you'll find the next quarter of an hour absolutely delightful'.[15]

These frames serve to offer maps of meaning – specific and culturally rooted ways of seeing – rather than referencing intrinsic or essentialist characteristics of particular sports; ice skating is not necessarily more aesthetically pleasing than Association Football, nor is it any less competitive. They are not mutually exclusive frames of reference. Indeed television's representations reference, albeit in different combinations, all these points of appeal. For example, while gymnastics is offered as 'artistic', it also offers action, entertainment and drama. The work of television's representation lies in part in its articulation of these various elements into a coherent, if complex, unity.

LINKS AND SETTING-UP

The menu is an important element of magazine assemblage in that it explains in advance the structure of the assemblage, and attempts to convince the audience of the high quality of the ingredients they are being offered. Menus are frequently illustrated with appetite-whetting clips, important in holding elements of the audience who may not be interested in the first item. Here is part of the menu from a *World of Sport*:

film of Hoddle: Glen Hoddle is Ian St John's principal guest in *On the*

Ball and as well as having his views on England's performance against Bulgaria, we'll also be seeing him in action

logrolling extract Logrolling is just one of the elements of the world lumberjacking championships and in *Sports Special One* at one o'clock, we'll be seeing this test of balance, plus the strength and agility of the climbers

wrestling extract The Iron Greek Spiros Ariam returns to the wrestling ring at four o'clock and Bobby Burnes, another villain of the ring, is also on the bill, but the main contest features the reappearance of the Dynamite Kid and the British light heavyweight champion Marty Jones

CU Dickie Davies Yes, some superb stuff there from two of the most talented wrestlers in the ring today. It really is an exceptionally skilful contest, one that I urge you not to miss. Right, all that's left for me to do is remind you about today's racing.[16]

Particular events are linked to particular points of appeal. The stress on the skill involved in the logrolling and wrestling could be seen as balancing a more prevalent way of seeing these events as, respectively, novelty and entertainment. The previous week the lumberjacking had been previewed as 'an amusing diversion'. Indeed, the dilemma for *World of Sport* was often to try and legitimise events that were trapped within the exotic/novelty frame. The next example, from *Sportsnight*, illustrates this process of setting-up operating through the typical sports mode of address, rooted in the donor/recipient relationship with the audience:

'So we have a completely new line-up for you – I hope you're going to find it enjoyable over the next hour and twenty minutes or so. Well, now, let me tell you what we have got for you. We've got highlights from the British Ice Dance Championships at Nottingham last week, where Robin Cousins also skated a quite marvellous exhibition – that's something to look forward to tonight, and with the All Blacks due to meet England at Twickenham on Saturday, we'll see how they proved they are fallible on the rugby field as they test that unbeaten record against the Northern Division. And we have for boxing fans a special feature on the career of Muhammad Ali, some of the most memorable moments both in and out of the ring, so that's something I think you're going to enjoy, and we shall have that for you at about half past ten. We shall be starting the action with the skating, but first let's get all today's football results from John Motson.'[17]

The programme offers action, enjoyment, stars (Cousins, Ali), narrative interest (the All Blacks), history as popular memory (Ali) and news (the football results). The importance of background and preview material to

TV sport is emphasised in the degree to which it becomes a point of appeal in itself, as in this item about a forthcoming Jim Watt fight:

> 'Incidentally, it'll be the fifth world title fight involving a British boxer this year and all five of them, I'm delighted to say, we've covered for you on BBC television. There'll be coverage of the weigh-in on *Grandstand*, and Desmond Lynam will be in Glasgow on Friday evening for a special edition of *Sportswide*, when Jim Watt and his manager Terry Lawless will be in the studio.'[18]

In other words, this link is an advance plug, not just for the fight, but for the preview material. And, in relation to the more important events, it is precisely this preview and post-mortem material that expands, adding layers to the whole process of setting-up.

Apart from the mere expansion of preview material, *Grandstand* has three ways by which it marks the place of events in the hierarchy of its sporting world. First, on the days of events which it takes to be most important, the programme is often presented and linked together from the site – rugby at Twickenham, the towpath at Putney on Boat Race day, or Aintree for the Grand National, for example. Second, the programme is often extended and starts earlier, as on Cup Final Day. Third, the main event is privileged by being previewed extensively before other items in the programme are mentioned.

PREVIEWS

In 1974, according to Andrew Tudor (in Buscombe 1975), support programmes contributed almost 30 per cent of total World Cup coverage, and preview and post-mortem material has continued to take up a significant percentage of the air-time devoted to big events. Where major events actually disrupt and transform normal patterns of scheduling (as during Wimbledon fortnight), they are often previewed by separate programmes. The setting-up processes in these programmes constitute a ground on which the past (the rituals and traditions associated with the event) and the future (the narrative questions opened up by the forthcoming event) are connected in points of appeal to the audience to arrange their leisure patterns so as to watch the event to come (see Wenner 1989b).

To follow this through, here is an example from BBC2's *Wimbledon Preview* in 1980. The programme began with a pre-title clip from the previous year's final: Borg wins the final point and sinks to his knees as the crowd cheer, his coach waves his arms in the air, the two players shake hands, Borg shakes hands with the umpire. The titles then came up – a Wimbledon 80 symbol superimposed over a panoramic view of the Wimbledon tennis courts.[19] From the start, then, the programme established the central reified moment of victory – the peak moment of the

Wimbledon fortnight, the winner of the men's singles. The isolating of this moment from the past heightened the ritualistic quality, with its various participants – the winner, the loser, the coach, the umpire and the crowd. The moment was located in the panorama of Wimbledon, which carried with it all the resonance of past tournaments and the one about to begin. David Vine's introduction immediately identified the event as one with a place also in the lives of the audience:

> 'Whatever your plans for the next fortnight, it's a pretty safe bet that the most famous sporting fortnight of the year is going to figure amongst them somewhere.'[20]

The programme established the central narrative question for the coming fortnight, namely, 'Who can stop Borg?', 'Can anyone stop Borg?' The men's singles was treated as much more important than either the doubles or the women's singles. This raises a complex question: to what extent are hierarchisations like this constructed by television, and to what extent does television merely relay, in reflective fashion, the pre-existent hierarchisation of the sport itself?

The narrative question was elaborated by clips and interviews with players, focusing upon McEnroe and questions about his temperament. The same process – raising of narrative questions, singling out of leading characters – was carried out for the women's singles (but not for the doubles) and then Vine, in summing up, repeated the appeal to the audience and its viewing pattern:

> 'We hope you'll be able to join us throughout the fortnight, as much as possible, and I know that we're certainly looking forward to it.'[21]

The preview for the 1980 Open Golf Championship followed a similar pattern. It opened with a long montage of golfers in the moment of success – holing putts, holding up the trophy, saluting the crowd, kissing the trophy, throwing hats in the air, and throwing balls to the crowd. The caption 'Who Will Win The Open?' was then superimposed – again raising the key narrative question. A historical section traced through the winners of previous Opens held at Muirfield. The referencing of a long tradition was here heightened by the changing formal properties of the representations – beginning with a gallery of past champions, such as Harry Vardon and James Braid, in black and white photographs, through newsreel film of Cotton in 1948, a telerecording of Player in 1959, and black and white film of Nicklaus in 1966, to Lee Trevino winning in full colour in 1972.

There followed a series of interviews with top players, establishing the expected leading characters in the forthcoming narrative, and interviews with all five BBC commentators, predicting who they expected to win.

After this, in the winding-up link, anticipation was linked to schedule in the final address to the audience:

> 'Well, we shall be opening up here for tomorrow morning at 5 minutes to eleven on BBC1 and we're looking forward to that, and we hope very much that you'll be able to be with us. And now from Muirfield on the eve of the Open, goodnight.'[22]

The final sequence of the programme was a lengthy repeat of the closing stages of the previous year's Open, following Ballesteros through the last three holes and ending with him receiving the trophy, which functioned as a prolonged appetite whetter. We have in these examples a typical combination of elements of previewing – a reminder of the peak moment of the event, a placing of the traditions, posing of the key narrative questions, introduction or reminder of the main characters who will be featuring, and an appeal to make the event part of your life for the next few days.

Barnett describes the experience of witnessing Botham making his 1986 comeback and getting two wickets at the Oval, and argues that there is a uniqueness about being there – television does not capture the shared momentary pause of wonderment (Barnett 1990: 154). To a large extent this is of course true, but such is the power and the ubiquity of television and its endless recycling of golden moments that the distinction can become blurred. I can remember clearly the being-there-ness of some sporting memories (England v. Portugal in the 1966 World Cup semi-final; Moorcroft beating Maree at Crystal Palace; and Botham's 355th and 356th Test wickets). But with many others (some races featuring Coe or Ovett, for example) I now have to think long and hard before I am sure whether I saw something in the stadium or merely on the screen.

Of course, television has no absolute control over framing; events also exert an influence, and sometimes the symbols by which the event will be remembered impose themselves over the initial frames offered by broadcasters. This happened in both Winter and Summer Olympics in 1988. In Seoul the positive drug test and subsequent disqualification of Ben Johnson overrode all other narratives, inscribing the Games into history as the Drug Olympics, even though there were more positive drug tests four years earlier in Los Angeles.

BBC's Calgary coverage was introduced with a montage of memories from earlier Winter Olympics, starting in black and white and graduating to colour. It was accompanied by the theme from *The Snowman*, a children's cartoon, which served to link the nostalgic memories on the visual level with connotations of snow, fantasy and magic evoked by the music. The montage was built partly around British interest, featuring Nash and Dixon (bobsleigh gold in 1964), and skating gold medallists John Curry (1976), Robin Cousins (1980), and Torvill and Dean (1984). But, as became evident in the opening programme, there was no real British medal hope around which to construct a patriotic position for the audience. In 1988 there was a vacuum, and as nature abhors a vacuum there was a rush of patriotic air, and in soared an eagle. Had Eddie 'the Eagle' Edwards not existed, the media would have had to invent him, which of course in a sense they did. Ski-jumper Edwards was expected to finish last in his event, but his genial 'have a go' attitude and his thick pebble glasses clearly provided the basis for a good media story.

In the absence of a medal hope, he at least offered national identification for a British audience. He was an entertaining interviewee until, taken over by his own image, he lapsed into self-parody. He was also a quirky eccentric with echoes of 'Those Magnificent Men in Their Flying Machines', and early twentieth-century newsreels of failed flight attempts. A major appeal of most Winter Olympics events is the possibility of thrills and spills, as the body is placed in jeopardy, and Edwards's lack of skill served to highlight the danger of the most spectacular of events. He seemed at times almost a sacrificial lamb, small, vulnerable and myopic, and, as he soared precariously into the air, we prayed to the gods, not for a good jump but for his very survival. For British television, Edwards rapidly became The Story of the 1988 Winter Games.

Chapter 8

Stars, narratives and ideologies

'Who cares who came third?'[1]

'Enormous cheers for the tiny Russian mother – a baby only two years ago, the Olympic medal four years ago, the world record this year again, and now the Olympic medal once more.'[2]

Star performers are characters within a set of narratives, and this process in turn provides the basis for the articulation of ideological elements of individualism, competition, gender difference, ethnic difference, work and pressure, and family, regional and national belongingness (see Laclau 1977: 143–200). Poulantzas (1973: 206–24) argues that ideology functions by fragmenting, masking and binding. It fragments events, actions and individuals by helping to mask real underlying patterns of social relations, and binds these fragments together in the form of imaginary coherences. There are many varieties of imaginary coherence, such as 'sport fans', 'ordinary people', families, northerners. The nation itself is, in Benedict Anderson's (1983) term, an imagined community. It is notable how important national identity is to the construction of sport, and, conversely, how important sport is to the construction of national identity. Cuba, the German Democratic Republic, South Korea and Kenya have all used sport to attempt to establish themselves on the world stage. It is striking that one of the first acts of Latvia, Lithuania and Estonia has been to establish Olympic Committees as a first step to entering the Olympic Games.

But set against this must be the growing prominence of individualism. Top sport stars no longer automatically put country first, as Davis Cup team captains know only too well. Internationalisation has opened up new opportunities that mean top sport stars are not just socially but also globally mobile. Television operates at both poles of the individual–nation couplet in its attempts to win and hold us.

Television has, in a sense, not a star system, but a personality system (Langer 1981: 351–66). In constantly selecting particular individuals to be foregrounded, in using individual stars as points of audience identification in both individual and team sports, television of course reproduces and reinforces a star system. But television also tends to turn stars into personalities. So sport performers have a threefold function for television: as stars they are the bearers of the entertainment value of performance; as personalities they provide the individualisation and personalisation through which audiences are won and held; and as characters they are the bearers of the sporting narratives.

In as much as character has a place within television sport, it is predominantly in the form of a star system. So part of the work of television sport involves the introduction of potential stars, the reinforcement of these stars as points of appeal, and the establishment of audience identification with their successes and failures. At the same time, stars always signify – and signify in ways beyond the structure of TV sport – the relation of individual and society (see Dyer 1979).

With regard to personalities, the routine professional practices of television tend to encourage a reliance on reliable contributors, people who can be expected to provide good television (see Elliott 1972, Kumar 1977). It is not necessarily the greatest stars who provide the best television material – a particular type of articulateness, lively, animated and punchy, becomes important. Don Revie, while in some senses the top star football manager of the 1970s, was never as successful a television performer as Malcolm Allison, Laurie McMenemy or Brian Clough (see Wagg 1984: 156–94). Keegan, on the other hand, was a star player who also succeeded in being a (somewhat anodyne) personality.

Performers become prominent in a broader sphere, embracing the world of chat shows, TV adverts, showbusiness gossip, or jet setting, society parties, etc. The initial reasons for public prominence become less foregrounded; celebrities are well known for being well known, in Boorstin's phrase (Boorstin 1961). Such celebrities, while generally emerging as stars or personalities, tend to reach a point where the prominence is self-sustaining; note, for example, the way that racing driver James Hunt and boxers Henry Cooper and Frank Bruno remained in the public eye after their retirement. It is precisely this passage from star to personality and celebrity that provides a means whereby top sport people attempt to negotiate the problems associated with end of career – collapse into obscurity as the star of yesteryear (and note that, with the exception of snooker and golf, retirement for most sports people comes in their mid to late thirties).

The importance of stars to the way television sets up sports is evident in the search for and focus upon stars and the fetishisation of victory and winners (Whannel 1986b). The star ethos inflects previews and post-mortem elements, where stars are used as tokens proving the value of the show. Discussion, negotiating conflicts between expertise and popularity, attempts to hold on to the two by presenting the expert as star and the star as expert.

There is a constant need to introduce new candidates for stardom – 'the word from the Romanian camp is that Melita Ruhn is their new superstar', 'the girl who's never before been in the top Soviet squad and has suddenly become its star' – and the overall stardom frame operates at several levels simultaneously. New stars are introduced, and we are reminded of old favourites, as our memories are reinforced and added to. The whole process is strongly linked to the need to build in British interest as a point of identification:

> Link: (Frank Bough): . . . but tonight there's a real chance of a first gold medal for Britain when Duncan Goodhew swims in the final just a little after 6.30 in the men's 100 metres breaststroke, fortified by the knowledge that he was the fastest qualifier in the heats.
>
> extract from 100 metres heat
>
> Brief interview with Goodhew.
>
> Link: (Frank Bough): Well, that as you will recall, all happened last night, and tonight's final of that event is due off shortly after 6.30. Another Briton in action tonight is Chris Snode, the Commonwealth Games diving champion, who starts his attempt on the springboard title with his preliminary dives.
>
> extract: one dive from Snode
>
> Link: (Frank Bough): Well, we'll see Chris Snode again later, as well as a boxer with a devastating punch called Joey Frost. You may remember that in last year's final, Frost produced the fastest ever knock-out in an ABA final. Look at this.
>
> extract from fight – knock-out in 15 seconds
>
> Link: (Frank Bough): Well, that's the way to do it, isn't it? And we'll see that in a few minutes.[3]

So the programme was set up in terms of the British stars and their chances. When Goodhew won, he became the 'man of the moment', 'what a great champion I think he's going to be', 'a great day for a nice man', 'an impeccably behaved captain'. Interesting was the way various characteristics were highlighted – in this case Goodhew's niceness (although in contrast Coleman endlessly talked about his aggression as a swimmer).

FRAGMENTATION AND MASKING

The way in which the representation of sport establishes a discursive field serves the function of separating and fragmenting. Sport is offered as a world of its own, separate and apart from the rest of the social world. This separation is marked in formal terms: just as, in the press, sports news appears in a separate part of newspapers, with its own hierarchy of news values, similarly on television, sport is separated within the news and in its own set of programmes. It is a world whose boundaries are rigorously policed – 'keep politics out of sport'. Questions of organisation, policy, finance and authority are rarely allowed to intrude into the representational spectacle.

Spectacle shifts attention from production to exchange. As an elaborate form of spectacle, the representation of sport, like spectacle in general, shifts the focus from the social relation of work to the commercial relations of the market-place, from the training ground to the stadium. Work is certainly referred to, but it is in the form of the hard self-sacrificial work necessary for uniquely talented individuals to realise their potential, rather than the socially organised and routinised production of public entertainment.

Individuals are represented as unique, separated from backgrounds, and from other people. They combine the gift of exceptional talent with the ability for remorseless application. Like Lowenthal's idols of consumption, they do not, unlike the idols of production, incite our envy, but only our admiration (Lowenthal 1961: 109–40).

The values upon which this world of stardom is built are primarily those of bourgeois individualism; in other words, an emphasis on individual achievement. This produces a contradiction around the coverage of team sports and the importance of team work, but one generally resolved in favour of the foregrounding of individual contribution. The ideal star is young, male and successful. The maleness of the concept becomes clearer when the qualities evoked and offered for admiration are analysed. There is a stress on a set of qualities traditionally associated with masculinity – toughness, aggression, commitment, power, competitiveness, courage and ability to stand up to pressure. Relatively unimportant by comparison are poise, balance, judgement, timing and dexterity. The need for 'masculine toughness' is underpinned by the constant reference to the pressure of top competition:

'and this is really what it's all about in an Olympic competition – pressure. And there's one man who simply revels in pressure and that's Daley Thompson – he loves it'.[4]

Sporting v. unsporting

If our heroes are determined, aggressive and able to withstand pressure, and achieve success only as a just reward for years of effort, they are also, ideally, models of sportsmanship, even when pitted against the unsporting.

Television constantly attempts to mark the boundaries between the sporting and the unsporting, to reinforce the correct conventions of sporting behaviour. However, the challenge of a rapacious professionalism to a hypocritical amateurism has changed these conventions and placed them under strain. Tennis is now characterised by a total professionalism and commitment to victory that occasionally causes the commentary, in response, to evoke a golden age: 'Oh dear, she's thrown her racket down again. I seem to remember years ago players would have said "good shot" to an opponent'.[5]

Boxing (and, in a more ritualised way, wrestling) makes great play of the sporting/unsporting frame. The Minter v. Antuofermo fight posed Minter as the classic boxer, against Antuofermo the brawler, with transgression of the rules (low punches, etc.) foregrounded.[6] However, use of this frame tends to be overridden by national positioning. Where the brawler is British, our attention is not so clearly drawn to the contrast.

The sporting/unsporting opposition is characteristically condensed onto British/foreign, where our 'own' competitors obey the rules in sporting fashion, unlike the foreign enemy. A contradiction is produced by the residual presence of a condensation of sporting/unsporting onto amateur/professional. There is still a trace of the notion of the professional sportsman as unscrupulous and amoral. The tradition of the amateur gentleman is still evident in the uneasiness with which professionalism is regarded in some quarters.

Old v. young

Contrasts are established between the old experienced performers and the young newcomers, although, as age inevitably tells (and in sport a lot earlier than in most other public spheres), and as television is always alert for new stars, youth is celebrated. Older performers are made only too aware that their dominance is inevitably in danger of eclipse by the next generation. In 1980 Brendan Foster was 'the old man of the team'.[7] The stress on youth – 'a young man with a promising future' – was particularly marked with female competitors, frequently described as 'only 16', 'only 15', etc.[8] One was the oldest lady in the competition at 23.[9] Indeed age is such an often-mentioned fact for women competitors it can attach itself, like a barnacle, to their very identity: 'I'm sure you remember her name, 16 year old Linsey MacDonald.'[10] A cult of youth is evident in the representation of sport, as in other areas of bourgeois individualism such as the fashionable world of fitness chic which celebrates fit, good-looking youth.

But young people are at first unfamiliar to an audience, so older, more established stars, and veterans, play an important role for television. Stephen Hendry, Tom McKean, Graham Hick or Andre Agassi may be the hot youngsters, but Ray Reardon, John Walker, Ian Botham and Jimmy Connors, whilst past their best, are all familiar figures who will draw an audience. Indeed, sport stars like Martina Navratilova, Jimmy Connors and Peter Shilton attract interest precisely because they have been around so long – they appear to be defying the ageing process.

Class

Both class and production are largely masked by this individual-based, performance-centred discourse. The class character of many sport cultures is particularly visible – one only has to compare the Boat Race with speedway; show jumping with darts; tennis with boxing. Yet in television representation it is rarely explicitly alluded to, and generally suppressed. The class difference between these sports on television is less evident than in the lived cultures themselves. The various components of the world of sport are generally offered as discrete, diverse and varied, but with little if any social context underpinning this variance. Only in certain major events with extensive background and preview material, such as Royal Ascot or the Rugby League Cup Final, does the class context emerge more clearly in vision.

Performers are rarely offered as classed individuals – differences that could be rooted in class are frequently displaced onto regional variation or individual idiosyncrasy. No two competitors can have ever been so closely or so regularly compared and contrasted than Seb Coe and Steve Ovett in the years between 1978 and 1982. Yet, of all the differences between them, class background is both the most evident and yet the least remarked upon by television.

Like all popular culture, the representation of television sport systematically treads and re-treads the ground of common-sense, drawing upon the language, axioms, aphorisms, beliefs and superstitions of everyday life, and working them into the form of more elaborated systematic practical ideologies (see Gramsci 1971: 324–5). It does this in particularly striking form in relation to the ideologies of gender and racial and ethnic difference.

Gender: masculinity and femininity

There is a close fit between sport and masculinity; each is a part of the other, so that prowess in sport seems to be, and is seen as, the completion of a young boy's masculinity.[11] By the same token, sport and femininity are seen as antagonistic. To be in sport poses a threat to femininity, and to be feminine poses a problem for sporting activity.[12] Duncan and Hasbrook (1988) suggest that media representation of female sport is likely to involve ambivalence. The media are attempting to validate and encourage audience interest in the particular event they are presenting while, at the same time, reproducing dominant images of gender that tend to emphasise men's superior strength and greater suitability for sport. This process is itself inevitably contradictory: Liz McColgan's 10,000m victory was rightly celebrated for its gutsy commitment, within an overall frame that implies that such attributes are still more appropriately 'masculine'.

The ambivalence is manifest in a number of ways. The audience is reassured that *despite* their involvement in sport, they are still real women, an assertion backed up by reference to family, husbands and children (the implication being that sport is a mere diversion). Where they are too serious, too self-evidently fit, and especially if they're not British, they may be implicitly admonished for being not real women, either physically (hence the notorious imposition of sex tests on some athletes) or sexually. Television will rarely allude directly to women's sexuality, but when the commentary referred to 'A marvellous and very feminine ladies' final in prospect between the two *married girls*'[13] the audience could draw upon a familiarity with 'shock horror' tales of lesbians on the tennis tour in the tabloid press to decode the remark.

In *Grandstand*, during a Marlboro International Trophy race, a woman racing driver was asked how she stayed fit enough to last the distance, and what her husband thought of it all. Neither is a question a male driver might routinely be asked. The driver, Desiree Wilson, had been racing for 14 years, since she was 12, and so obviously was very experienced. She won a race at Brands Hatch, which, it was pointed out, was a very difficult course (difficult for a woman?) and when she finished in 'a fine third place', it was called a 'terrific achievement because she is quite small and it requires a lot of strength to handle these cars'.[14]

Not only is there a constant implication that sport is a bit aberrant for a woman, but, even for top performers, it is 'natural' that other things come first: 'Since Chris married, tennis hasn't been quite at the top of her priorities – which is quite natural.'[15] It is the very qualities seen as so essential for sport that are constantly suggested to be a bar to women: 'She is the sort of girl one associates with the type of person who doesn't want to dominate anybody . . . and in American Tennis if you don't learn to dominate you don't compete at all.'[16] If a woman does show any qualities of toughness or aggression, these are frequently marked as masculine traits:

'Well there are many men doubles players who'd like to have a return of service like that.'[17]

'I wouldn't want to be unkind to her, but I'd say she almost swims like a man – she's certainly got a man's physique.'[18]

'If you saw the training schedule that Louise Miller goes through – it would frighten many men.'[19]

When Ingrid Kristiansen led for the first half of the 1987 London Marathon and then dropped back, the commentary kept saying that she was 'paying the price for over-aggression', as if a mere woman had to be punished for such presumption.[20] And this kind of toughness is often set against feminine beauty as if the two were incompatible: 'Petra Schneider, not the prettiest of swimmers, but my god, she's tough.'[21] These elements of a gender ideology were often articulated with political ideological elements. Tough, non-feminine qualities were often evoked for East European athletes. One long jumper was 'a big powerful East European woman', and the Russian rowers were 'a big and powerful team of ladies'.[22] By contrast, the women we were most confidently invited to identify with were those, mostly western, who have all the 'correct' traits of femininity, which are constantly drawn attention to: 'a leggy Sonia Lannaman'; 'Tessa Sanderson, another of the beauties in Britain's team'.[23] TV seems particularly fond of femininity in its 'little girl' form. A young woman tennis player was recently described as being of 'tender years', and the coverage of gymnastics highlights this theme:

> 'Gymnastics has always been one of the Olympic showpiece sports but in recent years it's been even more popular. Mainly because of the women, and mainly because they're not women but young girls'.[24]

> 'And here we have the tiniest girl in the whole competition [the commentator mentions her height and weight]. She really is a little speck. I think she might win a few hearts here – 14 years of age'.[25]

The appearance of sexuality in gymnastics is quite complex, and depends in part upon the culture and coaching conventions of gymnastics itself. The sport is certainly well aware of its television audience. There is a combination of little girl cuteness, precocious sexuality, elements of Hollywood in some of the music, elements of burlesque and oblique reference to showgirl-type routines, and Eastern and Arabic influences. The references to 'girls' are typical of a wide range of sport coverage. At times, television's attempts to mark the aberrance of masculine traits in a woman, the naturalness of femininity and the true place of women as part of a family, all at the same time, veer close to parody in their strenuous efforts to hold on to all ends of the chain, as in this ITV voice over a basketball item:

> 'The ITV team have come across some fairly unusual characters here in Moscow, none more so than in the basketball arena. If you like your ladies on the tall side look no further than Juliana Semanova – the most effective woman basketball player in the world. The 28 year old Russian stands 6 foot 11 inches and towers over team mates and opponents alike. . . . Semanova tips the scales at a modest 17 stone and wears specially constructed shoes, size 18 . . . on court she's an awesome proposition, but off it she's just another fun-loving girl who enjoys pop music and

wants to start a family, perhaps a basketball team of her own. English literature plays a part in her life, she cites Charles Dickens as her favourite author. And Semanova's ambition – to pit the skills of the women's team against the men. Well the men haven't taken up the challenge yet, and perhaps you can't blame them.'[26]

In men, of course, any appearance of femininity often has to be explained away, as in this Murray Walker comment on a motor cyclist: 'see the long hair poking out from under the helmet, but don't let that fool you, he's very tough indeed';[27] and inadequate performance can be derided by reference to women: '65 seconds for the first lap . . . that's slower than the women would run at this race'.[28].

Race and Britishness

The representation of black people in sport also draws upon and articulates elements of common-sense and elements of racist ideologies. Cashmore (1982) has analysed the way the myth of 'natural ability' is used to suggest that blacks are lazy because they don't need to work at it. Wiggins (1989) has reviewed the historical context of the debate over supposed 'natural ability'. Lashley (1990) examines the way sporting opportunities for blacks are limited by their lack of access to powerful positions. Maguire (1988) investigates the degree to which black footballers are stacked in the peripheral speed-based positions and kept away from the more dominant tactical midfield roles. A recent collection (Jarvie 1991b) explores many of these issues further. Crystal Palace chairman, Ron Noades, recently demonstrated one strand in popular common-sense when he was inter- viewed for the Channel 4 programme, *Great Britain United*.[29] He reeled off a set of stereotypical attitudes – not many black players can read the game; in winter you need hard white men to carry the artistic black players through – and suggested black players had nothing to offer management because strength and speed were not needed. Of course these views stood exposed in the context of the programme, but interestingly were also widely condemned in the press, including some tabloids.[30]

As with gender, there is a degree of ambivalence around images of race in sport on television. While sport offers a fund of positive images of talented black athletes succeeding, it also does serve to reproduce elements of stereotypical attitudes. On television this is often articulated in terms of natural ability and tactical naivety. When three Ethiopians constantly exchanged the lead in a Moscow Olympics distance race this was repeat- edly ascribed to tactical naivety, in contrast to the disciplined running of the Finns. It could equally have been regarded as an inspired bit of tactical running that put the Finns off their stride and produced a win for Ethiopian Yifter. It has been subsequently widely rumoured that the 'dedication and commitment' of the Finns extended to the distasteful, if not illegal, practice of blood-doping, and Finnish runner Vaino was stripped of a Los Angeles Olympic medal after failing a drugs test – so much for experience.

But these articulations are contradictory. Analysis of representations of black people on television suggests that, in contrast to the images of social problems, inner city riots and the racist discourses of crime and immigration, sport coverage offers a striking contrast. Here alone is a whole range of positive images of black people being active, fit, talented, self-determining, successful and popular. Internationally, particularly in athletics, leading black competitors like Ed Moses, Carl Lewis and Merlene Ottey have dominated their events. Black boxers in general have been dominant, but it was Muhammad Ali whose own highly visible public persona did most to articulate this to black pride and cultural identity. In cricket, Viv Richards, Joel Garner and the West Indian team in general have similarly dominated the sport.

Yet the contradictions are always present. Sport, like showbusiness, has always been an escape route from the ghetto, while simply reinforcing old stereotypes, such as 'all blacks are good for is sprinting and tap dancing'. Although sport constitutes a socially acceptable arena for black visibility, any overt challenging of dominant assumptions does not go unpunished. Ali was exiled for his opposition to the Vietnam war, but it is clear that his membership of the Black Muslim movement had as much to do with his suspension by the boxing establishment. The American sprinters Carlos and Smith who staged a Black Power demonstration in Mexico in 1968 had their careers wrecked. Neither Carlos and Smith nor Ali received any significant approval in the sporting media, where the general attitude was one of condemnation.

On the national level, clearly sport has been an arena of cultural visibility for black Britons, particularly in athletics, boxing and, to an extent, cricket. This has been articulated in liberal–integrationist discourse as part of the process of becoming British. But it is possible that such successes have also been significant in the defining and articulating of a black cultural identity. West Indian success at cricket has clear and strong cultural resonances among black Britons, as the joyful waving of the 'blackwash!' banner to celebrate a 5–0 Test victory over England demonstrated. When soccer team West Bromwich Albion had three highly successful black players in the 1970s their support notably drew on the local black community to a greater extent than the all-white Aston Villa side of the same area. In terms of cultural identity, neither blackness nor Britishness is a fixed, stable element, and sport and its representations are one site on which the way these elements are articulated is in process of transformation (see Gilroy 1987, 1990).

The media deal with this in various ways. Sometimes blackness is in effect masked in the same fashion as class – it is not referred to on the verbal level, although unlike class it is of course instantly visible. If television tends to mask blackness as a cultural factor, it has also tended to be silent about the presence of racist chanting and barracking at football, and more recently at cricket. But there is clearly an underlying structure of Britishness that seems to make it more possible for those performers (Frank Bruno) who do not constitute a challenge or a threat to whiteness to become popular stars. The more assertive Lloyd Honeyghan is one of the few sport performers to have taken a public stand against the iniquities of apartheid, giving up a world title and much money rather than fight a South African. He seems unlikely to become the form of popular hero that Bruno has become, which seems to suggest a hidden structure in the representation of star personalities. A *Radio Times* cover (29/7/78) showing Tessa Sanderson, Sharon Colyear and Sonia Lannaman in bikinis running through surf in Jamaica rendered the three as doubly distanced: the picture suggested the Caribbean (they are 'not really British') and they are not in athletic context. Distanced from sport, they are on display, objectified, no longer active sporting women but women to be looked at, available for the male gaze (see Figure 8.1). The televising of Daley Thompson's whistling during the national anthem can be similarly read, through his blackness, as signifying a distancing from the less problematic patriotism of a Seb Coe.[31] Even in the multi-cultural sporting context, black Britons all too easily become culturally invisible. At the 1987 World Athletic Championships, over 30 per cent of the British team were black, yet an advertisement for the Olympus sports shop showed a shop full of sports stars, all of whom were white.

Work

The production of the sporting performance is partially masked. Work is frequently referred to and training sometimes shown, but only within a discourse of commitment and dedication. The huge industrial process that now underlies top-level sport – the organisation and management of events, the employment of officials, the obtaining of sponsorship, the deals with clothing manufacturers such as the giant Adidas, the contractual commitments of players – in short, the dense and complex web of social and economic relations that produces the spectacle, receives little attention. Like all specialist journalists, those who cover sport for television have a close relation with those whose activities they represent. Such relations make for good reportage and minimal critical journalism.

Along with the stress on commitment, toughness, aggression and ability to withstand pressure goes a stress on the hard work necessary to prepare, and the portrayal of victory as a deserved reward for that work. When Goodhew won his swimming gold at Moscow, the commentary emphasised the effort and years of hard training.[32] Sharron Davies's silver was won

LONDON (BBC Radio London: page 50) 29 July – 4 August 1978   Price 13p

RadioTimes

Fun and Games

Before the Commonwealth Games (full coverage
from Edmonton, Canada, on BBCtv and Radio from Thursday)
Tessa Sanderson, Sharon Colyear and Sonia Lannaman,
three of Britain's athletic hopes,
went to Jamaica. See back feature

GREAT SUMMER OF SPORT
COMMONWEALTH
GAMES

Figure 8.1   Radio Times cover (29/7/78) showing three British athletes. The 'Fun and Games' title, the bikinis and the surf all contribute to a suggestion that this is not really serious competition as far as the 'girls' are concerned. The placing of these three in a Caribbean environment creates a distance from Britishness, despite the sub-heading description of them as 'three of Britain's athletic hopes'.

despite 'a really tough time . . . illness . . . psychological pressure . . . months of torment and disappointment', and 'crowned four years of hard work'.[33] What is masked by this kind of emphasis is that presumably all the other competitors put in years of hard work too and gained no reward for it. This is precisely one of those elements of sport discourse that can be most successfully articulated into an individualist ideology of endeavour – winners are celebrated, losers disappear. And along with work and toughness comes the constantly cited pressure. 'It's all part of the swimming competition scene.'[34] 'There is extra pressure on our team as they set out to retain the toughest of all Olympic titles.'[35]

> 'So the pressure is really on her as she comes up to do her second vault. A great deal of pressure on her – into her second vault and it's got to be good. It's amazing how she can come into a routine with all the pressure on her.'[36]

Coping with this pressure, it is constantly underlined, requires aggression, commitment and power. It is the 'masculineness' of these skills that contributes to the contradictions set up and constantly reproduced between femininity and sport. It is only in the supposedly artistic sports that desirable qualities are those of femininity. This is seen at its height in gymnastics, where the discourse of the commentary, in highlighting grace, elegance, poise and balance, elevates the aesthetic at the expense of the contest. There is a notable stress on perfection, which precisely puts the notion of 'competition' in crisis, one commentator wondering 'just how much further they can push the barriers in their sport'.[37] The entertainment value of this art, rather than the desire to see who wins, is often the centre of the appeal to the viewer: 'The frontiers of the sport were pushed almost to the limit, but for the viewer, as I say, it was sheer enjoyment.'[38] This is not to say that other elements are absent. Strength, physical power and danger are still alluded too, even if their presence is not prominent. The double bind for women in sport is that they are generally portrayed as not strong enough, or lacking dedication and commitment, but where they possess these qualities they are often seen as unfeminine.

UNITING

Having separated individuals from the social context and masked their class belongingness and position within social relations, the ideological operation provides new unifying coherences. There is a dual operation at work. Athletes are established as star performers, and values are attributed to their work, with youth, toughness, aggression and ability to withstand pressure being foregrounded. But television must also work to transform stars into personalities, people with recognisable human characteristics that we can identify with, as a way of winning and holding our attention.

There are two main ways that television sport is able to articulate character – by relating the individual to the personal, and by linking the individual to the wider collectivity. The relating of the individual to the personal characteristically stresses some form of family link and places the individual in the context of that family connection, in the process marking gender difference firmly. The linking of the individual to the wider collectivity involves an articulation of region, nation or race, and draws upon national identity.

Individual into personal: the family

On the visual level there are frequent cuts between a performer and a watching family. So we see footballers' wives at Wembley, Frank Bruno's mother, Nick Faldo's wife, Liz McColgan's husband, and Sergei Bubka's extended family. Bjorn Borg's coach appears visually almost as a surrogate father – cut to at the same moments as a parent and producing the same reactions. We see Martina Navratilova's (female) partner in shot in similar familial circumstances, but on the verbal level the relationship is not explicitly alluded to. This lack of reference to non-heterosexual couples or relationships is another instance of masking, except that television is able to assume our intertextual knowledge of gossip about lesbian tennis players in the tabloid press.

In fact the practices of television produce an interesting visual blurring of the distinction between parents and coaches. Ice skating is set up so as to catch competitors in shot sitting down with coaches (who often look like, and sometimes are, parents) while the judges' scores are revealed. The blurring of roles of parent or partner and coach are particularly significant in the case of women, whose success is so often attributed to a man, and whose success and moment in the spotlight so often have to be shared with men:

> 'She's been very well programmed by her coach, Tommy Boyle'.[39]

> 'Coached by her husband, she's got a 7-year-old son and he'll be watching this on television.'[40]

> 'She's going to celebrate, I think, with retirement, and marry her coach.'[41]

Families always have to be happy ones – Sharron Davies was asked 'What did your dad say before the race?', but no hint was given to viewers that the often oblique references to anguish and torment actually referred to Sharron Davies's difficult relationship with her father.[42] Family and partner responsibilities are in conflict with sport involvement but not in a simple manner. If the dominant inflection is that women are not perfectly suited for sport, do it as a hobby and will end up in the home, there is also an emergent element, inflected by the rise of the women's movement, that is at the least open to a reading supporting a more positive view of women and sport. Representations of women in sport provide a stock of potentially positive images of women being physically active, fit, successful and demonstrating that being female and reaching the top in sport are not necessarily incompatible, even if the verbal anchorage produces a more contradictory reading. The following example seems to me to be open to different readings:

> 'And if the 1980 Games have proved anything, I think they've proved that women have finally and fully arrived in the world of international sport. If you look at Kasankina in the women's 1500m – she's a double gold medallist from the last Olympics, took time out to have a baby, came back on the track, gives a devastating display, in a time that would have won the men's event in 1920'.[43]

While this does in the end validate Kasankina only by reference to a man's performance, it also acknowledges that there is no absolute conflict between having a baby and being a top sport performer, and no reason why mothers should not return to their work. Yet on television her identity as a mother somehow begins to supplant her identity as an athlete:

> 'Enormous cheers for the tiny Russian mother – a baby only two years ago, the Olympic medal four years ago, the world record this year again, and now the Olympic medal once more.'[44]

It is characteristic that women are praised and returned to the domestic practically in the same breath. In 1991, in the build-up to the 10,000m at the World Athletics Championships, the contest between Liz McColgan and Ingrid Kristiansen was dubbed 'the battle of the supermums'.[45] The success of sporting individuals is unique because they are unique, yet whilst being extraordinary they are also ordinary – like the rest of us they have parents, partners and children, whose admiration will be part of the prize. This again is a feature of the idols of consumption; they did not get where they are through unfair advantage – in the end they are just like us.

Individual into collective: national identity

The primary collective identity to which individuals are attached is of course the nation. National identity is a major point of identification for the audience, even though, given the peculiar and contradictory amalgam that constitutes the British state, a uniquely uneasy one. The very name is unstable – England/Great Britain/British Isles/United Kingdom – and the distinction between Britishness and Englishness is characteristically blurred.

Television coverage produces images of the nation and addresses its audience in terms of national belongingness, referring to 'our' chances, 'speaking for us all' and celebrating 'a great day for Britain'. The language of chauvinism is ever present – 'great stuff for Britain', through the ups and downs, 'yes, disappointment there for the whole country',[46] and the attention of viewers of the Moscow Olympics was often drawn to 'the small British contingent in this giant communist crowd'.[47] Even in individual sports, a collective frame intervenes, linking performers to national identity. When motor racer Nigel Mansell was leading the Canadian Grand Prix in 1991, it was 'great news for Mansell, great news for Williams, great news for Britain'.[48] The national focus frequently amounts to tunnel vision. In the television build-up to the 1500m semi-finals at the Seoul Olympics in 1988 on Channel 4, out of a total of 11 minutes and 47 seconds, 8 minutes 52 seconds were devoted exclusively to the British runners.[49]

Regional identities are evoked too, but often framed by popular nationalism – the genial Geordie, the battling Brummie, and the crafty Cockney may all be competing, but in the end they are all part of that rich diversity of Englishness. Individual sports like darts and snooker make great use of regional identities, via accents, etc., and refer individuals to the nation-components of the British state, 'The Scottish extrovert meets the gentle giant from Wales'. In the graphic illustrating forthcoming matches at the Butlin Darts, each player's name was followed by a little flag symbol – England, Scotland, Wales.[50] Similarly the State Express World Challenge Cup used a graphic of snooker balls with national flags on them. Regional identity can be neatly and instantly sutured to national identity – 'That's the way, that old bulldog spirit – these Liverpool boys know how to do it'.[51] Here, in one neat move, elements of localism, masculinity and Britishness are articulated together.

All this is not accomplished without conflict. In the Jim Watt v. Robert Vasquez fight, the fighters arrived behind the Union Jack and the Stars and Stripes, and 'God Save the Queen' and the US anthem were played. As Watt is Scottish and Vasquez of Mexican parents, the USA v. Great Britain frame is an uneasy one.[52] Scottish football matches in the 1970s were marked by noisy barracking of God Save the Queen, the fans expressing their own preference for that Scottish nationalist anthem of the 1970s, 'Flower of Scotland' (Cosgrove 1986: 99–111).

This is where representing sport becomes problematic: there is a contradiction not simply between localism and nationalism but around a British national identity in which the part (Englishness) characteristically signifies the whole, appropriating and standing for the subordinate Celtic national identities of Welshness, Scottishness and Irishness. It is a contradiction resolved in various ways, from the veneer of impartiality when England play Scotland/Wales/N. Ireland, and the partisanship of England v. a foreign nation, to the appropriation of Scottish success under the signifier of 'British'. Typically, a dominant Englishness either incorporates or marginalises the Scots, Welsh and Irish. Scottishness is itself a complex amalgam, shot through with the imposition of invented traditions (see Trevor-Roper 1983, Jarvie 1991a). Ireland too, with its particular relation to Britishness, its complex combination of political, religious, nationalist and republican tensions, has in consequence a split sporting identity (see Sugden and Bairner 1986). Such tensions are not necessarily directly reflected in the sporting field – during the 1990 World Cup Irish team manager, the Englishman, Jack Charlton, became a popular hero in Dublin, whilst Irish ex-footballer and journalist Eamon Dunphy, who publicly criticised the style of the team, became so unpopular that in one Dublin pub, when his face appeared on TV, the drinkers began singing 'If you hate fucking Dunphy clap your hands'. The signifiers of national identities in sport are not necessarily straightforward, as this confused set of tensions between national belongingness and team identity suggests.

On English television, international competition is most commonly set up as Britain/England v. the rest. Characteristically this draws upon the ideology of fair play and sporting behaviour, whereby it is sporting Brits against the not so sporting rest. Foreigners are either quaint, funny and incompetent or, if they regularly beat us, take it far too seriously, benefit from levels of state and/or private support not open to the poor British, and probably use drugs. There is also a broader cultural frame at work that counterposes serious, competent Europeans and westerners with fun-loving, disorganised blacks, and the third world generally.

Whereas British athletes are characterised by their admirable qualities, foreigners are often shown either as over-resourced (as in this slightly bizarre comparison: 'These days it's the long standing traditions of Henley and the Boat Race against the resources and organisation of the East Europeans'[53]) or as comical. Television's 1980 Olympic coverage gained amusing mileage from a Hungarian celebrating in flamboyant fashion, a Tanzanian hockey goalkeeper who let in a vast number of goals, and a Mozambican swimmer who took two and a half minutes to finish the 200m.[54] It's worth reflecting that our gymnasts probably look a bit comical to the Romanians. Irish jokes surfaced in the shape of the pentathlete who went the wrong way[55] and the tracksuit with OYLMPIC on it.[56] The mobilisation of racist stereotypes for comic effect perhaps saw its nadir when the Indian hockey team were said to be on a bonus of 100 popadoms a man.[57] Even where other nations were successful they could be trivialised. 'It was a great day for a Pole with a pole' – he won the gold medal.[58] After winning the 200m the Italian was described as 'with his eyes staring, almost in a frenzy'.[59] Our own Seb Coe has been known to look a little strange in the moment of victory, but this passes without such derogatory comment.

The construction of foreigners in television sport offers two contradictory versions of otherness. Where foreigners are of inferior performance compared with the British they are regarded as a joke, as incompetent, as naive, or as not taking it seriously. But where foreign performance is superior, this is often ascribed to the unfair advantages of greater state support, as in the Eastern bloc, greater resources, as in the USA, the use of drugs, or simply taking it all too seriously. Only the sporting Brits have got the balance right. Where no British competitors can be found to identify with, television adopts a variety of strategies to help hold our attention. When at Moscow in 1980 there were no Britons involved in the boxing, a British angle was found by having Joey Frost at the ringside to comment on his chances against the winner – 'And I wouldn't have thought Joey Frost would be too worried by what he saw there', and, during another fight, 'clearly there's a potential opponent for Joey Frost in the welterweight division'.[60] Irish competitors were sometimes enrolled as surrogate Brits – 'There's no British interest in this but Eamonn Coghlan and John Treacy going for Ireland'[61] – and so were Commonwealth competitors, as when a commentator, clutching at straws, proclaimed, 'In the absence of a British competitor our hopes lie with the Australian girl'.[62] Even a family connection can be invoked:

> 'The most heart warming of all victories, certainly all the athletes thought so, was in the steeplechase. There was Bronislaw Malinowski, half a Scot through his mother, coming out at the very last minute to take the gold he so richly deserved'.[63]

By contrast, the greater separateness of black Britons from national identity is notable. Frank Bruno may be 'ours', but can the same be said of boxers Lloyd Honeyghan or Dennis Andries? Television appears more able to appropriate a white Pole with a Scottish relative than a black Briton.

The royal nation: a state made popular

Sport is one of those sites on which popular ritual and state and royal pageantry sometimes meet. In the case of FA Cup Final Day the popular aspects of the ritual are in the ascendancy, and the presence of the royals is relatively marginal. At Ascot and Badminton the royal family assume centre stage. Royal Ascot in 1980 had a ceremonial opening with a parade down the course, white horses, red-coated riders, and the Band of the Welsh Guards playing the anthem as the parade reached the Queen Elizabeth II stand. The Queen, Prince Philip and the Queen of Denmark were in the first carriage, Prince Charles and the Queen Mother in the

Figure 8.2 TV Times cover (28/3/87). Racing provides a prime site around which the monarchy can be located as within and part of popular cultural practices.

second with the Grand Duchess of Luxembourg and the Prince of Denmark. The crowd gave three cheers, and on television Jan Leeming was brought in to discuss the dresses.[64] At the Badminton Horse Trials images of class privilege were everywhere. The event takes place on a huge private estate with a large country house in the background. We saw Mark Phillips, Prince Charles on a horse, the Queen with her host the Duke of Beaufort, the Queen and Prince Charles in the stable yard, Anne and Mark, Prince and Princess Michael, the Queen and Edward, the Queen and Colonel Whitbread.[65]

All of this was naturalised by a verbal level that treated the occasion like any other sport event. Television on the verbal level remains silent about, and hence masks, the massive sense of a privileged elite that is only too apparent on the visual level. It manages and handles the contradiction between class privilege and the popularity of the monarchy, generally accomplishing it with effortless ease. This articulating of popular pleasure and royalty through television sport is well illustrated by a *TV Times* cover featuring the Queen Mother at the races, with a story about the 'Royal Champion: The Queen Mother and her Beloved Horses' (see Figure 8.2). Under the sub-heading 'Queen Mum's a winner in more ways than one', an article inside celebrates her relation to the people: 'A quarter of a million people were present that day and it seemed as if a quarter of a million voices were yelling and screaming for the Queen Mother's horse.'[66] The royal family has increasingly turned to popular television to strengthen its populist appeal – as in appearances by Princess Anne on *A Question of Sport*, and Prince Andrew and other royals on a special charity version of *It's A Knockout*.

NARRATIVE: THE CASE OF COE AND OVETT

The coverage of the Coe–Ovett 'story' during the Moscow Olympics of 1980 provides a good case study in the process of narrativisation. Clearly television did not invent this story, or create its importance within the scheme of things. It did, however, draw on it heavily as part of its appeal to viewers. In doing so it constantly foregrounded the events precisely as a story, which can be understood in terms of the workings of the hermeneutic code (Barthes 1974: 19). The hermeneutic code poses the initial enigma of a narrative, and gives the text its forward progression towards the resolution of the enigma. So as not to answer the question too soon, a number of strategies are adopted. The most relevant here are constant reformulation of the question, the promise that there will be an answer, and the provision of a partial answer. As opposed to fiction, in television sport the event itself is clearly not structured by the conventions of narrative, apart from the basic competitive structure of sport that results in winners and losers. But in the way television is able to draw upon the inherent hermeneutic of sport events, to reorganise, to re-present it, it can be said to be narrativising.[67]

Television coverage of the 1980 Moscow Olympics was dominated by the Coe–Ovett story. It could of course be argued that the prominence given to this story was merely right, proper and natural. After all, Coe and Ovett are two of the most successful British athletes ever, they were currently world record holders at their main events, and almost unprecedentedly joint holders of the 1500m world record. They had virtually never raced each other and were about to meet in both the 800m and the 1500m in the world's premier athletics event, the Olympic Games. Is this not a good story by any standards? To agree that it is an extremely good story does not mean accepting that its dominant position in the coverage is simply natural. On the contrary, the factors that make it, for British television, a major story are rooted in cultural assumptions open to analysis.

The high value placed on notions of 'greatest', be it fastest, highest or longest, ensures a focus upon world record holders. The Olympic Games is supposedly a competition that determines the best. The strong emphasis placed on British competitors enables audience identification. Sport itself and television coverage of it are both male centred. There is a strong tendency to treat men's events and men's sports more seriously than women's events and women's sports. We see athletics as the premier Olympic sport. This does not mean that it has the same level of prominence in different countries – to the Romanians, for example, gymnastics may appear far more important. Track events are generally given more television prominence than field events. One reason could well be the lack of a tradition of world-class British competitors. But also track events fit the conventions of TV sport more adequately – the competitive aspect is more directly and immediately visible. Finally, British television has always emphasised the middle distance events, often called the 'blue riband' events. This is no doubt influenced by the tradition of good runners and the mystique of Bannister's 4 minute mile, but again it can be suggested that these events fit the needs of television particularly well.

So a middle distance race between two male British world record holders in the Olympic Games is certainly a good story. Indeed, it fits so many of the criteria for prominence that the focus on Coe and Ovett during the second week of the Olympics amounted at times to tunnel vision. Very little time was devoted during the previews to discussing the other runners in the 1500m. In outlining the structure of the Coe/Ovett narrative, I will not distinguish between ITV and BBC, in part because the conventions of television sport are broadly common to both, and in terms of their handling of this narrative the similarities seemed to be more significant than the differences.

1 Posing the question

The Coe and Ovett contest was a major feature of the Olympic coverage right from the opening programmes, in which the central question 'Who will win?' was immediately posed, with an implicit enigma 'which is the greatest?' Coe and Ovett were inscribed from the start as the characters, the contenders; in other words, the question was not who would win the 800m/1500m, but would Coe or Ovett win. Subsidiary questions developed the story, drawing upon contrasts in personal style. The first tangible event was the arrival of each. Coe 'conducts himself impeccably',[68] Ovett was 'greeted like the star he is',[69] the man who has 'done things his way'.[70] The implied good guy/bad guy contrast was invoked. An opposition of experience/youth was introduced, on the basis that, though there was little difference in age, Ovett had had more competition. The heats and semi-finals were comfortably won by Ovett and Coe, and both were regarded as 'going well'.

2 Partial answer

Ovett's victory in the 800m altered the position by giving a partial answer to the question. This called for a reformulation of some of the questions, but also marked a point from which recapitulation of the story could be offered. This happened both within the Olympic highlight programmes and in news bulletins.

3 Periodic organisation (1)

It was a 'golden day for Britain' and a 'triumph for the strong silent man who hates publicity'. The contrast was made between Ovett with 'the gold he wanted so much' and Coe offering 'the briefest of handshakes'. There was talk that the East Europeans tried the only way they knew to stop Ovett (i.e. physically) but 'he's big enough to look after himself' and 'wasn't having any nonsense'. The 'strong silent man had spoken with his feet as he always threatened to do'. Finally we were reminded that this was only a partial answer; 'now we wait for the race of the century part two'.[71]

4 The answer revealed

The 1500m was described as a fantastic run by Coe. After the 'misery of last weekend, now everything is golden again'.[72] Two themes emerged: Coe got 'the revenge he wanted' and Ovett 'takes the defeat well'.[73] A major feature of this resolution was that, while the question 'Who will win?' was resolved, the larger enigma, 'Which is the best?', remained unresolved. This fitted the need for a continuing Coe–Ovett story that could go on providing a point of identification for viewers. Both channels remarked on this: 'the arguments will go on',[74] 'the argument remains, which one is greater'.[75]

5 Periodic organisation (2)

The race was over and the narrative resolved, but not yet completed. The story was in fact re-told in precis form in post-mortem programmes and news bulletins and also in the final highlights programmes. It was of course implicitly a fairy-tale ending. Not only did it produce two gold medals for Britain, not only did the (good guy) hero triumph over adversity, after suffering defeat, crisis of confidence and illness, but the bad guy, magnanimous in defeat, turned out to be a good guy after all. Additionally, in television terms not only was the story a great success in itself, but, in that the final enigma of 'Who is better?' remained unresolved, the continuing story was given a greater impetus for following years.

Rivalry

Reducing the race to a competition between two people presented it as an individual head-to-head contest. Metaphors used to describe this drew upon other models for head-to-head conflict, such as boxing, bullfighting, duelling, war and gladiatorial combat. The race was called a battle, a heavyweight championship, a duel. Winning the 800m was first blood to Ovett. Coe and Ovett were the gladiators, they were at the moment of truth. Coe's victory was revenge. Much was made of the rivalry between the two. ITV put together an edited sequence of preparations for the 800m semi-final with a voice-over suggesting that Coe and Ovett were not on speaking terms and were ignoring each other. Coverage in the media echoed the style of world title boxing coverage. There is some evidence that audiences respond more to commentaries that foreground tension between participants (Bryant *et al.* 1977). The framing of events in terms of head-to-head confrontation – Coe v. Ovett, Decker v. Budd, Fatima Whitbread v. Tessa Sanderson – has been a growing feature of television sport during the 1980s.

Experience v. naivety

After Ovett won the 800m, the contrast of his experience and Coe's naivety was mobilised. Ovett was 'battle hardened', the 'master tactician', the 'man who stamps his authority on a race', 'always in command'. Coe by comparison was said to lack experience and, after the defeat, to lack confidence. He was called tactically naive, his 800m was a tactical disaster, and it was suggested that his preparation may have been inadequate.

Within the context of the narrative, the doubts over Coe's experience and confidence constitute problems. Coe, as a character in the narrative, has to overcome these if he is to triumph.

Aggression

The emphasis on such qualities as toughness, commitment, aggression and ability to withstand pressure is a typical feature of the representation of top-level sport. The presence of these qualities in Ovett and possible absence of them in Coe were part of the post-800m reformulation of the story. The subsequent course of the narrative was structured by the need for Coe to acquire these qualities. The first reformulation referred to his lack of aggression and the need for him to become physically involved. The second referred to him gaining in determination, learning aggression and showing signs of aggression. In particular, his brief imitation of a sparring boxer after the 1500m semi-final was taken as a sign of the success of this learning process. The resolution of the narrative provided the proof of the value of this learning process, Coe's victory being taken as a token of his new-found ability to compete.

That the need to learn aggression, or to be aggressive, should be foregrounded in this way conforms to a more general pattern. Study of sport coverage more generally shows that while there is a wide range of qualities invoked – toughness, aggression, commitment, power, courage, ability to withstand pressure, and also balance, poise, judgement, timing, dexterity, speed, accuracy, concentration, flair, imagination – there is a tendency to evaluate more highly the first six of these. In turn these qualities conform closely to conventional constructions of masculinity. There are many factors that have inhibited the progress of women in sport – lack of facilities at school, the hidden curriculum, limited or male-based sport facilities, a lack of leisure in the sense that men have known it.[76] But important, too, is the systematic underpinning of gender difference that the representation of sport provides.

THE BIG SHOWDOWN

The dominance of the Coe–Ovett story provided a perfect overall narrative structure for the Olympic coverage as a whole, offering a way of constantly forging points of identification for the viewer. Moscow offered only a partial answer to the key narrative question, each athlete winning the event that the other was expected to win. In 1981 the two continued to break records whilst avoiding each other. Media coverage and public interest in a confrontation grew in tandem. Athletics amended its rules to allow payment to athletes by means of trust funds, and three races featuring Coe and Ovett were planned for 1982. The event advertised on the *Radio Times* cover of 17 July 1982 (see Figure 8.3) was to be the first race of the three. This cover, while not itself a photograph, references and mobilises our familiarity with the codes and conventions of sports photography. It is an attempt to capture for us a photograph that does not exist and so carries with it a promise – the promise of utopia. The cover offers us a golden moment still to come: Coe and Ovett battling it out down the home straight.

It is, I think, an exceptional image, and it is worth briefly highlighting its salient points. It shows two runners in white, whose position, height and apparent weight are very similar. The picture emphasises muscularity. Their eye lines meet in a striking mutual stare. The absences too are striking – no numbers on the vests, no colours denoting sponsors or national affiliation (apart from a residual trace of red and blue in the stripes on the sides of the shorts), no other competitors, no ads, no officials, no trackside equipment, and the crowd a mere blurr in the background. The athletes burst out of the frame towards us. The spectacle is perfectly presented for our eye with all extraneous detail erased, as if we had suddenly been blessed with tunnel vision.

The picture mimics photography in many ways: the angle, framing and cropping are all characteristic of athletics photography, as is the way the painting mimics the out-of-focus blue blurr of the crowd produced by telephoto lenses. But the *Radio Times* cover is not simply an attempt to capture the realism effect of photography. The rendering of the two runners as physically equal (Coe is in fact shorter and slighter), the elimination of extraneous detail, the almost eroticised stress on muscularity, and the slight hint of caricature, all proclaim the painting. This gives the confrontation a mythic dimension without finally undermining its realness. It promises an ideal moment, and one precisely not available in photographic form.

There is also more than a hint of reference to the Greeks – athletes in white, with connotations of purity and the amateur tradition; but also connotations of gods, Titans, clashes and mythic confrontations. At the time this picture appeared, the British audience was being offered another representation of athletics, also featuring the story of the confrontation between two rivals, both British. The film *Chariots of Fire*, appearing in the wake of the Moscow Olympics, echoed the phenomenon of the Coe–Ovett rivalry by tracing the story of Eric Liddell and Harold Abrahams, who, like Coe and Ovett, both won Olympic gold. The film opens and closes with athletes in pure white, invoking again the pure amateurism of Greek athletics. (This is largely a myth. The Greeks made no firm distinction between amateur and professional, and the Greek Olympians often gained spectacular rewards; Kidd 1984. The term 'amateur' in sport is essentially a product of the attempt of the Victorian bourgeoisie to exclude the working class from their leisure activities.) *Chariots of Fire* eventually

GREAT SUMMER OF SPORT

Radio Times

The big showdown begins

Sebastian Coe and Steve Ovett
meet in the 3,000 metres.
Full coverage on Saturday BBC1
and Radio 2. Inside:
the record-breakers

Figure 8.3 Radio Times cover (17/7/82) promoting the race that never happened.
All surplus detail has been eliminated to focus on the narrative drama, with the two
protagonists portrayed as physically similar, with muscularity emphasised and eye
lines matching.

turned up on television in 1984 as part of the build-up to the Los Angeles Olympics, and BBC's Los Angeles coverage used the *Chariots of Fire* theme music for its title sequence. There is a complex process of inter-textuality at work here, with factual and fictional representations echoing each other.[77]

The *Radio Times* cover was the work of illustrator Mark Thomas, who intended the doomladen navy blue background to produce a stormy setting for the clash of the Titans. Thomas received an unusually elaborate briefing from *Radio Times*. It called for the two to be portrayed in identical fashion, dressed in white, racing for the line, straining for the tape, and bursting out of the frame, with eyes meeting. There should be no sponsors' colours or trademarks, and no national identification. They supplied Thomas with over 100 photographs and slides of the two by way of reference. Only the Moscow 1980 pictures showed the two together.

The showdown offered the utopian fantasy of two great athletes battling it out all the way to the finish, precisely as Roy of the Rovers offers the utopia of heroic football in which our team triumphs against the odds (see Tomlinson 1983). It offered the pleasure of competition. It promised an answer to the long-running Coe–Ovett narrative. At a time when athletics was becoming commercial while still calling itself amateur, it handled the contradiction by invoking virginal white purity. It offered a simple drama-tised world – no distractions, no ads, no money, no politics, and an answer to our questions imminent.

Ironically, it was not to be. An injured Coe was forced to withdraw. Taken ill the week before, Ovett ran well below his best. We did indeed see a 'big showdown', with two athletes battling all the way to the tape, but instead of Coe and Ovett it was Dave Moorcroft and Sydney Maree. This precisely demonstrates one central contradiction of television sport. Television constantly attempts to build our expectations and to frame our perceptions, yet ultimately does not control the event itself.

TEARS OF A CLOWN: THE MAKING OF GAZZA

If, seen through the British perspective, the stars of the Moscow Olympics were Coe and Ovett, and the shadow of the Decker/Budd incident lay across the Los Angeles Games, the star of the 1990 World Cup was undoubtedly Gazza. The process was rendered more dramatic by its speed. Before the competition started he had yet to attain a permanent place in the team, despite a growing press campaign. In the event, just as England started poorly and got better and better, in what was a disappointing and at times a depressing competition, so Gascoigne, while other stars like Gullitt and Maradona flopped, got ever more self-assured and was increasingly prominent.

Almost all stars require one single dramatic televisual moment to set the seal on their progress. For Seb Coe it was the moment of victory in the 1500m, for Ian Botham his Headingley innings in 1981, for Dennis Taylor his dramatic victory over Steve Davis in the 1985 World Championship. For Gascoigne a more idiosyncratic moment became mythologised. Towards the end of England's semi-final he received a booking which would ensure that, if England qualified for the final, he would miss the game. As this realisation sank in, tears welled up. It was a moving moment on television, but only when the image of Gazza crying appeared on a tee-shirt all over the nation shortly after the competition, with the caption 'There'll Always be an England', did Gazza become, in the Barthesian sense, a myth (Barthes 1973).

Which signifying elements made this particular object so popular? Gazza served to condense a number of things: a re-emergence of skill and talent in an otherwise fairly average if highly competent team; an idiosyncratic and at times wayward figure in the mould of Botham, Higgins and Best; a clown who can also cry; a true patriot (men's public tears are not always granted legitimacy, but tears shed in the cause of chauvinism surely qualify); on top of all this, the narrative place of the tears, shed at the very moment when for the first time, almost unbelievably, hopes surfaced that England might actually win the whole competition. Finally, Gazza as myth required that England fail, for, if they had won, the image of his tears would surely have been eclipsed by other images. Crucially, the ability of television to produce golden moments, consumed by a whole nation, aided this instant production of myth (see Whannel 1989).

Part III

Cultural transformations

Chapter 9

The case of athletics

Athletics has integrity and a clean and healthy image. Athletics is all about winning.

> (John Russell, marketing director of Peugeot-Talbot,
> in press conference preceding Peugeot-Talbot Games, 17/7/85)

In effect Budd and Slaney were not so much paid for a race, as to make a television appearance.

> (John Rodda, *Guardian*, 1/11/85)

The recent history of athletics reveals graphically the way the interlocking forces of television and sponsorship have been transforming sport. The turning point for athletics came at the start of the 1970s. Staff cut-backs and other stringent economies had pulled the Amateur Athletic Association (AAA) through a financial crisis, a move from the White City to Crystal Palace gave the sport a more modern, up-to-date appearance, and new record-breaking stars, in particular David Bedford, began to catch the imagination.

By 1972 the AAA was solvent and had found a new sponsor in the Nationwide Building Society, which was to support the AAA championships for the next ten years. The move to Crystal Palace provided athletics with a new, growing audience. The development of more internationally televised events and increased illicit payments for the top 'amateurs' spawned a travelling athletic circus. With the emergence of a series of world-class performers, Britain was particularly well placed to take advantage of this international growth.

By the end of the 1970s, it was clear that athletics had a lot to offer as a television sport. As the premier Olympic sport it received unique attention every four years. The success of top British stars like Seb Coe, Steve Ovett, Daley Thompson, Fatima Whitbread and Tessa Sanderson made it possible to provide the audience with a point of identification around national interest. As a mixed sport, with a mixed gender following, it fitted neatly into a strategy aimed at the 'family audience'. And, as a sport with multiple events, it offered a wide range of potential stories.

British athletics had been televised by the BBC from the 1940s until 1985. Coverage in the early days was infrequent, but the public interest generated by BBC film of Roger Bannister's sub-4-minute mile world record in 1954 and television coverage of a dramatic race between Russian Vladimir Kutz and Chris Chataway were the beginnings of athletics as a popular television sport.[1] Even in those days there were interesting conflicts of interest. Athletics official Jack Crump and ex-Olympic champion sprinter Harold Abrahams, who negotiated TV deals on behalf of athletics, also had contracts to commentate on athletics for the BBC.

During the 1960s BBC sport coverage attained high professional and technical standards. David Coleman, *Grandstand* presenter since 1958, emerged as a commentator who became the voice of athletics for the television audience at the 1960 Rome Olympics. British success at Tokyo in 1964, the growth of satellite coverage and the introduction of colour from 1968 were all boosting the popularity of television sport generally. The BBC still had a dominant position in sport, but after the 1967 franchise re-allocation had created London Weekend Television (LWT) (a company with a major stake in sports coverage) ITV began to attempt to challenge this dominance.

ITV finally won the exclusive contract in 1984 after 12 years of trying. In 1972 John Bromley had failed to convince the British Amateur Athletic Board (BAAB) that ITV would give athletics adequate coverage, and the BBC kept the rights. In 1976 the BBC was able to renew its contract for another four years at a cost of just over £250,000. In 1980 the BBC again renewed the contract for another four years, at a cost of almost £2m, bidding from ITV helping to force the price up.[2] More than any other single factor, it was the emergence of Coe and Ovett and the rivalry between them, from 1979 onwards, that helped to transform British athletics, and their much-publicised races made athletics into a major television sport.

Athletics was at last beginning its slow move to open professionalism. Undercover payments to top athletes had been an accepted, although secret, part of the sport for a long time. But the challenge of Packer to the cricket authorities had alerted the athletics world to the danger of an outside entrepreneur establishing a rival professional branch of the sport (several previous attempts had foundered). A change in International Olympic Committee (IOC) rules meant athletes could now be paid training and other expenses, and compensated for lost wages.[3] The privately funded Sports Aid Foundation was established in 1978 to provide training and living expenses for top British athletes. In 1980 an AAA sub-committee recommended cash prizes, appearance money and benefit from advertising to athletes.[4] In 1981 the International Amateur Athletic

Federation (IAAF) established permit meetings, in which promoters could pay appearance money. The money could not go directly to the athlete but was held in a trust fund, administered by the national association, and could be used to provide the athlete's expenses, the balance going to the athlete on retirement.

In May 1984 ITV offered £8m for exclusive rights to televise British athletics for five years. Within the BAAB the AAA was holding out for £10m. There were worries about ITV's commitment to sport, and loyalty to the BBC was also a factor. The BBC raised its bid to £9m, Bryan Cowgill of Thames was brought into the negotiations and ITV's new bid of £10.5m then seemed likely to win the day, BAAB secretary Nigel Cooper commenting, 'It does look as though the sport could have money pouring out of its ears'.

The one factor that looked as if it could sabotage ITV's chances was the sensational news that it was to withdraw from the 1984 Olympic coverage, having failed to come to an agreement with the Association of Cinematograph and Television Technicians (ACTT) over pay and conditions. But earlier in the year the Independent Broadcasting Authority (IBA) had changed the rules over advertising. Sponsors would now be allowed to advertise before, during and after the coverage of events they were sponsoring. The International Management Group (IMG) and other agents could see that sponsors were likely to favour events on ITV in future and it was pointed out to the athletic authorities that an ITV deal could be worth more in sponsorship.

By July the deal was signed, ITV announcing its intention to make athletics 'a real national sport'. John Bromley called it 'the biggest boost for morale in the history of ITV sport'. A special unit was established to cover the sport, under producer Richard Russell, who commented, 'We believe that there is a lot more to coverage than the rather formal approach of the BBC, which is basically aimed at giving you exactly the same view as if you had the best seat at Crystal Palace'.[5] The BAAB called for bids from sport agents to handle the sponsorship deals. IMG, West Nally, Keith Prowse and Alan Pascoe all put in bids.[6] To the surprise of many, the contract went not to the established giants IMG or West Nally, but to ex-athlete Alan Pascoe's Alan Pascoe Associates (APA).

Deals with Kodak, Pearl and Peugot-Talbot meant APA rapidly reached its commitment to provide £600,000 per year, Pascoe commenting that there were still events available, 'but we are asking a lot of money to project athletics in its new image . . . sports sponsorship is no longer a somewhat naive jab at name improvement or prestige getting. It is a very sophisticated marketing tool'.[7] Great stress was laid on the 'family image'. Peugeot-Talbot approved of the 'squeaky clean image', and McVities chose to sponsor athletics because it smelt right. John Bromley later commented: 'The thing about athletics is that it's got good demographics.

It caters for everbody, young and old, men and women. What's more, unlike football, it's clean family entertainment. Finally, it's got heroes you can identify with' (Aris 1990: 122–3).

ENTREPRENEURSHIP AND CONTRADICTIONS

This financial influx has been of great material benefit to athletics, but the resultant transformation also heightened the contradictions between amateurism and entrepreneurship. Athletics gained an income in 1985 of £2.1m from television fees and around £1.5m from sponsorships.[8] From this the British Athletic Promotion Unit (BAPU), led by ex-policeman Andy Norman, paid over £350,000 in subventions to athletes. Agents typically take fees of around 25 per cent, so APA may have made over £200,000.[9] In arrangements where agents receive an agency fee from one party (the sport) and a service contract from another party (the sponsor), there is clearly a potential for misunderstanding and suspicion, if not conflict of interest.[10]

The increased importance of television and sponsorship has also been transforming international athletics. In the last few years the IAAF has established a link with International Sport and Leisure (ISL), an offshoot of Adidas, which also has links with the World Cup and the Olympics. It has introduced many new competitions: the World Athletics Championships, the Marathon World Cup, the World Junior Championships, and the IAAF Grand Prix scheme, intended to bring together the major permit meetings in a coherent series that could popularise the sport to a wider audience and bring in TV and sponsorship revenue.

The Grand Prix (GP) scheme is a contradictory system. It attempts a form of capitalist rationalisation aimed at a more efficient exploitation of the popularity of athletics, but it also attempts to regulate and control the free market of European invitation meetings.[11] In 1985 the IAAF received $4.5m from a three-year contract with NBC to cover IAAF events.[12] Meanwhile Ted Turner's cable network got in on the act by establishing a Goodwill Games as an alternative Olympics,[13] and an international consortium backed by Italian cable television interests planned a European Community Games. Currently there are plans to stage the world championships every two years instead of every four. The number of top-level events is expanding rapidly. One result of the increased rate of penetration of sporting organisations by capital has been a form of inflation, already seen in dramatic form in tennis. More money from television and sponsors produces more events, but the number of top stars remains limited; as Cliff Temple has argued, 'the problem is that there are now too many meetings, egged on by sponsors and TV pursuing too few genuinely crowd-pulling athletes'.[14]

In the first year of the ITV contract, athletics spent around £400,000 on payments to athletes, and 'long serving and honourable honorary officials suddenly found themselves at the helm of a multi-million pound industry'.[15] The first draft of the ITV contract, which like all such documents was not made public, reportedly called on the sport to use 'financial inducements' to get top stars for televised events, although the phrase was supposedly later changed to 'best endeavours', a great British euphemism. The growth in the forces of entrepreneurship meant that the traditional control of old-style officials was challenged by the rising power of the meeting promoters, who had the responsibility of delivering star-packed meetings to television. In 1985 Andreas Brugger spent around £320,000 on one meeting in Zurich, and David Bedford said that the International Athletes Club (IAC) meeting costs around £140,000 to promote.[16] Athlete Jack Buckner argued that the money was distributed very unevenly: 'Money in athletics does not go very deep. The majority is taken by the superstars at each event and everyone else fights for the crumbs . . . this system is maintained by the media whose coverage further emphasises the domination of a few superstars'.[17] The Grand Prix system itself found it difficult competing with the competition to attract athletes. Over 20 per cent of Grand Prix races had to be declared void because there weren't sufficient athletes from the top 50 rankings.[18] Only 6 of the 16 Grand Prix meetings were able to stage the required number (12) of point-scoring events.[19]

The new economic forces working upon athletics have not eased tensions between the various organisations. The traditional role of sport organisations in fostering a broad base has been in conflict with the new entrepreneurial pressure to produce quality at the elite level. The International Athletes Club has been one focus of contradictory tensions. As a form of trade union for elite athletes it nevertheless had aspirations to improve the position of the grassroots. At the same time, as promoter of its own events it also had to manoeuvre, with mixed success, through the cluttered field of sponsors, advertisers, brokers and television producers. After originally opposing the IMG bid to handle athletic sponsorship, it then did a spectacular U turn, remaining aloof from the BAAB deal with APA and choosing instead to work with IMG itself. It managed to lose the longest-standing sponsorship in athletics, Coca-Cola pulling out of its 17-year involvement in the IAC meeting because of an unwillingness to share the limelight with GP sponsors Mobil. The partnership with IMG failed to bear fruit and, in the great sponsorship race, IAC was left on the starting blocks, still hunting for a sponsor, while all around it the revenue flowed into athletics.[20]

Women's athletics had always been faced with a tension around the decision to retain a separate body (the Women's Amateur Athletic Association – WAAA), with consequent marginality, rather than be absorbed completely into the AAA or the BAAB and so lose control of women's events. The complex and loose federation of athletics organisations produced fixture clashes. The second day of the 1985 WAAA Championships in Birmingham (sponsor TSB) clashed with the Oslo GP, making it hard for women athletes to obtain permission to go to Oslo. The WAAA meeting was part of the ITV deal and the WAAA got £100,000 of the TV money for the championships and one international. John Rodda pointed out that, for that money, ITV expected a much higher level of competition than had been the case in recent seasons at the women's championships.[21]

Meanwhile the Scottish WAAA had managed to negotiate a sponsor deal involving vest ads, only for the traditionally minded WAAA to overrule them and bar it. Women's athletics was caught in a classic double-bind. Agreeing to unity and hence absorption within one single mixed governing body would mean a loss of control and autonomy. But independence meant marginality and impoverishment, exacerbated by the apparent desire of the WAAA leadership to protect women athletes from contamination by commerce.

The BAAB and the AAA also stumbled over the hurdles of sponsorship management, weaving an erratic path. They considered and ultimately rejected a £200,000 offer from British Nuclear Fuels and, in the light of the subsequent Chernobyl nuclear disaster in the USSR, were no doubt heartily glad they did so.[22] They then barred an agreed deal between Haringey Athletic Club and the Health Education Council featuring the slogan 'Be a Pacesetter – Don't Smoke'.[23] Here, as elsewhere, a patrician disdain for commerce was locked into a tug-of-war with the entrepreneurial invasion.

THE HEAD TO HEAD THAT HAD TO HAPPEN

One of the major events of the 1985 athletics season was the confrontation between Mary Decker and Zola Budd, described by ITV presenter Jim Rosenthal as 'the head to head that had to happen'.[24] It had to happen, in a sense, as a result of an unresolved narrative tension. Mary Decker went to the Los Angeles Olympics with an outstanding record but never having won an Olympic medal, partly as a result of the US boycott of Moscow. Zola Budd, a highly talented athlete from South Africa, went to Los Angeles shrouded in the controversy produced by her obtaining British citizenship in world record time, and using it as a flag of convenience in order to dodge the boycott of South African sport. The two collided in the 3000m final and Mary Decker fell. Budd ran on to finish seventh. Endless television repetition of the incident and extensive post-mortem debate in the media completely obscured the result of the race, won by Maricica Puica of Romania, with Britain's Wendy Sly gaining the silver medal. On the *TV Times* cover for the week of the race, Zola Budd is portrayed as 'racing to bury the memory of the Los Angeles Olympics' (see Figure 9.1).

ITV was keen to make an impact in its first year, while American

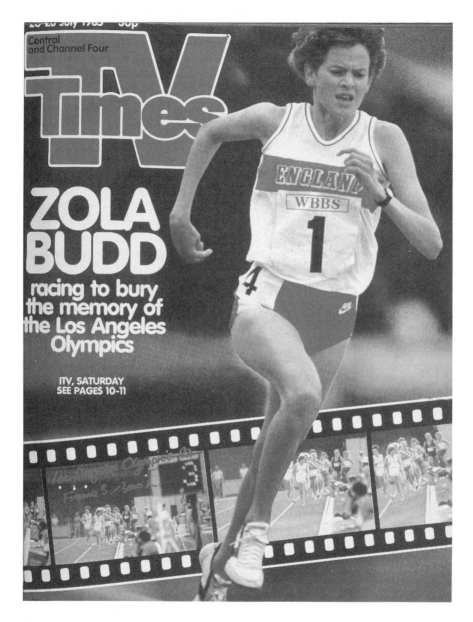

Figure 9.1 The *TV Times* cover (20/7/85) sets up the Decker v. Budd race almost as an exorcism of the nightmare memory of the Los Angeles race in which Mary Decker fell over Zola Budd's heels, picked out in film stills. Note the anxiety to mark South African Budd's Britishness by choosing this picture of her in an England vest.

television sought to bring its audience the triumph that Mary Decker's fall had deprived them of. Eventually the race was slotted into one of the highlights of the 1985 British athletics calendar, the Peugeot-Talbot Games at Crystal Palace. This meeting, already arranged as usual for a Friday night, had to be extended to a second night, allowing the Decker–Budd race to be screened live in ABC's *Wide World of Sports*.[25]

In the televising of the event in Britain, the Decker/Budd 'confrontation' completely dominated the coverage of the second night of the Peugeot-Talbot Games. In the 56 minutes of transmission time, material directly relating to Decker and Budd took up almost 33 minutes, including the race, which was just 8 minutes 32 seconds. Of 15 events in the stadium, only six were televised at all. The six events shown to TV viewers included the last two laps only of a men's 3000m, and two very brief excerpts from field events. Only two of the eight women's events were screened.

Two very distinct selections were at work here. First, the women's 3000m was foregrounded as the only event of any real significance, and second, Decker and Budd were the only competitors of key importance. Very little time was spent giving any information about the other runners, two of whom finished ahead of Zola Budd. Interestingly, the normal graphic format for results, showing 1st, 2nd and 3rd, had to be amended for the post-race result in order to include Zola Budd who finished in fourth place.[26]

The event did not meet with universal acclaim. *Running* called the Decker/Budd race 'a crashing bore' and commented: 'the quality of the athletics often seemed to be in inverse proportion to the amount of public relations and media hype . . . treating athletes as prize fighters in opposite corners – complete with comparisions of their bodyweight – cheapens the sport and will make many rue the departure of the BBC from the domestic scene.'[27] In the *Guardian*, John Rodda wrote that the decision to extend the meeting to a second day, taken after two-thirds of tickets were already sold for the Friday, looked like sharp practice and had attracted the attention of the Advertising Standards Authority and the Office of Fair Trading.[28] Further controversy was generated by the absence from the race of Olympic champion, Maricica Puica, who was keen to run but, it is believed, was offered only a derisory £2000. Later in the year it was revealed that Budd was paid £90,000 and Decker £54,000. Thames TV International handled the overseas sales of the broadcasting of this meeting on behalf of ITV. American network ABC alone is believed to have paid £180,000, providing the revenue to pay Decker and Budd. Budd's fee was widely believed to be at least four times greater than any previous fee to an athlete for a single event.

ADVERTISING AND POLITICS

The establishment of Zola Budd as a popular heroine portrayed her as an innocent victim of events, and, ironically, the apartheid issue and the collision with Mary Decker, by placing Zola Budd so centrally in the public eye, merely served to dramatically increase her earning power. Early in 1985, when Wendy Sly beat Zola Budd in the USA, Sly got £4900, Budd around £27,000.[29]

The representation of sport commonly involves a de-politicisation, an attempt to preserve sport as an arena devoid of politics. This can of course never be fully accomplished, as all events signify in ways that can be articulated into political discourse (see Nowell-Smith 1978, and Wren-Lewis and Clarke 1983). The Zola Budd affair placed the de-politicisation of sporting discourse under great pressure. There is an uneven and contradictory process, in which television preserves a much greater separation of sport and politics than does the press. Right at the start of 1985, one major national daily was already suggesting that Zola Budd had 'run one ring too many round Britain's citizenship laws' and was losing the goodwill of the British public. It proclaimed that 'her latest wishy-washy statement, promising to live in this country during the athletics season, is little short of an insult'.[30]

The BAAB, whose early commitment to Budd was enough to send its secretary all the way to South Africa to plead with her not to turn her back on Britain, was sharing this feeling in its insistence that she establish proper residential status. Budd herself agreed to be interviewed only on the condition that politics not be raised, which sadly did not deter *Running* from featuring a lengthy profile.[31] She refused every opportunity to make any statement disapproving of apartheid, a silence open to only one interpretation.

The evacuation of politics reached a crisis for broadcasting in July 1985 when the Dairy Crest Games in Edinburgh were not transmitted because ITV Sports said signs placed in the arena by Edinburgh City Council, saying 'Edinburgh against Apartheid', contravened IBA regulations against political advertising. The Edinburgh Council refused to remove them, and the transmission was cancelled.[32] Dairy Crest expressed disappointment that the sport's clean, healthy and uncontroversial image had suffered quite markedly.

The British Athletics Promotion Unit, which was insured against TV cancellation, announced its willingness to compensate Dairy Crest.[33] The Council offered to remove the banner if a spot was offered in the Channel 4 transmission to explain its case, but this was refused.[34] The BBC says it would have made the same decision.[35] It is clear here that the de-politicisation of sport, whilst largely produced by the routine practices of broadcasting, is also reinforced by the state. The outcome of a national–local tension within the state, manifest here, was resolved by the authority of the IBA, in effect a state regulatory body.

TRANSFORMATION: STARS IN THEIR EYES

Athletics has been going through a process of transformation both economically and culturally. The connection between these two levels is more complex. If, in Williams's (1980) sense, the process of determinations involves the setting of limits and the exerting of pressures, it is quite clear that the economic forces produced by the combination of television and sponsorship do constitute a driving power upon these transformations. These forces set limits and exert pressures upon the processes whereby the athletics calendar is drawn up, the programme of events for each meeting is established, and the competitors for each event are arranged.

Athletics has always had a star system, undercover payments and promoters anxious to organise head-to-head clashes to attract crowds. But now it is not the crowd but the television audience that has to be attracted (note that, while 11 million watched Decker and Budd on TV in Britain alone, Crystal Palace, sold out the previous night, was less than half full). This is a significant distinction: the television audience is different – athletics fans are only a small proportion of it and the conventions of television produce a form of entertainment distinctly different from the entertainment available to the live spectator. This is not to make a value judgement; both forms of entertainment can be judged in their own terms. It is merely to point out that the organising principle for top-level athletics is now inevitably the need to provide television entertainment of consistent quality.

In this sense the matchmaking role has become a crucial relay between economic and cultural levels, linking the market value of stars and their cultural centrality as the bearers of the narratives around which audience identification is forged. As the focus of all the tensions and contradictions involved in the production of uncertainty of a consistent quality, ex-policeman Andy Norman's lot was not a happy one. At the Peugeot-Talbot Games in 1985, Steve Cram, who broke the world record for the 1500m three days earlier in Nice, decided not to run against Coe. Coe, wanting a tough race, then got transferred to the 800m on the morning of the race, to run against Cruz. On hearing this only one hour before the race, Cruz pulled out, and in punishment Norman then got Cruz barred from his next three races.[36]

More significantly, the Ovett career, which Norman did much to manage and promote in its early stages, ended in tears, shed publicly on ITV. The affair typified the complex enmeshing of the financial interests of television, sport and sponsorship, the secretive manner in which such relations were forged, and the way in which the roles and responsibilities of sport stars were being re-worked.

At the 1989 AAA meeting, attempts were made to set up yet another big showdown – the first meeting between Coe and Ovett on a British track. Coe was committed to run in order to qualify for the Commonwealth Games team, whilst Ovett, whose form had been in decline ever since 1984, was not keen. Ovett eventually agreed to run, but only because, as he later claimed, he was offered money (anything from £4000 to £20,000 according to some press reports) by Andy Norman and assured that Coe was also being paid. Ovett found that Coe was not being paid, and, feeling that he had been manipulated and Coe cheated, tried to pull out. At this point, pressure was put upon him by Andy Norman, by two other athletics officials and by ITV, which was reported to have threatened to sack him from its commentary team if he did not run.[37] Ovett ran, not surprisingly in mediocre fashion. Coe was tripped on the penultimate lap and, amazingly, got up to catch up and eventually win. Ovett then broke down and wept on a television interview, whilst hinting at what had gone on. The subsequent enquiry found that, while Ovett had been offered money, they couldn't determine who had done it (!).

Tensions over race plans became common as the inflation of athletics increased. More meetings, more promoters and more money in television revenue and sponsorship continued to pursue the small number of global stars available, as television attempted to reproduce audience-attracting uncertainty while ensuring a high and consistent quality of entertainment. The athletics authorities, themselves torn between entrepreneurial zeal and paternal benevolence, continued the struggle to manage the free-market forces that they had unleashed. Clearly, more heads-to-heads had to happen, and over the following years Fatima Whitbread v. Tessa Sanderson, Steve Cram v. Said Aouita, and Ben Johnson v. Carl Lewis all became the focal point of athletic coverage. It is clear that athletics in the mid 1980s was still only at the beginning of a major transformation. Mark McCormack believed that athletics could be to the 1980s what golf was to the 1960s and tennis to the 1970s – the boom sport:

> Arnold Palmer was the right person to represent at a time when the sport of golf was growing by leaps and bounds. A decade later with our representation of Laver, then Newcombe, and then Borg, we were able to repeat this success in tennis, and now, again ten years later, we are positioned to do the same thing in running, though no stratospheric superstar has yet emerged in this sport.
>
> (McCormack 1984: 237)

Like many other sports, athletics at the highest level is being transformed by the new economic conditions that television and sponsorship have produced, and by the cultural tensions and upheavals that have resulted in the challenge to traditional amateur paternal authorities by the new entrepreneurial forces of sponsors and agents. In all areas of athletics – the international federation, the International Athletes Club, women's athletics, club athletics – the effects of these contradictory tensions are being negotiated. Underpinning this is the need to ensure that television continues to get what it wants from athletics.

There are, however, signs as we move into the 1990s that athletics is already beginning to suffer from the same form of sporting inflation that has overtaken tennis. Fuelled by the demands of television and sponsors, more and more events are established in the calendar. Promoters, increasingly forced to compete to attract the limited number of top stars, are obliged to increase the rewards on offer. Weary stars jet from meeting to meeting, rarely able to deliver the much-promised world records, despite highly co-ordinated pacemaking. In a greedy desire to grab all the television and sponsorship money going, the IAAF has now decided that it will stage its world championships every two years. The irony is that unwillingness of athletes to devote too many seasons to major championships at the expense of the more lucrative permit meetings, together with audience over-familiarity breeding boredom, may devalue the very entertainment value the IAAF seeks to market.

In tennis, the International Federation began to lose control to the top players and their agents (see Mewshaw 1983). Top players like Bjorn Borg could earn so much from exhibitions that the pressure of the regular tournament circuit began to lose its allure. In athletics, the authorities, under pressure from television and sponsors to guarantee the presence of stars, are increasingly having to battle with runners who, as well as being subject to injury and keen to avoid too many dramatic head-to-head confrontations, wish to make their own racing programmes and often find continental events more attractive than British ones.

The traditional amateur paternal forms of sport organisation were of course themselves always profoundly contradictory, containing a class-ridden elitism, an uneven degree of semi-democratisation, a commitment to voluntarism and service, and the economic function of distributing resources to the less commercially viable sectors of sport and thus maintaining a broad base. The commercial challenge is equally contradictory in that, while providing the means of economic survival for many sports, and producing an entertaining and pleasurable spectacle, it has concentrated resources at the elite levels, made sport a branch of the advertising industry, made sports over-conscious of image and the needs of television, and heightened the tensions between the uncertainties inherent in sport and the need of entrepreneurs to offer guaranteed entertainment. This whole process, profoundly re-making sporting cultures, should lead us to ask the question 'Who is sport for?'

Chapter 10

The road to globalisation

It's Berlioux's job to keep commercialism out of the Olympics; it's Dassler's job to make sure every athlete bears the Adidas name in large letters on every piece of clothing and equipment. Therein lies the conflict.

(Peter Ueberroth 1985: 136)

'Improved insoles played a very important role and you know when I'm speaking about insoles I'm referring to financial rewards for people using shoes'.

(Horst Dassler of Adidas, in *Selling the Games*,
Flashback for Channel 4, 1987)

The Olympic marketing programme is totally new. Only those who move quickly and act decisively are going to keep one pace ahead of the competition and benefit from the dramatic image enhancement that it provides.

(International Sport and Leisure,
promoting the TOP programme, 1986)

'What better partnership than an activity that makes people thirsty and a product that quenches thirst so deliciously?'

(Gary Hite, vice president,
International Sports, The Coca-Cola Company, 1988)

Twenty years ago, if you suggested that the World Cup might be staged in the USA, it would have seemed as likely as a Polish Pope. Now that both those things have happened it might seem wise to keep one eye on the sky in case of flying pigs. At first sight the very idea of staging the World Cup in the USA seems ludicrous. Football might fairly be thought of as the world game, massively popular everywhere . . . except in the States, where at least three attempts to launch the game have foundered. But, seen from within the sports business, it makes perfect sense. The USA is *the* big market, and although the Federation of International Football Associations (FIFA) is already rich, making soccer an American television sport would bring in massive new earnings from television fees, advertising and sponsorship.

Once all this is understood, staging the 1996 Olympics in Atlanta also seems infinitely rational. Athens mounted an emotional bid, articulating themes of tradition, history and the myth of Ancient Graecian athletic purity, as well as insisting with ceaseless and ultimately counter-productive repetitiveness that the centenary Olympic Games just *had* to return to their birthplace. In the midst of a conflict between tradition and modernity, the choice of Atlanta has revealed that, even in the gerontocracy of the International Olympic Committee (IOC), modernity is getting the upper hand. Baron de Coubertin's heart may be buried in Greece but the soul of the Olympics is gone westwards. With Olympic sponsor Coca-Cola and media mogul Ted Turner of CNN cheek by jowl within its city limits, Atlanta seems as good a place as any for the modern Olympic spirit.

The spread of modern sport provides an interesting example of globalisation. One November night in 1985, in torrential rain, I passed an open window to hear the familiar tones of John Motson describing a match between Everton and Arsenal. Nothing very unusual, except that the temperature was 87 degrees, and the room was in Malaysia. The largely Chinese audience knew far more about English football than the domestic Malaysian version. Not only has television football become a global phenomenon, but a western-oriented view of the sport has successfully been extended to much of the world (Geraghty, Simpson and Whannel 1986).

This globalisation of sport is of course only part of a much broader process of globalisation, firstly of markets, trade and labour, and secondly of culture. This has produced a world media system, an international sport system and, in the last 20 years, the emergence on a global scale of the phenomenon Stephen Aris (1990) has named 'sportsbiz'. It has become commonplace to assert that the last 20 years have seen the transformation of the Olympic Games into a global television spectacle by the financial power of the American networks, especially ABC. How have we arrived at this point?

According to Robertson (1990: 19), the crucial take-off period of globalisation was between 1880 and 1925. International sport in its organised form is little more than 100 years old. The first English cricket side to tour Australia went in 1861, but the first Test Match was not until 1877. The International Olympic Committee was formed in 1894 and staged the first modern Olympic Games two years later. But the Games were a rather casual and ad hoc affair and it was only after the turn of the century that international sport began to take on an organised form. FIFA, the world governing body for football, was formed in 1904, although it was another 26 years before it staged the World Cup for the first time. The International Amateur Athletic Association was formed in 1912, and many other sports formed international governing bodies in the opening two decades of the twentieth century. While international sporting contact developed rapidly between the wars, it took the emergence and development of jet travel to allow it to begin to assume its modern form.

The growth of sporting competition gave birth to the sport clothing and equipment industry, with the emergence of Slazenger, Lillywhites and Dunlop. In America, a meat-packing firm called Wilson suddenly realised what it could do with all the gut it was throwing away and took the first step to becoming one of the giants of tennis racket production. And in a small town in Germany in 1948 a shoemaker called Adi Dassler saw the future of sportswear and formed Adidas. He then quarrelled bitterly with his brother, who left the family firm, crossed the small river that runs through Herzogenaurach and set up a rival factory, naming his firm Puma. Adidas rose to pre-eminence by investing massively in ensuring that over half the world's top sport stars wore its gear, and by the 1980s Adi's son Horst Dassler had become a pivotal international power broker, who, according to one observer, taught Havelange how to sell the World Cup and Samaranch how to market the Olympic Games.[1]

In the move in less than 100 years from the horse-drawn carriage to the jet, sport also moved from being a rich man's hobby and poor man's relaxation, to being a major cultural form and a part of the entertainment industry. If the jet was important to this process, television was crucial. Television was at first slow to spread. Green (1972) estimates that by 1950 there were 5 million TV sets worldwide but still only Great Britain, the USA and USSR had TV. Just 20 years later there were 250 million sets in 130 countries, and since the early 1970s television has spread rapidly to Africa, Asia and Latin America. Television, especially American television, became such an effective audience winner, and consequently so attractive to advertisers, that it was able to pay increasingly astronomic sums for those few events, like the Superbowl and the Olympic Games, that could win and hold vast audiences (see Tomlinson and Whannel 1984).

Changes in the world economy in the 1970s and 1980s included a trend towards de-monopolisation of economic structures and a deregulation and globalisation of markets, trade and labour. The globalisation of capital required a new category of professionals – international lawyers, corporate accountants, financial advisers and management consultants (see Featherstone 1990). In sport, the weakening of traditional amateur paternalism and the growth of entrepreneurship spawned the sports agents and promoters who constitute sportsbiz.

Of all forms of cultural imperialism, television sport is particularly well fitted for globalisation. Entry into international sport has become a key signifier of modernisation in the third world. According to Don Anthony (1980), in Juba in the southern Sudan in the mid 1970s, the only paved road led from the airport to the stadium. The staging of a major event like the

Seoul Olympics constitutes a *rite de passage* into the modern (western) world. Schramm (1964) felt that the growth and spread of television would provide the means of modernisation and development for the third world. However Fejes (1981) argued that the media had not so much speeded development as heightened dependency upon the west. Third world countries have become dependent upon the developed world both for the technology and for the bulk of programme material, producing a striking pattern of dominance by the major media producers of the west, primarily the USA (see Schiller 1971, and Tunstall 1977).

Boyd-Barrett (1977) stated that the flow of media material was uni-directional, moving from the major countries of the west to the third world, with very little material moving in the opposite direction. Underlying the whole unequal cultural exchange is the imbalance of economic power between the developed world and the third world (see Nordenstreng and Varis 1978). Golding (1977) argued that third world media producers derived their philosophies of broadcasting from western countries. Professionalism becomes imitation. Broadcasting thus tends towards a global uniformity of style.[2]

During preparations for the 1978 World Cup in Argentina, representatives from the European Broadcasting Union (EBU) discovered that Argentinian football coverage used a completely different set of camera positions from that accepted in Europe. Bill Ward, head of EBU's 1978 World Cup operations group, commented: 'We didn't want to upset the hosts, but the standard of coverage was just not up to European expectations. So we took extracts from British and European coverage, held seminars for the Argentine cameramen, directors and producers, and pointed out all the faults in our own work. On this basis they accepted the system we adopt.'[3] Indeed, so impressed were the Argentinians with the European conventions of football coverage that they even altered three brand new stadia to accommodate the 'correct' camera positions. Goldlust (1987: 97) argues that 'the examples of sports television produced by the wealthier and technologically more sophisticated services – those of the North American commercial networks, Western Europe and to a lesser extent Australia – have become the leading models of media professionalism throughout the world wide industry'. This process was dependent on the rise of American television sport since 1960. The massive sums that became available to the Olympic movement from the 1970s, and the commercialisation of the Olympics and the World Cup established a model for the intense capitalisation of sport.

THE US EXPERIENCE

In the late 1940s and early 1950s such American television sport as there was featured sports like wrestling, roller derby and boxing. There was almost no coverage of baseball, football or basketball, the poor technical quality of the period favouring small-scale individual sports. From the beginning there was a willingness on television's part to enhance the entertainment element of actuality; one commentator used to break pieces of wood to simulate breaking bones, and rub balloons to simulate groans during wrestling broadcasts (Rader 1984: 37–9).

Gillette, seeking a good vehicle to target male consumers, had been active in sports advertising and sponsorship since the radio era (Johnson 1971: 224). It saw television sport as the wave of the future. Its long-running TV show, *The Gillette Cavalcade of Sports*, 'did not merely cover a contest, it presented an attitude about the contest – and by extension, an attitude about America, and about the Gillette Blue Blades as a sort of steel-coated embodiment of American optimism' (Powers 1984: 55–62). Advertising agency Dancer, Fitzgerald and Sample also saw the potential of television sport, and used baseball coverage under the title of *ABC Game of the Week* to promote Falstaff beer in the midwest (Powers 1984: 71). In short, the driving force behind the formative moments of American television sport came from advertising agencies and their clients (see Parente 1974).

ABC Sports: up close and personal

At the end of the 1950s the American Broadcasting Company (ABC) had no major sport events and was third in the ratings, a long way behind the National Broadcasting Company (NBC) and the Columbia Broadcasting System (CBS). Although the smallest network, ABC was an aggressive competitor that was making more subtle use of market research, catching on to the importance of demographic profile long before the other networks. Identifying youth as the audience section least loyal to the old giants NBC and CBS, ABC went for a youthful image, to be built partly around sports. In 1960 it was a well-timed move. Powers argues that the youthful theme echoed the Kennedy idealism of the new frontier, the sporting emphasis echoed the Kennedy's image of muscular athleticism, and, 'shrugging off the darker morbidities of the Cold War and McCarthyism', the country was in a mood for newness and regeneration (Powers 1984: 118–21).

ABC discovered that, instead of broadcasting events because people were interested in them, it could make people interested in the events because they were on television (Powers 1984: 153). The slogan 'The Thrill of Victory, the Agony of Defeat' emerged as an epigrammatic description of the intended approach (see Sugar 1980). The phrase was to become a motto for ABC Sports along with 'up close and personal' (see O'Neil 1989). Like *Grandstand*, *Wide World of Sports* became a whole depart-ment within ABC, providing a valuable training and initiation into Roone

Arledge's particular version of broadcasting professionalism. But financial pressures meant that the programme depended on minor and marginal sports – cliff diving, rodeos, demolition derbys and logrolling for a substantial portion of its content. In addition it was a video programme and had to sell itself hard to compensate for the lack of immediacy – NBC rubbed it in by advertising itself as the network of live sports. However, it built an audience, a reputation and contacts and by the early 1980s was earning around $200m annually for ABC (Klatell and Marcus 1988: 159).

ABC was in the forefront of the attempt to make sport more dramatic and spectacular. It put microphones inside golf cups, on basketball hoops, on referees, and even inside the Olympic Flame to catch the sound of it being lit. And it put cameras on jeeps, on mike booms, in risers, on helicopters, cranes and airships. Commentators were instructed to find the drama, to bring out the story line, and it is worth noting that Arledge himself studied literature at Columbia University and was much influenced by the teaching and narrative theories of Lionel Trilling and Mark Van Doren (Powers 1984: 134–5). Arledge spelled out his attitude in a 1960 memo which asserted that, rather than take the game to the viewer, TV must take the viewer to the game, and ended in block capitals, 'In short – WE ARE GOING TO ADD SHOW BUSINESS TO SPORTS'.

American football and the Superbowl

Along with the rise of ABC Sports the big success of the 1960s was the emergence of American football as the dominant American television sport. By 1962, the cost of television rights to the Championship game had risen from $200,000 to almost $1m (Powers 1984: 84). In 1960 the established National Football League (NFL) was challenged by the American Football League (AFL), 'the first utterly self-contained professional sports league that had been formed with the intention of surviving on television revenues' (Powers 1984: 153).

Audience figures for football went up by 50 per cent in the early 1960s and, as television demand mounted, NFL Commissioner Pete Rozelle was well placed to take advantage of the intense competitiveness to ensure a high price. Eventually CBS paid $28.2m for two years of NFL, and the following year NBC paid $36m for five years of AFL, giving the 'second-class' league real credibility for the first time. In mid 1966 the two leagues merged in a formula based, according to Johnson (1971: 139), on the comparative quality of their respective television markets.

Rozelle established the Superbowl, a new final match between the two champions. In order to bestow the aura of authenticity to this instant invention of tradition, Superbowls were identified by Roman numerals. Rozelle also got Congress, via legislation promoted by Senator Long of Louisiana, to exempt the new league from any anti-trust move, and, perhaps not entirely by coincidence, New Orleans was subsequently awarded an NFL franchise (Powers 1984: 181). In 1970 the Superbowl was watched on TV by 70 million people, more than double the number who voted to make Richard Nixon president two years earlier (Johnson 1971: 18). By now the combined amount paid by the three networks had reached an annual $46m and the rights to college football were going for $12m (Johnson 1971: 51).

Having consolidated the NFL position and established the Superbowl as the jewel in the crown, Rozelle now turned to the task of finding a prime-time slot for the game, eventually getting ABC to show live matches on Monday nights (Powers 1984: 183–4). Arledge recognised that, in scheduling football in prime time, ABC would have to establish a much broader demographic profile – a younger, more female, better-educated audience than the predominately male audience for afternoon games. He put great effort into establishing personality presenters, foregrounded individual dramas and human interest, and in general further developed the 'up close and personal' style (Klatell and Marcus 1988: 143). Starting in 1970, ABC soon found itself with a 30 per cent audience share, and a runaway success which changed the social habits of a nation; according to Rader, cinema attendances slumped, hookers left the streets, restaurants closed their doors, bowlers rescheduled their leagues, and gamblers and bookies rejoiced (Rader 1984: 115).

As ever, the Arledge approach ensured that the show was more important than the event, with dramas, evocative close-ups, multiple instant replay and slow motion. American football, with its regular pauses between brief moments of frenetic action, proved to be perfectly tailored to television's need to forge audience identification around close-ups of key individuals. The choice of the controversial Howard Cosell ensured that the programme would catch the imagination of the nation and provide the fuel for conversation and argument; indeed Powers (1984: 188) refers to him as 'the ultimate anti-star'.

The golden decade

Golf and tennis too were rapidly winning a television audience. In 1968 Lamar Hunt founded World Championship Tennis (WCT), and in 1972 NBC signed a deal to cover eight of its finals on Saturday afternoons. In that year a dramatic final match between Laver and Rosewall caught the imagination of the American public and launched tennis into a golden decade of expansion. In 1970 cigarette advertising on television was banned by Congress. As in Britain, tobacco money began to flood into sport sponsorship and one of the immediate beneficiaries was women's tennis, which gained substantial support from Kim and Virginia Slims. By 1976 there were 70 tennis tournaments on television, compared with 7 in

1971 (Powers 1984: 222). The appetite for top sports, the emergence of sports agents and assorted hustlers and the rise in public prominence of the women's movement all combined to produce one of the most bizarre of all made-for-TV events, the 1973 'Battle of the Sexes' in which Billie Jean King responded to the challenge of ex tennis champion, 53-year-old Bobby Riggs, that he could beat any woman. Held at the Houston Astrodome, with Howard Cosell commentating, King 'arrived at courtside in an Egyptian litter borne by a flounce of semi-naked men, and presented Riggs with a live pig' and then beat him in straight sets (Powers 1984: 237). This ersatz event was watched by 30,472, the largest ever tennis crowd, and by 50 million on television.

Protest though they did about the terrible cost and the bitter competitiveness, all three networks were as eager as ever to bid huge sums to capture major events, and during the 1970s the dramatic growth in the scale and scope of American television sport continued. Along with it came a host of problems. The increased money flowing from advertisers via the networks produced an insatiable demand for new events. Sports agencies flourished, made-for-television events and trash-sports sprang up like mushrooms and the need to sell all this to the public produced a series of scandals.

During the tennis boom in the early 1970s CBS had a series of head-to-head matches with huge prize money, publicised with the slogan 'winner-takes-all'. By 1977 it had emerged that the players were offered guarantees and the House Communications Sub-Committee investigation into TV Sport found it guilty of making fraudulent claims (Powers 1984: 241). The money flowing into College football also had a corrupting influence, as colleges competed to attract and hold talented players (Powers 1984: 226). Maverick entrepreneurs made many attempts, mostly unsuccessful, to launch new made-for-TV leagues, such as the American Basketball Association (1967), the World Hockey Association (1972) and the World Football League (Powers 1984: 237). Billie Jean King and her husband were also involved in the ill-fated World Team Tennis, which was established in 1973 but never managed to win over television, advertisers or live spectators.

The 1970s were the golden age of trash-sports, of which the original and most successful was *Superstars*, devised by Barry Frank, then head of Trans World International (TWI), and sold to his former boss Arledge (Rader 1984: 129). It started an 11-year run on ABC in 1973, and spawned numerous spinoffs and copies that proliferated throughout the 1970s. Only by the early 1980s did the sub-genre begin to run out of steam in the wake of declining public interest.

American football continued as the major attraction. It reaches a disproportionately large percentage of 18–49-year-old men in higher income brackets, a group difficult to target in any other way. One estimate is that 7 per cent of CBS's $300m profit in 1981 came from advertising during pro football (Rader 1984: 122). American football rights for the five years from 1982 changed hands for a staggering total of $2bn, triggering a players' strike and boardroom panics. But the massive income from advertising has ensured a continued willingness to pay high fees. The Superbowl is watched by 100 million people in North America, and ads cost up to $1.1m per minute (Aris 1990: 126).

Rozelle's achievement has been to get the clubs to act like 'a modern corporate combine'. In other words, it's a form of monopoly capitalism – the most distinctive feature of the NFL is that all teams get an equal share of revenue, with the single exception of income from executive boxes (Aris 1990: 133–7). Rozelle realised the danger – that if clubs did their own TV marketing, some teams would do better than others and unity could be shattered, so he kept the clubs united by skilfully dividing the networks. Baseball, too, was benefiting from network competition: the 1983 baseball TV contracts were worth $1bn, as compared with $190m for the previous four-year contract.

GLOBALISATION AND THE OLYMPICS

The huge and affluent American television market gave the major networks, CBS, ABC and NBC, the financial resources to bid ever-greater sums for US rights to the Olympic Games. These auctions, dominated by ABC from the mid 1960s to the mid 1980s, produced a huge new revenue source for the Olympic movement (see Table 10.1), but made it increasingly dependent upon the networks.

In effect, US television pays for the Olympics, and plays a major role in influencing how they are run, including the layout of site and stadia, the

Table 10.1 US network payments for Olympic television rights ($m)

Summer Games				Winter Games		
Year	Place	Network	Amount	Place	Network	Amount
1960	Rome	CBS	0.39	Squaw Valley	CBS	0.05
1964	Tokyo	NBC	1.5	Innsbruck	ABC	0.59
1968	Mexico City	ABC	4.5	Grenoble	ABC	2.5
1972	Munich	ABC	7.5	Sapporo	NBC	6.4
1976	Montreal	ABC	25.0	Innsbruck	ABC	10.0
1980	Moscow	NBC	87.0	Lake Placid	ABC	15.5
1984	Los Angeles	ABC	225.0	Sarajevo	ABC	91.5
1988	Seoul	NBC	300.0	Calgary	ABC	309.0
1992	Barcelona	NBC	420.0	Albertville	CBS	240.0

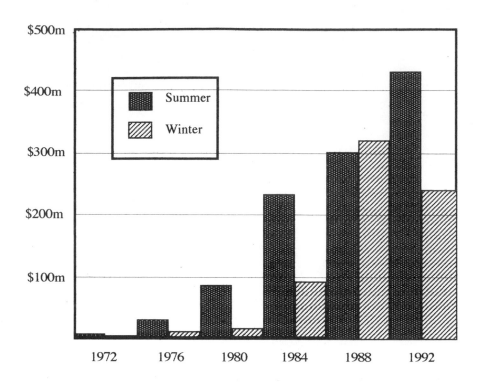

Figure 10.1 Amounts paid by US television networks for the Olympic Games in USA television rights.

nature of ceremonies, the choice of events and the timing of events. The Koreans introduced daylight saving time to try to accommodate television schedules, and the Games were moved forward to avoid a clash with World Series baseball. When ABC agreed to pay $309m for the 1988 Winter Games in Calgary, many people felt that things had got way out of hand. Riding high on the back of what proved to be an overoptimistic forecast of ad revenue, and fired up by a dramatic competitive bidding process as intense as any poker game with millions at stake, ABC, in its determination to retain its 'Network of the Olympics' image, overplayed its hand (Spence 1988). True, Calgary was exceptionally attractive – perfectly placed to be broadcast live during East coast prime time, and filling the quiet gap in the sport schedules between the end of American football and the start of the basketball season. But there was very little chance of ABC recouping all of its $309m in ad revenue, especially when, shortly after the bid, the US economy plunged into recession.

Making the best of a bad job, ABC had the Games extended to fill three weekends to increase its ad potential, but in the event still lost around $50m. The real casualty was Seoul. Hoping for more competitive bidding, and calling for bids as high as a preposterous $900m, Seoul was confronted by an ABC with empty coffers, a moribund CBS, and an intransigent NBC which went up to $300m and stopped dead, forcing Seoul eventually to agree to a face-saving deal which promised more if ad revenues soared above unpublished thresholds.

The location of the Olympic Games has become a major concern of American television. Live action is always far more popular, but only in a few parts of the world can the Olympics be relayed live in East coast peak time. (The East coast has the largest concentrations of population and is consequently the most lucrative target area for advertisers.) Europe is fairly hopeless, while the West coast of the American continent (e.g. Los Angeles) is ideal. Seen in this light, it is easy to see why Atlanta will be a popular choice with the networks.

In the wake of Calgary the American television industry began making very bearish noises about the future of Olympic rights fees. In fact the fees have proved as resilient as ever, partly because of CBS's determination to use the Olympics to boost its prestige, although it is also worth noting that the IOC was believed to have rejected a bid of $500m from ABC for both Summer and Winter Games in 1992. This is a revealing indicator of the current scope of the Olympic Games: how many executives in how many corporations ever find themselves in the position of receiving an offer of $500m, far less rejecting one?

However, the bearish noises of American television had two significant effects. First, the IOC became intent on raising the proportion of fees paid by the rest of the world. In 1988, ABC had paid around $1.67 per TV household compared with 17 cents by European nations (Wilson 1988: 23). There was a loudly expressed view in American television that Europe was getting a free lunch. Second, Samaranch was quick to realise the danger of having all the Olympic eggs in one basket, and the IOC began to investigate new sources of finance.

The IOC is itself a strange body, the last sort of institution one would expect to be presiding over the most prominent regular global event of our times. Its awkward attempts to come to terms with modernity can be illustrated with reference to the characteristic features of its last three presidents. Avery Brundage (1955–1972), a rich man who treated administration of the IOC as a rich man's hobby, mustered a last defence of amateurism, and was a classic example of the benevolent (and sometimes not so benevolent) paternalism of traditional sports administration. When Brundage retired, the IOC had $2m. Lord Killanin (1972–1980) presided over a period in which the Olympic movement appeared to lurch from crisis to crisis. He inherited the spectre of terrorism, the Munich massacre of 1972 ensuring that for the foreseeable future security would be a major consideration for all Olympic sites. Subsequent Olympics in Montreal and Moscow were hit by boycotts, and the grandiose plans and poor financial control of Montreal ensured a massive deficit of over $2bn that the citizens of Montreal are still paying for. Such was the scale of the financial liability that only two cities, Tehran and Los Angeles, even bothered to bid to stage the 1984 Games. Despite this, and largely thanks to the growth in television fees, when Killanin retired, the IOC had $45m in its coffers.

The appointment of Juan Antonio Samaranch as IOC President in 1980 marked a new era in which the Olympic movement began for the first time to grapple with and attempt to come to terms with modernity and commerce. He was the first full-time president, travelling thousands of miles in his desire to visit every country with an Olympic Committee. While emphasising the need for caution, given the nature of the IOC, he increased its role, expanded its staff and premises, promoted the growth of sponsorship, and in general introduced the notion of administration as rational capitalist management.

However, the IOC is still predominately a rich man's club, and an old man's club, that could fairly be described as an autocratic, aristocratic, patriarchal gerontocracy. In 1986 one-third of its members were over 70, half were over 65, and only six had been born since the Second World War. There were only 5 women, but 13 major aristocrats, including 4 princes, 3 lords, 1 princess, 2 sheikhs, 1 count, 1 Grand Duke and 1 ex-king. The IOC functions in many ways like an eighteenth-century gentlemen's club. Members are not elected by any external constituency; they are chosen by the IOC itself. They represent no one, certainly not their country of origin; indeed they are regarded as ambassadors from the IOC to their country. This is the body that chooses, every four years, the site of the Olympic Games. In 1986, 13 cities spent £130m on bidding to stage the Summer or Winter Games in 1992. Hosting the Games is now part of a whole development strategy for a city.

At the 1986 IOC Session, it was decided that, after 1992, Winter and Summer Games would no longer be celebrated in the same year. The decision was welcomed by most of those involved. The IOC felt it would give greater prominence for the Winter Games, the National Olympic Committees (NOCs) felt that it would be easier to raise money for the two separately, sports agents felt it would make the Winter Games more lucrative in sponsorship terms, and the major sponsors welcomed the marketing opportunities presented by global events occurring every two years. But the decision was prompted by the intervention of American television, who made clear their desire to spread the burden of raising ad revenue over two separate years.

The success of Peter Ueberroth's 1984 Los Angeles Olympic Committee in generating a 'surplus' marked the rise to prominence of corporate sponsorship in the Olympic movement. The 1988 Olympic income from TV and sponsorship was $855m (Aris 1990: 155). Ueberroth made over $100m in sponsorship, compared with previous games which made $5–10m. Los Angeles made a 'surplus' of $227m (profit is not allowed under the Olympic Charter) and the IOC was furious when it realised it had no power to claw this surplus back, or even to have a say in how it might be used.

Los Angeles was seen by some as a turning point and its success was certainly partly responsible for the greatly heightened competition to stage the Games, and the vast sums spent in campaigning. But Los Angeles was in a rather aberrant position. The citizens of Los Angeles had voted to put no public funding into the Games, which were staged by a private corporation for the first time. At this time it was assumed that the Games were a guaranteed loss maker, and this expectation meant that Ueberroth could drive bargains with all his suppliers (Ueberroth 1985, Reich 1986). The organisation depended heavily on voluntary labour, and the city picked up many of the massive peripheral expenses for security, transport organisation, etc., which consequently never appeared on the balance sheets. A close scrutiny of the financial projections of bidding cities often reveals an irrational optimism (Bateman and Douglas 1986, Bourke 1991).

The IOC had already determined that it would organise sponsorship centrally, but this presented major problems – in particular, the NOCs held the rights to exploit the Olympic symbol in their areas. ISL had to organise the TOP programme to sign up all the NOCs so that ISL could negotiate global contracts on their behalf. The TOP programme is a form of global capitalist rationalisation, using sport as advertising and offering monopoly access to the Olympics and product exclusivity in 43 product categories, which means Kodak can buy into the film category and prevent any rivals, such as Fuji, from being involved. Coca-Cola was a prime mover in urging the development of such a programme.

ISL did a presentation for the IOC in 1983; controversially no one else was invited to tender, and it got the contract in summer 1985. IOC secretary Monique Berlioux, hostile to any outside involvement except as mere consultants, was forced to resign. ISL hoped to make around $150–200m from corporate sponsorship for the 1988 Games, and offered a guarantee of $15m. In the event, TOP had mixed success, selling only 28 product categories to nine companies – Coca-Cola, Visa, 3M, Brother, Philips, Federal Express, Kodak, Time Inc, and Panasonic – and making around $125m. It discovered that not many multinationals genuinely wanted global marketing. McDonalds and Mars said it was too expensive, and American Express said it was too ambitious (Aris 1990: 171). ISL was set up and owned by Horst Dassler, boss of the giant sports clothing firm Adidas, until his death in 1987. Revealingly, Dassler has acknowledged that ISL was not intended solely or even principally as a means of making money, but was created partly as a means of staying on good terms with and keeping good relations with the organisers of major events and the officials of the international federations, who of course are important contacts for the Adidas business.

So the financial power of television was now being challenged by a new source of revenue from sponsorship. If the Olympics between 1964 and 1984 were shaped according to the needs of television, the Olympics from 1988 may increasingly be shaped by the promotional needs of corporate capitalism. Samaranch is on record as saying that arena advertising will not be allowed, but as sponsorship becomes more central to Olympic finance the pressure to give sponsors' names the much greater exposure that arena advertising would provide may become irresistible. The Olympics of course have a great logo – it's instantly recognisable, signifies international-ism and excellence, and, even in these commercial times, still carries among its numerous connotations the mythic notion of the purity of Greek idealism (see Kidd 1984). In the USA, only the McDonalds logo is more recognisable (100 per cent against the Olympics' 99 per cent). ISL's research suggests that companies are less interested in particular Games and more in the Olympic image. Almost half of people interviewed in the USA, Singapore, Portugal and West Germany thought the Olympic rings indicated that a product was of good quality (Wilson 1988: 28).

Staging the Olympics also provides the pretext for linking corporate self-promotion and communal internationalism: an advertisement for Calgary proclaimed, 'Let's show the world how great we are, Calgary'. The Olympic world is increasingly dominated by the language of entrepreneur-ship, with phrases like 'modern aggressive marketing', 'tailor the events to their business objectives', 'top-of-the-mind awareness', 'share of mind equals a share of market', 'defensive positioning' tripping easily off the tongues of the men in blue suits.[4]

Coca-Cola has been involved with the Olympic movement since 1928 and is quite clear that it is the association with the prestige and ideals of the Olympic movement that attracts it. In 1988 it utilised the Olympic Torch for its new Olympic logo, 'The Flame Burns Brighter . . . Coca-Cola'. The new Coke song, 'A Message of Hope', appeared in a television advertise-ment with a 1,000-voice choir singing in 16 different languages. Coca-Cola president Neville Kirchman spoke of a 'strong wish for world unity' and said: 'Our corporation commissioned the music and lyrics to represent the hopes and dreams for peace of young people everywhere.' One is forced to wonder whether it is just human fellowship, or also the market-place that features in this utopian dream of unity. The song was written by Ginny Reddington and Tom Dawes, who, the press pack proclaimed, already have many Coca-Cola hits to their credit, including 'Coke is It' and 'the Winning Taste of Sprite' (remember that one?). The song evoked fears of the future before offering the utopian solution in which 'we will all be

Figure 10.2 IOC President Juan Samaranch gives Olympic medal to Coca-Cola boss Roberto Goizueta.

there, Coca-Cola to share'. This then is the new Olympic internationalism – there we are with our Coke in one hand and our Visa card in the other. The IOC now presides over a highly successful enterprise for profit production, whilst still retaining the structure of an eighteenth-century gentlemen's club; in such a situation it is not surprising if contradictory tensions reproduce and multiply.

SPORT INTO THE 1990s

In the 1960s, sports agents like McCormack built their power initially on representing top stars. By the 1980s sports agents were forging new links with governing bodies, which were being forced to come to terms with commerce. West Nally played a significant role in the gradual move to open professionalism in the athletics world. In 1980 it paid the IAAF $400,000 for a three-year deal to promote a series of Golden Events, which was to include a clash between Coe and Ovett.[5] It played a key role in the first World Athletics Championships in 1983, selling the television rights, film rights, sponsorship and ground advertising. As in the 1984 Olympics, sponsorship was sold to a small number of companies, which West Nally said it hoped would bring 'dignity as well as profit to the event'.[6] The European Broadcasting Union paid nearly $1m for the television rights. Sponsors like Coca-Cola, Iveco, Kodak, Canon and TDK paid around $1m each, as well as presumably providing what they could in the way of 'dignity'. The audience was believed to have topped 1000 million.[7]

Adidas boss Horst Dassler originally worked closely with Patrick Nally, and only set up ISL after they parted. In what Aris describes as the first multinational sport sponsorship, they helped establish the World Youth Football tournament, FIFA president Juan Havelange providing the product, Dassler the contacts, Coca-Cola the money and Nally the salesmanship (Aris 1990: 167).

Juan Havelange came to power in FIFA by promising the third world countries that he would expand the tournament, but to include 24 teams in the 1982 Finals he had to find finance. Dassler and Nally, through their firm Société Monegasque du Promotion Internationale (SMPI), guaranteed 130m Swiss francs. It was the most successful marketing operation in the history of any individual sport, but made only $4m more than the massive advance. In 1982 Nally and Dassler parted company, Nally feeling his legwork was being used to make Dassler ever more powerful, whilst generating no real profits (Wilson 1988: 183). Dassler and Havelange had got together to revolutionise the marketing of the World Cup; and then taught Samaranch how the business worked and, Aris claims (1990: 160), also got him his job as IOC President – Dassler delivering the third world vote and Havelange controlling the Latin bloc. Aris refers to Dassler as the Godfather of sportsbiz.

But in 1987 Horst Dassler died, and Adidas (but not ISL) was acquired by the French mogul Bernard Tapie, who made little secret of his keenness to play at the big table, talking of France gaining the World Cup in 1998 and Paris the 1996 Olympics, thanks to his influence.[8] But Adidas was being overhauled by Reebok and Nike, which had been quicker to invest in cheap Asian production facilities, and Tapie was hitting finance problems and discovering that Dassler's influence didn't necessarily come automatically with Adidas ownership. In the globalisation of sport it was ISL, not Adidas, that occupied a pivotal position between the sport institutions, the television networks and the multinational corporations.[9]

The international prominence of major sporting events now gives them immense opportunities for cashing in through marketing and corporate hospitality. At Wimbledon in 1973, tickets produced the bulk of income. Since then, Centre Court prices have quadrupled and ground admission is up tenfold, yet now ticket sales are only 20 per cent of income, 60 per cent coming from television and 20 per cent from other sources. In 1982, US TV got Wimbledon to move the men's singles to Sunday, and by 1987 it had a TV audience of 350 million in 80 countries, bringing an income of £9m. The Committee has chosen to preserve the aura of exclusivity by rejecting title sponsorship, competition sponsorship and arena ads, which could be worth £5–10m, choosing instead to accept the International Management Group's suggestion to concentrate on marketing and licensing the name and the logo. As a result you can now buy clothes, shoes, wallets, belts, luggage, bone china, preserves, sheets, blankets, towels, stationery and calendars with the Wimbledon brand. Hospitality facilities were first marketed in 1975, and with 44 units, hired by more than 100 companies, a table for eight sells at £2000 per day. Each marquee holder is guaranteed 16 tickets daily (Wilson 1988: 39–40). Over 13,000 championship tickets go to corporate hospitality each year.

McCormack's main competitor in tennis is Donald Dell and ProServ, founded in 1976, representing 150 athletes in 9 countries, with a turnover of $25m. ProServ set up the 1982 European Community Championships (Antwerp) offering as a gimmick prize the Diamond Racket, 1600 diamonds in the shape of an E, worth $1m. Aris (1990) comments that 'the crowds who come to see it are oddly silent, as if overawed by the sight of so much wealth'. Such events arise as the result of careful market research. Dell was looking for a city with good communications, a large (and affluent) catchment area, a suitable arena, a friendly tennis association with good TV sponsor contacts, and no competing rival tournament. By 1987 it was ProServ's biggest earner, the most lucrative indoor championships in the world, televised in 37 countries.

As the field gets more and more crowded, sponsorship, especially in North America, has increasingly been seeking out up-market sports like yachting, show jumping and polo, of which potential sponsors BMW commented that every player and spectator was a potential BMW owner. The Australian success in the America's Cup suddenly made the event more dramatic and heightened its national interest, with the USA desperate to win the trophy back. The resultant media blitz has transformed an elite event into a global popular one, to the discomfort of the more traditional sector of the yachting establishment who rather resent their yachts being turned into giant floating billboards.[10]

Exporting sports in an attempt at globalisation became a dominant trend in the 1980s. American football, Australian Rules, sumo, and even cricket are all targeting new potential markets. Baseball has a whole long-term strategy for marketing the game in Europe, its Commissioner commenting cheerfully, 'It'll take a while but we'll get you in the end'.[11] Barry Hearn has attempted to establish snooker in Thailand, Hong Kong, Malaysia, Singapore, Brazil and China. A new European American Foootball League has been established. FIFA, in perhaps the most audacious bid for globalisation, has decided to stage the next World Cup in the USA in 1994, and is now faced with the prospect of winning the allegiance of the American public and, more crucially, the major networks. The lack of interest from US TV has pushed Havelange into floating bizarre suggestions for 'reforming' the game, by making the goals wider. As the qualifying rounds are already under way, we could yet see the first case of goalposts literally being moved after the game has started.

Chapter 11

Field of representations

'We are the ladies of the 80s
We build our bodies to beat the best'
(Slogan of all-woman dance troupe, in
Sport and Leisure, July/Aug 1987)

'I've got the Big G, boys, the big G.'
(Daley Thompson, to camera,
at the Los Angeles Olympics, 1984)

Television does not invent ideological elements, although it certainly transforms, dis-articulates and re-articulates them in new and distinctive ways. But these sets of ideological articulations are only part of a broader field of representations from which television selects and combines. This field is structured by a complex pattern of dominant, residual and emergent cultures (see Hall 1977, Laclau 1977, R. Williams 1977).

The world of sport and of sport broadcasting is still marked by residual elements from the formative period of the late nineteenth century. In particular there are traces of the ideology of the public schools and the muscular Christians, and the amateurism of sporting organisation. The public schools and the muscular Christians stressed a particular form of masculinity, involving toughness, physicality, character forming; the ethos of fair play and sportsmanship; teamwork, co-operation and self-sacrifice; and the greatness of the Empire, with Imperial Britain as civiliser (see Mangan 1981, McIntosh, 1952). The British sport organisations established in this period were characterised by their commitment to amateurism, and claim to sole legitimacy, by the social authority by which they were able to impose their dominance, by their voluntaristic character, and by the paternal benevolence of their public attitude.

It was in this period and around these institutions that, in a variety of ways, sport became inscribed as an apolitical domain, apart from normal social life, an arena separate and distinct from political turmoil and to be defended against it. These residual traces are still evident within broadcasting in many ways. They can be seen, for example, in the privileging of toughness and aggression as qualities. The code of sportsmanship is evident in the references to 'boorish crowds', and in the nostalgia for days 'when players would have said "good shot" to an opponent'. The Empire lives on in the belief in Britain as the sporting nation *par excellence*. The BBC's sporting calendar still exhibits a privileging of amateurism in the prominent presence of Rugby Union internationals and the Boat Race. In its separation of sport from other areas of social life and lack of critical journalism, broadcasting tends to perpetuate a paternal assumption that 'institutions know best' and helps preserve sport as a world of its own, outside politics.

However, since the late nineteenth century, sport at its highest level has clearly become a major form of popular entertainment, and television is associated with modernity and development, allowing sport to expand. The growth of television, the launching of colour television, and the spread of communication satellites all added to the spectacle. Sport represented modernity and rational progressivism. It was becoming internationalised, spectacularised and professionalised (Critcher 1979: 161–84). Increasing focus fell upon the role of national teams and their importance for national prestige. This became a major impetus for the expanded role of the state in sport provision generally and for the attempt to foster an elite in particular, from the late 1950s (J.E. Hargreaves 1986: 182–204). Broadcasting both reflected and promoted these trends.

The individual has always occupied a slightly odd place in British sport, and the tension between sport as team game and sport as individual achievement is generally present. A form of individualism rooted in rugged self-reliance harks back to the 'barbarian ' or aristocratic field pursuits – hunting, shooting and fishing – and the Victorian obsession with exploring and mountain-climbing. The discipline and endurance needed for some forms of sporting activity brought a stress on commitment and self-sacrifice, foregrounded in military sport and in the military version of physical training. This form of PT became a major influence on boys' education from the early twentieth century as ex-army PT instructors went into education.

From the late 1970s, with the hegemonic collapse of the welfare state/social democratic ethos and the rise of Thatcherism, monetarism and Reagonomics, the growing force of an emergent individualism rooted in neo-liberalism has been all too evident. Sport has become a road to success and self-improvement, a process evident in the reshaping of tennis, snooker and athletics. There has been a growing emphasis on single-minded commitment and rigorous training, and the emergence within sport of a strong work ethic.

This individualism is heightened by the entertainment contract, by the tendency to reward people as individuals rather than as team members.

Television has been a major force in the development of an international star system in sport. Top sport stars have become major celebrities. The increasing financial returns available to top sport stars have made sport success seem like one more path to self-reliance and self-sufficiency, and provide a highly public form of success.

In the last 20 years fitness has become fashionable. A new image of a physically active femininity has challenged older images of female frailty – a challenge impossible without the critique of gender relations provided by the rise of the women's movement. Physical activity in women has become not merely permissible, but represented as desirable – sexual attractiveness has become articulated with fitness.

One dominant trend during the 1980s was the emergent emphasis on style and consumption. The born-to-shop generation sought to define themselves by their choice of commodity – you are what you buy (see Tomlinson 1990). Sport was fashionable, so sport clothes were fashionable, and the fashion world increasingly borrowed from the world of sport. It's fashionable to be fit – but even more important is to look fit by wearing the right clothes. It's competitive – and it's important, not simply to be fit, but to be fitter than others, as exemplified by the popularity of forms of fitness that really push the body (squash and aerobics), the development from jogging and fun runs to the marathon cult, the new emphasis on pain and 'the burn'. It is a new form of 'Il faut souffrir pour être belle' – only now 'one has to suffer to be *fit*'. There are clear links with Thatcherism and the need for national suffering to produce national recovery: the medicine will not taste nice but it will be good for us.

FITNESS CHIC

The emergence of representations of women as active, and the attempted recuperations it produced, contributed to an increasing elision of the worlds of sport and fashion in the form of fitness chic. It is in the context of the representation of women as active that sportswear has been dramatically transformed into fashion. With the rise of the women's movement and changing definitions of femininity, women have come to be represented as fit, healthy and active, although the process was always somewhat uneven and contradictory (see Bolla 1990).

This in turn produced an ideological recuperation, whereby the styles of sport were in turn rendered fashionable, inflecting the connotations of action back towards display. Female sporting performance was represented in the form of the fashion feature, as in one preview for the London Marathon, headed 'HERE'S WHAT THE WELL DRESSED MARATHON RUNNER WILL BE WEARING TOMORROW'.[1] It was notable that cigarette brands that targeted women, such as Kim and Virginia Slims ('You've come a long way Baby'), chose to put money into sponsorship of women's tennis – a sport that reaches an affluent market sector, both live and on television, and enables the visual reconciliation of women as active and women as display.[2] Fashion styles borrowed from sportswear, and advertising copy emphasised activity:

> Until today leisurewear lacked DASH! Fashion is about lifestyle and DASH is for living in. It puts fashion into function, with styled-up shapes, creative colour schemes and super fabrics that have no inhibitions. DASH has vitality, its youthful, shaping-up to the wearer, not an age group. Prices are competitive . . .[3]

Yes, even the prices were competitive! Advertisements for the new leisure wear attempted to address a range of consumers, both active and passive. Clova tracksuits were 'stylish yet comfortable'. Sportswear didn't mean you actually had to expend energy, and leisure itself was fun. In the Sporty's Fun Suit, 'You can go anywhere in this twosome and feel perfectly at ease. Whether it's doing something active outdoors or a hectic evening's disco dancing', whilst 'whether you're aiming to get into the record books, or simply the athlete who's far keener on keep-fit classes, you'll look good in the Guinness tracksuit'. A White Horse ad featured leisure suits 'perfect for that energetic run, a gentle stroll to the pub, or for simply relaxing at home'.[4]

There was a need to pull fitness and pleasure together. After all, television's representation of sport made it clear that real fitness didn't come easily, as a hotel ad pointed out: 'Keeping fit and having fun don't always go together. Especially when you're travelling on business. At Holiday Inn we're changing all that. Most of our British inns now have a mini-gymnasium that we call Gym'n'Tonic.'[5] But fitness also required hard work and was a serious business. An Adidas poster featuring Daley Thompson reclining on a sofa in a stylish tracksuit was headed, 'What to wear when you're in serious training', and an Olympus advertisement showing a woman tennis player, with a male player in the background, captioned, 'When You Play To Win, Dress To Kill', proclaimed: 'Anyone who's serious about his game knows that if you're well turned out, somehow your tennis turns out better too.'[6] And being fit was highly competitive. The text on one Adidas ad attempted to hold together sportswear as fashion and fitness as a serious commitment, 'If you're serious about running, if you're determined to improve your performance, if you're dedicated to quality, if you're concerned about comfort, there's really only one choice.'[7]

Indeed this advert marked a remarkable and rapid transition. Fun running began as a grassroots alternative to the deadly serious competitive world of televised sport. But in a few short years it spawned a serious competitiveness, an obsession with 'PBs' (personal bests) a new elitism ('have you done a marathon yet?') and a phenomenon known as 'compulsive running'. In short, it became a major site for precisely the competitive individualism of top-level televised sport. That this ideological theme marked a broader transformation was highlighted by a milk ad featuring highly active people including athlete Linford Christie, with the slogan, 'Milk . . . for the way we live *now*' (my emphasis).[8] The way we live now is in awareness of the competitive ethos and the need to be fit and prepared simply to survive.

THE WORK ETHIC

The growth of top-level sport, the increase of financial returns, the rationalisation of coaching methods, the heightened importance of national success (driven by the East–West tensions of the Cold War), and the rise of a new individualism together produced a strong work ethic in sport – an emphasis on rigorous training and Brohm's 'taylorisation of the body', an attempt to wring maximum productivity from the human frame (Brohm 1978: 57).

This hard work is now punishing too; indeed physical punishment has become a signifier of hard work successfully performed. A page spread in the *Observer* showed all Bryan Robson's career injuries (he is on crutches with arm in sling and legs in plaster; 'his intrepid playing style has always made injury likely . . . Robson's body has been battered from head to toe').[9] And television constantly articulates the need for toughness ('Don't let that fool you, he's very tough indeed') to survive in top sport. Indeed, sportswear can be sold on this masochistic basis. An ad for Olympus showed a runner in a barren, parched landscape and promised 'We'll take you to hell and back'.[10] The film *Rocky* makes great play of the physically punishing nature of training. The ideological statement would appear to be, It's a tough life, you have to prepare yourself in order to compete with, and defeat, other individuals. The ethos was encapsulated in commonsense in the aphorism, 'no pain, no gain'.

Traditionally in dominant modes of representation women look good while men work hard, but now women have to look good *and* work hard; and in addition are expected to work hard at looking good. This is the underlying message of work-outs and aerobics: go for it, feel the burn. The body is subjected to a new discipline. An advert headed 'Fashion That Body' offered the Jackie Genova Workout Kit – colour co-ordinated leotard, belt, tights, legwarmers, plus Jackie Genova's own book *Work That Body*. *Work Out*, a free newspaper devoted to total fitness, was launched in June 1983. The new ethos was best caught by an all-woman dance troupe, whose act involves work-out routines, when they adopted the slogan, 'We are the ladies of the 80s, we build our bodies to beat the best'.[11]

ENTREPRENEURIAL CULTURE

It seems no accident that it is advertisements that were in the forefront in the emergent theme of fitness chic. In the context of the growth of sponsorship and television, the rise of a new competitive individualism produced by economic stringency and the ideology of Thatcherism, the cultures of sport have become highly entrepreneurial. The entrepreneurial culture both draws on and feeds the image of sport: athletics has 'integrity and a clean and healthy image. Athletics is all about winning'.[12]

Advertising appropriates the sense of importance, the authoritativeness and the aura of tradition and history of major television sport events. Rolex's Wimbledon sponsorship endeavours to associate its product with excellence: 'Meticulous in timing, refined in execution, the hallmarks of a great player are also the trademarks of Rolex'.[13] It draws heavily on the values and demands of top-level sport that television stresses – determination, toughness, dedication, timing, hard work and competitiveness. An advert for Rank Xerox copiers features a picture of determined-looking runners with the text:

> Some time ago Xerox set out to develop a new state of the art. Copiers that would combine the sophistication of the computer age with the durability needed to survive the pace of everyday office life. Which is why, when it comes to copying, we make the running. The marathon race is one of the toughest challenges the human body can face. To complete the course takes a lot of determination, dedication and hard work. So it's entirely appropriate that we chose today to launch our new range of copiers.[14]

Commerce draws upon sport for the images it offers of success and national prowess:

> In international squash the speed and skill of Jehangir Khan has become a legend. His determination to win has carried him to the very top of world competition. The will to succeed can be seen throughout Pakistan. In sport, engineering, industry, art and architecture. PIA has set for itself equally high standards. And is determined to achieve them.[15]

Sport in turn has to be businesslike, and it is no surprise that sports that fit this corporate image have prospered. Golf's image of respectable competitive individualism helped sell the game to corporate America. Aris describes it as 'the archetypal middle class sport where business could be combined with pleasure in agreeable surroundings' (Aris 1990: 16).

> Golfers are an agent's dream. Sober, responsible, untemperamental men like Britain's Nick Faldo or Australia's Greg Norman make ideal corporate front men. They can be relied upon to be nice to the sponsor;

In world competition, he trusts his skill.

In flying, he trusts PIA.

In international squash, the speed and skill of Jehangir Khan has become a legend. His determination to win has carried him to the very top of world competition. The will to succeed can be seen throughout Pakistan. In sport, engineering, industry, art and architecture.

PIA has set for itself equally high standards. And is determined to achieve them.

Flying to major cities in four continents. Operating a modern wide-body fleet with smooth efficiency. And hospitality that's an age-old tradition.

Celebrities like Jehangir Khan travel across the world many times each year. And have a wide choice of different airlines. Yet they choose PIA. Again and again.

PIA
Pakistan International
Great people to fly with

IAL (PAK)—84

PIA FLIES TO 62 DESTINATIONS ON 4 CONTINENTS: ABU DHABI•AMMAN•AMSTERDAM•ATHENS•BAGHDAD•BAHRAIN•BANGKOK•BANNU•BEIJING•BOMBAY•CAIRO•CHITRAL COLOMBO•COPENHAGEN•DAMASCUS•DELHI•DHAHRAN•DHAKA•D.I. KHAN•DOHA•DUBAI•FAISALABAD•FRANKFURT•GILGIT•GWADAR•HYDERABAD•ISLAMABAD•ISTANBUL JEDDAH•JIWANI•KANO•KARACHI•KATHMANDU•KUALA LUMPUR•KUWAIT•LAHORE•LONDON•MANILA•MOENJODARO•MULTAN•MUSCAT•NAIROBI•NAWABSHAH•NEW YORK PANJGUR•PARIS•PASNI•PESHAWAR•QUETTA•RIYADH•ROME•SAIDU SHARIF•SHARJAH•SINGAPORE•SKARDU•SUI•SUKKUR•TEHRAN•TOKYO•TRIPOLI•TURBAT•ZHOB

Figure 11.1   Pakistan Airlines advertisement.

to turn up at those boring dinners for the company's salesmen and other promotional events; generally to behave themselves – unlike the tennis hoodlums. The market for golf equipment is huge and highly competitive and the game itself is one with which the corporation man strongly identifies.

(Aris 1990: 40)

And in sports like golf and tennis corporate hospitality has grown rapidly by offering the 'new elite' privileged access to events. Aris argues that maintaining the veneer of exclusivity is an important dimension to this marketing. Advertising attempts to link itself to the aura of success that is at the heart of that most reified moment of television's representation of sport, the victory ceremony. A British Telecom advert, headed 'KEEP PRESSING FOR GOLD', featured a large picture of Tessa Sanderson on the victory rostrum at the 1984 Olympics with her gold medal, and the text stressed Telecom's role in bringing the event to Britain via satellite: 'With events like these British Telecom is bringing both news and business to Britain'.[16]

This advertisement appropriated British Olympic success to link patriotism and business. Sport was denoted by the image of sporting success, an image that is a distinctive product of television representation. These qualities are linked to those of business, signified here as patriotic, as helping the nation. It is no accident that this advertisement, from a newly privatised company, should be so concerned to effect an imaginary resolution of the conflict between commerce and patriotism, illustrating graphically the hegemonic reworking of images of the nation, with entrepreneurship placed firmly centre stage.

CONTRADICTIONS

Of course, all these elements are not part of one cohesive field. On the contrary, it is their simultaneous but contradictory existence that produces some of the tensions characteristic of the field of representation of sport. Take, for example, the *Radio Times* cover for the week of the World Athletics Championships of 1987. It portrayed two athletes, one black and one of Turkish-Cypriot origin (Daley Thompson and Fatima Whitbread), as spearheading the British challenge, and offered an image of woman as athlete a long way distanced from the bikini-clad athletes Tessa Sanderson, Sharon Colyear and Sonia Lannaman pictured on an earlier cover. At the same time, the slogan 'Enter the Gladiators' appeared to place a tough, uncompromising macho combativeness even more to the fore. Clearly blackness, Britishness, physicality and femininity are not unchanging terms, but are subject to negotiation and contestation. Just as the field of popular culture as a whole is riven with tensions and contradictions, so is

COMPLETE 10-DAY GUIDE TO BBCtv and Radio

AUGUST BANK HOLIDAY

RadioTimes

218
Oslo

358

ENTER THE GLADIATORS

**Fatima Whitbread and Daley
Thompson spearhead the
British challenge at the World
Athletics Championships in
Rome. Full coverage on
BBCtv and Radio 2 from
Saturday**

Figure 11.2   Radio Times cover (29/8/87) showing Fatima Whitbread and Daley
Thompson. Femininity, blackness, national identity and physicality are all caught
here in the midst of a process of renegotiation. This is an uneven and contradictory
process, and it would be hard to characterise this simply as either a positive or a
negative image.

the sporting world. Indeed it is precisely these tensions and contradictions that have been placed under pressure by the transformations of the last 20 years and in the process many of these tensions and contradictions have been re-formed.

Uncertainty v. predictability

Uncertainty is built into the structure of sport itself. Sport as an entertainment is, among other things, a form of commodity. Capitalism's need to reduce the uncertainty of the commodity, to guarantee the presence of entertainment value, comes into conflict with this – producing at one and the same time an attempt to use the uncertainty of sport to win and hold an audience, while winning and holding the audience by ensuring that the promise of entertainment can always be fulfilled.

Amateurism v. professionalism

The gradual penetration of sport by capital, accelerated by the rise of television and the growth of sponsorship, undermined the amateur ethos, if only because top players perceived the hypocrisy whereby everyone but they could earn money. The crisis in the Olympic movement during the 1980s was precisely a product of this tension (see Guttman 1984). Economically, television and sponsorship placed the old amateur ethos under increasing strain.

Sportsmanship v. victory

As a subsidiary contradiction to the previous one, the existence of large monetary rewards, the dependence of careers upon success and the fore-grounding of sport as a form of national prestige have placed the ethos of fair play under great strain and produced the sense of a morality in crisis, with questions of drug-taking, unsportsmanlike conduct and cheating fore-grounded. Television continues to recycle the fine old amateur principles of sportsmanship, and celebrates a good loser. Unease can be detected over losers who fail to fulfil their role – as in the 1985 Snooker Championship, when a shattered Steve Davis plainly had no heart to utter the appropriate 'good loser' lines; or at the Moscow Olympics when Coe was supposedly rather graceless in defeat. McEnroe has constantly been pilloried by British television for no greater offence than failing to adopt the codes and conventions of an English sporting gentleman. (This is particularly hypocritical as television is shrewd enough to know that its audience demands to see re-runs of the latest scenes involving McEnroe or Alex 'Hurricane' Higgins.) At the same time it also validates and valorises the tough, determined commitment to victory of a Daley Thompson or the cocky arrogance of an Eric Bristow. In so doing, television is in part merely relaying dominant acceptable attitudes in the sporting world itself. In the 30 years following Roger Bannister's 4 minute mile, the ethos of the English sporting gentleman has been challenged by the new individualistic drive for success.

Nationalism v. individualism

While top-level sport has indeed foregrounded national identity and national prestige, and hence chauvinism, the rise of the entrepreneurial ethos and the penetration of sport by capital have produced a countervailing individualism. Top performers in the same teams are competing against each other for star status and hence earning power, which potentially weakens team commitment. International representative competition is often less rewarding than other events. For example, in tennis, the Davis Cup has become devalued as an event, as many top tennis players prefer to play more lucrative tournaments or even exhibitions. The British athletic authorities have found it hard to ensure that top athletes turn up for internationals, when individual international invitation meetings can offer so much more money. The clash between club and country in football has been accentuated by the growing international mobility of individual star players.

Television has aided the growth of a star system in sport, enabling sport stars to become personalities and celebrities. Plainly, television celebrates nationalism and national identity, and mobilises viewer identification with British chances. It would feel great unease with any sportsman who denied the importance of 'playing for my country'. Yet in the way it constantly focuses on the individual, de-emphasises teamwork and team tactics and seeks to lift star individuals from out of the background of the team, it serves to reproduce the contradiction it has helped to heighten.

Tradition v. modernity

Sport roots itself in tradition, in the cyclical recurrence of its ritual occasions – the Cup Final, the Olympics, the Derby, the Boat Race, etc. But the increased dependence on sponsorship challenges this tradition. Sponsors need to rename events or establish new ones in order to foreground their brand names. They come and go. Gillette supported cricket for ten years and the Gillette Cup had gone from being a rather controversial new innovation to seeming almost part of the bulwark of cricket tradition as against newer upstarts like the Benson and Hedges Cup. Suddenly, overnight, it was gone, to become the NatWest Trophy. Similarly, Football's League Cup became for a while the Milk Cup, and its league became the Canon League, both short-lived sponsorships. Other meaningless events, such as the Leyland Daf Cup and the Zenith Data Systems Cup, have proliferated. These examples are characteristic of the tensions within sport between tradition and modernity.

Television celebrates, reproduces and has done much to invent and inscribe the traditions of British sport. It is hard to imagine, for example, how an obscure rowing event between two universities could ever have become a national occasion without the BBC. It is hard to imagine Wimbledon without imagining the BBC coverage and the voice of Dan Maskell – as near to the Centre Court as most of us will ever get. It is hard to believe that Rugby Union internationals could ever seem quite so important without the BBC. While these traditions always seem unvaried and cyclically recurrent, they can be added to with ease; the World Snooker Championship has had less than ten years of coverage and already seems like a permanent fixture. Similarly the one-day cricket finals and the World Athletics Championships are now written firmly into the annual calendar, illustrating well that process Hobsbawm and Ranger (1983) dubbed the invention of tradition. Yet it is television that has made possible the forces of sponsorship that tend to undermine and challenge this tradition by creating new events, and renaming and reshaping old ones.

Patriarchy v. feminism

As a result of the increased acceptability of physical activity for women, the traditional masculine domination of sports is inevitably beginning to come under pressure. The struggle of women athletes to get the International Olympic Committee to introduce a women's marathon, and the growing struggle of women snooker and darts players against patriarchal power are indications that this will be a contradiction of growing importance in sports.

In this context television must be seen as one of the bastions of patriarchy. Its scale of values marginalises women's sport. Its producers and commentators are still almost entirely male,[17] and its representational practices tend to reproduce traditional concepts of femininity. But this is clearly going to become a site of struggle. In the coverage of the second World Athletics Championships in 1987, commentators were more than once heard correcting themselves after referring to athletes as 'girls' rather than 'women', possibly in response to recent criticism in a television documentary on the portrayal of women on television. And television sport offers, at least potentially, a fund of positive images of physically active women to set against the rather greater patriarchy of the world of sporting institutions and their values.

Sponsorship is also potentially contradictory here. Women aged 18–35 are a prime target for advertisers, and corporate sponsors wishing to reach such a group have shown considerable interest in the sponsorship opportunities offered by television coverage of women's sports. Women's professional golf and tennis became established largely because of this interest.

So television's representations of sport reproduce, in complex and contradictory fashion, elements of a field of representations which is itself complex and contradictory. It continues to articulate residual elements (from the golden era of public school sport and muscular Christianity) together with emergent elements (the new competitive individualism). In some areas (the personalised and individualised star system) television plays a leading role, in some (fitness chic) it is more marginal. But in terms of images of sport itself – what it is, what it stands for, and what its key values are – television occupies a position of dominance. This is not simply a matter of concern for television professionals. As long as sport continues to be restructured according to the needs of television, it is a matter also for those who have a stake in the diverse sporting cultures that make up what has become television's 'world' of sport.

Chapter 12

Audiences and pleasures

The great strength of media studies has been its emphasis on understanding media products and their effects both in terms of the moment of their production and of their consumption. The development of the field has thus far worked forward from politics and production processes, through programme analysis to the present concern with audiences. What is now needed is a new synthesis of the relations of production and consumption in the light of the critical insights and empirical evidence harvested from the current interest in audience studies.

(Scannell 1990: 7)

Technological advance and globalisation have produced a spectacularisation of the televisual image of sport, bringing high-quality live pictures of major events to a global audience. While it is relatively easy to comprehend the transformation this has produced in the organisation, production and cultures of sport, understanding the cultural impact on the audience is a far more complex matter. Good empirical evidence on television sport viewing has still to be gathered, and all that can be done here is to map out some directions of enquiry.

For the most part television sport is a reliable, rather than a spectacular winner of audiences. But the special major events have a unique capacity to win and hold huge audiences even well outside normal peak viewing time. On occasions the Olympic Games and the World Cup get British audiences of 15 million plus. The Grand National, the World Snooker Championships, *Sports Review of the Year* and Wimbledon tennis consistently top 10 million. Over half the population regularly watch some · television sport (Marles 1984).

Football was for a long time the most consistently popular regular sport, with *Match of the Day* and *The Big Match* getting audiences of 8 million or more during the 1970s. But as football declined during the 1980s it was increasingly challenged by snooker and, on occasion, athletics. However, the more recent revival of football since live coverage has kept it at the top. ITV's *The Match* is currently consistently getting over 6 million.

Most large television audiences are fairly heterogeneous, composed of class, age and gender ranges in rough proportion to the population as a whole. In general the television audience has slightly higher proportions of women, older people and working-class people. Just as soap opera, often thought to be a female-oriented form, still gets a substantial proportion of male viewers, the male-centred form of sport still has a fairly large female audience. Audiences are measured by presence in the room. Audience figures do not distinguish between those who have chosen to watch a programme, and those who are merely present. Recent research on viewing and the family has rightly foregrounded the question of how the set is actually watched, or not watched, how viewing decisions are made, and who controls the switch (Morley 1986, Collett and Lamb 1986).

Some marked differences in gender preferences can be detected, however. In 1988 the sports with the highest proportion of adult males were rugby, cricket, baseball, football, American football and golf, but in no case were adult men more than 56 per cent of the total audience. The sports with the highest proportion of women in the audience were skating, tennis and equestrian sports, all with audiences including over 53 per cent adult women. This appears to echo the supposed masculine/feminine orientation of these sports. Yet if audience size is taken into account, far more women watch the major sports – football, cricket, athletics, snooker, golf and racing. Only tennis has both a high proportion of women and a high overall audience.[1]

There are also some marked differences in class. The audience for television sport, like the population as a whole, is predominantly working class. The largest proportions of social class AB are to be found in the audiences for rugby, ski-ing, tennis, golf and cycling, whilst those sports with the largest proportion of CDEs are wrestling, darts and boxing. In examining age, the most significant difference appears in youth viewing (ages 16–24). The sports that attract the highest proportion are baseball, swimming, American football, sumo and cycling, which are almost exclusively Channel 4 sports.

Yet the percentage figures can again be misleading. Examining the total figures for the year 1988 reveals that in every demographic category the most-watched sports were snooker and football, along with the Olympic Games and multiple sport programmes such as *Grandstand* and *Sportsnight*. Amongst both men and women, and in social classes AB, these four were followed by cricket, athletics, racing, tennis and golf. Amongst CDE viewers, wrestling edges golf out of the top 11, and, amongst youth, American football and wrestling come above racing and golf. The similarities are striking, emphasising again the heterogeneous nature of the audience for television sport. A major determinant here is that if a sport gains a lot of air-time, not just because of popularity but because of relative cheapness (e.g. racing, cricket), it will almost by definition get a large mixed audience. We need to know far more about which members of households choose to tune in to which sports, and what degree of resistance this produces from other members.

Steven Barnett (1990) points out that sport audiences for major events fluctuate widely, and suggests that factors like scheduling, channel loyalty and the presence of British interest intervene (see Goodhart *et al.* 1975). BBC audience research (BBC 1976) has revealed that the presence of England in a football match can add some 10 per cent to the audience, while Scotland adds 5 per cent. Barnett draws on the Target Group Index (TGI) which investigates, among other things, which sports people like to watch, and argues that watching television is, increasingly, a default activity, which people choose when they have nothing better to do, an assertion which Peter Collett's fascinating work on audiences seems to support.[2] In the 20 years 1969–1989 show jumping, wrestling, swimming and horse racing have dropped out of the top 10 most popular sports on TV, to be replaced by snooker, darts, cricket and motor racing. Two mixed sports have gone, whilst all four new sports are, on TV at least, male only.

Barnett (1990) says there has been a substantial decline in levels of absolute interest, and only snooker and athletics at their 1989 levels would have made the top 10 in 1969. He argues that 'there seems to be irrefutable evidence of a major decline over twenty years in viewers' enjoyment of the so-called major sports', although there has been a growth in interest in some minor sports, not all of which are included on the TGI. The BBC (Marles 1984) has detected a similar decline between 1979 and 1983. Barnett concludes that the sports audience is a soft one. There is a tendency for casual viewers to watch only certain major events. Casual viewers are of course crucial to audience building, and they are most likely to change their habits because of the schedule, the type of competition, the possibilities of national success, the presence of personalities, and other factors.

Audience feedback in letter form, in *Radio* and *TV Times*, on *Points of View* and in the tabloid press often indicates a hostility to sport amongst women, and there is certainly good reason that such a male-defined and dominated domain might produce such hostility. At the same time there is some evidence that significant numbers of women do not merely watch but also enjoy a range of television sports, not just those, such as athletics, tennis, skating and gymnastics, with female competitors or an 'aestheticised' dimension; but also sports such as snooker and golf. Major events like the Olympics and World Cup football appear to have had some success in engaging and holding female viewers. BBC research (1976) found that during the World Cups in both 1966 and 1974, the female audience grew from 25 per cent to 40 per cent during the course of the competition. But far more research is needed to give us a greater understanding of the dynamics of the family and gender relations when it comes to making viewing decisions about television sport.

Institutional research by broadcasters has been of two main types. A massive and sophisticated process of head-counting, based on metered sets augmented by diaries, produces detailed information on the numbers of viewers, but does not distinguish between those who have chosen to watch and those who are merely in the room. Indeed, as Collett's research revealed, a set can often be switched on with no one in the room. Augmenting this, the BBC for many years has compiled the Appreciation Index, a multiple-choice survey that probes the level of viewer enjoyment. While the figures can be interesting, they tend to demonstrate, not surprisingly, that viewers tend to enjoy the programmes they choose to watch, and the multiple-choice answer reveals little about the nature of these pleasures. In addition, both BBC and ITV commission regular ad hoc studies into particular aspects of broadcasting and its audience.

Academic research was hidebound for many years by the hypodermic model, rooted in a mechanistic assumption that a given stimulus would produce a given response. The development of more sophisticated effects research from the 1940s revealed that attitudes were hard to change, and that media messages were more likely to reinforce them than change them. Work on agenda-setting suggested that, while the media didn't tell people what to think, they were adept at telling them what to think about. Attention shifted from asking what the media did to people, to the question of what people did with the media. Much of this research was flawed by a rather atomised and individualised societal model. The development of the encoding/decoding model gave rise to the first attempt to explore how media language structured the range of decodings an audience might make.

This pioneering work on decoding had two notable problems. First, the subjects viewed the programme in groups in non-domestic situations, a limitation Morley (1981) fully acknowledges (see also Lewis 1983, Jordin and Brunt 1986). Much subsequent work, including Morley's own, has explored the domestic viewing situation, the family and the ways viewing decisions are made.[3] Analysing baseball, Roberta Pearson (1988) has argued that, just as the texts of sport are more open ended, so is the audience a more active one, more involved with the process of offering or producing alternative interpretations of the action. It is worth noting that, of all television programme types, sport broadcasts are probably the most likely to be viewed also in larger groups in the home, and in communal public spaces like bars and hotel lounges. I have heard accounts of widely differing viewing experiences from people who watched games in the 1990 World Cup in homes, bars and hotel lounges in France, Belgium, Ireland, England, Scotland and Italy. Any future investigation into the audience for television sport needs to take this communal context into account.

A second problem with Morley's original model stems from the concept of decoding, rooted as it is in the notion that images are 'read'. This works best with those areas of media production – news and current affairs – where meaning and the cognitive dimension are of prime importance. But with sport, as with other forms of entertainment, feeling, emotion and the affective dimension are also important. The pleasures of viewing are complex and multi-faceted and cannot be totally understood from within the decoding model.

PLEASURES

Pleasures are peculiarly resistant to analysis, and present particular challenges to empirical testing. The first step is to challenge common-sense assumptions of pleasures as transparent or self-evident, needing no explanation. The production of popular culture is striving to generate profit, but can do so only by offering a product – entertainment – chosen by its audience as having a real use-value. The field of popular pleasures is a function not simply of mass production but of a more complex exchange between producer and consumer, in which both profitablitity and meaning are the site of struggle and negotiation.

Pleasure has both a psychic and a social dimension. There are basic mechanisms that produce within us the sensation of pleasure, which various forms of psychoanalysis from Freud to Lacan have attempted to identify. Such explanations, applied to popular culture, have led to significant insights and influential arguments (Marcuse 1955, Mulvey 1975). Psychoanalytic accounts alone, however, can be prone to trans-cultural, trans-historic tendencies, and risk the danger of a psychic reductionism, in which all ideological domination stems from entry into language, or from acquisition of gendered subjectivity (Hall *et al.* 1980: 117–76).

It is crucial to retain here the social dimension of pleasures, which never appear in abstract form, but always in the shape of particular structured experiences, specific cultural forms, with their specific histories and modes of production and consumption. Pleasures cannot, then, simply be viewed as a set of commodities on display, from which the free consumer merely selects. They actively address us, hail us and seek to position us.

The political dimension of the pleasure of popular culture has been the subject of intense debate. It has been seen as a distraction, a form of bread and circuses, as potentially educational (Brecht 1964), as potentially utopian (Dyer 1978), or as revolutionary (following Marcuse, the Paris situationists, see De Bord 1977). But these qualities may not simply be a function of the pleasurable experience itself – they may be produced in different forms by different modes of consumption. Again, the social organisation and ideological construction of pleasure are sites of struggle and contestation. The meaning of pleasurable experiences is never simply dictated by those who produce them, or those who consume them.

PLEASURE AND SPORT

Pleasure depends in part upon the interplay of repetition and difference, clearly a central element in the structure of sport competition. For instance, in snooker, the structure of each frame is determined by the repetition of the rules for potting balls and the difference of performance, strategy and luck contributed by the players. Barthes distinguishes between the cosy and comfortable familiarity of '*plaisir*' and the more disruptive, engulfing experience of '*jouissance*' (Barthes 1975). *Jouissance* is certainly present for performers at peak moments (e.g. Coe at Moscow) and possibly occasionally for live spectators. Standing on a crowded football terrace after your team has scored a goal involves both euphoria and a temporary disruption of view and perspective as the crowd leaps and surges, but, for the television audience, *plaisir* is the more common experience. Television sport viewing may enthral, but rarely in a disruptive and disorientating way.

Dyer discusses entertainment in terms of the categories of energy, abundance, intensity, transparency and community, categories that clearly provide a way of analysing the sport experience (Dyer 1978). There is the energy provided by the crowd noise, by the physical movement, speed and athleticism. Abundance is evident in the size of the crowds, the lavishness of the spectacle and the presence of star performers. Intensity is a major element – in the uncertainty, the emotional involvement of participants and spectators, the sense that everything is at stake, the feeling of being almost unable to watch (a common comment from viewers of the final moments of the Steve Davis/Dennis Taylor snooker final of 1985). Transparency is provided by the realness of the spectacle, the commitment of the players and the actuality quality of sport as opposed to more fictionalised or rehearsed forms of entertainment. Community is also an important element in the involvement of spectators, and the mobilisation of local, regional, national or emotional identifications. Like other forms of entertainment, sport offers a utopia, a world where everything is simple, dramatic and exciting, and euphoria always a possibility. Set against this of course is the fact that, for the typical sport fan, failure is a more common experience than success. Sport entertains, but can also frustrate, annoy and depress. But it is this very uncertainty that gives its unpredictable joys their characteristic intensity. Sport events offer a liminal moment between uncertainty and certainty; unlike fictional narrative, they are not predetermined by authorship, nor can they necessarily be predicted by cultural code or even specialist knowledge. So they precisely offer the rare opportunity to experience genuine uncertainty. This is part of the unique fascination of genuinely live events as opposed to those that merely offer the appearance of liveness.

Terry Lovell (1980 and 1981), drawing on Raymond Williams's elusive and allusive term 'structures of feeling', proposes the concept of structures of pleasure. Soap operas, for instance, offer the female audience validation, reassurance and utopianism (Dyer, Lovell and McCrindle 1977). If the pleasures of sport viewing have a structure, then identification is central to it. While there are clearly aesthetic pleasures in merely watching a sport performance, the real intensity comes from identifying with an individual or team as they strive to win. Taking sides appears important to the experience of watching sport, even where no obvious local, regional, national or emotional affiliation offers itself. Hence the search for a surrogate Brit is not simply about nationalism, but about the need to secure an appropriate figure for audience identification in order that the pleasure might work.

Alan Lovell (1975) talks of pleasure points, and a taxonomy of the pleasures of viewing television sport is clearly needed. Such a taxonomy can certainly start by listing the forms of pleasure that textual analysis identifies: familiarity with conventions (genre), identification, nationalism, narrative and resolution, star watching, spectacle, immediacy, thrills and spills (the body in jeopardy), physicality/sexuality/eroticism, gazing at the body, and so on. However, such a list needs to be not simply empirically tested against the complex responses of actual audiences, but subject to reformulation in the light of such tests. There is a need here to establish the cultural and historical specificity of sport as entertainment; to chart more exactly TV sport and its relation to its audience. Wenner and Gantz (1989) have examined the behaviour and attitude of television sport viewers, and found that watching to find out the fate of a favourite team or individual was the strongest motivation for watching, followed by a liking for the drama and tension. But of course research in this area faces problems both of theory and of method. You cannot adequately explore the nature of popular pleasures solely by asking direct questions; people are not necessarily reliable sources on the nature of their pleasures, which cannot always be easily comprehended or articulated.

Several writers have drawn attention to the common occurrence of sexual metaphor in sporting language. Morse (1983) refers to American football, with its deep penetration and end zones. Easthope (1989) talks of snooker's deep screws and kisses on the pink. Tudor comments of English football that 'compared to many continental cultures we subscribe to an orgasmic theory of football; the foreplay only has meaning if it is climaxed with goals' (Buscombe 1975). Sport, as a form of display, clearly has an erotic dimension that is at once instantly visible and, in television's discourse, deeply suppressed. Most sports place the body on display, make it available as a form of visual spectacle, yet the erotic power of such display is never alluded to and even aesthetic beauty is referenced only in those few 'aestheticised' sports, such as ice skating and gymnastics.

Laura Mulvey (1975) analysed narrative cinema in terms of the dependence of its visual pleasures on scopophilia (erotic pleasure in looking) and voyeurism, producing a spectacularisation of women for the male gaze. But television sport arguably also places male bodies on display and renders them available for both a female and a male gaze. Indeed, on the visual level, athletic bodies are not simply displayed but almost lovingly dwelt over, repeatedly and in slow motion. Drawing on Laura Mulvey's work on visual pleasure, Duncan and Brummett (1989) discuss TV sport in terms of fetishism, voyeurism and narcissism. Their account of the process of viewing pleasure is somewhat speculative and abstract but does succeed in drawing attention to the voyeurism inherent in television's growing tendency to bring us the views we are not supposed to be seeing, such as shots of stressed managers and glimpses inside the dressing rooms.

Margaret Morse (1983) offers a more substantial and developed application of psychoanalytic theory to the representation of sport. She argues that sport discourse is unique in that its object is the male body. The strong cultural inhibition against looking at the male body can be attributed to a deep-seated reluctance to make the male the object of scopophilia. Yet the gaze at maleness is necessary to the construction and constant replenishment of a shared cultural ideal of masculinity. How is it that spectator sports can license such a gaze and render it harmless? She suggests that there is a careful balance of play and display and every look of man at his exhibitionist like is transformed into a scientific enquiry into the limits of human performance; hence the obsession with records and statistics.

Morse argues that, whereas the pleasures of the stadium are communal, a football game on TV is received in privacy by an isolated, usually male viewer who must forgo the pleasures of the crowd. The extremely long lenses with narrow angles flatten space, and, along with instant replay, contribute to a considerable deformation of the stadium point of view: spatial compression, temporal elongation and repetition emphasise only points of action and body contact to the detriment of the overall geometry of the game.

The frequent repetition means that the game is no longer occurring in a world subject to the laws of ordinary linear and uni-directional time, and this transforms a world of speed and violent impact into one of dance-like beauty. Whereas the stadium-goer is a participant in a ritual, the TV viewer looks at a phantasmic realm never seen in any stadium. This fantasy has to do with the passage into manhood, a period of ambiguous sexual identity. The construction of a masculine image of power and beauty plays an important role in that passage. Laura Mulvey's analysis of the opposition between narrative and spectacle provides a framework for the discovery of how a masculine image is constructed for the male gaze.

The visual field has become primarily spectacle; particularly during action replay, the narrative *per se* ceases. Male icons are direct objects of the gaze of the camera and thus of the television viewer, the mark of pure spectacle, but, unlike the female figures in Mulvey's article, alone and frozen, these multiple, at times fragmented, male figures move, often with a machine-like, deliberate slowness which is the attribute of perfect machines. Sport on television, then, offers a ritual space where man can overcome his separateness from nature, God, other men and his own body and achieve grace, signified by slow motion. Slow motion then realises the fantasy of the body as perfect machine with an aura of the divine. The most typical relation of women to sport and this phantasm of male perfection is avoidance through lack of interest – but women are also unwelcome in the inner sanctum of sport; the female gaze is that of an outsider.

Morse offers a complex and absorbing account which warrants further debate and exploration. The opposition she suggests between the communal stadium experience and the isolated male television viewer seems to me to have problems. Much TV is watched in groups – sport probably more so; indeed sport is more likely to be watched in communal viewing situations, whether in sitting rooms or bars, than most forms of television. Most large television audiences include a significant portion of women, whose viewing situation is not necessarily that of an outsider. Morse states that the primary identification of the sports spectator in the stadium is not with the team but with the crowd itself, a situation certainly not very evident at Anfield or other major soccer grounds. She says television is one of those solitary pleasures like novel reading, but this seems to discount the important social dimension of television – watching it with others and talking about it the next day. Her suggestion that the visual field has become primarily spectacle, particularly during action replay when the narrative ceases, is, I think, incorrect. My own sense of sport viewing is that, for most people, the desire to know what happens next, to follow a narrative and to discover a final resolution is a central and indispensable part of the mechanism of identification. The pleasures of television sport viewing, whilst built around this identification, seem to me to be many and various, and cannot be reduced to the scopophilial gaze of the spectator, male or female, at the body.

However, it has to be said that much discussion on the audience for television sport is speculative. There is a need for more detailed empirical ethnographic work. The first step might be to endeavour to refine a taxonomy of the pleasures of sport viewing, through a combination of interview and participant observation. The work of David Morley (1980, 1986), David Morley and Roger Silverstone (1990), Ann Gray (1987) and Dorothy Hobson (1982) offers a useful frame of reference for further work in this area.

Chapter 13

Final thoughts

What then has sport offered to television in return for such support? Has it sold its ethics, sacrificed its morality, mortgaged its soul? Has it changed its rules, modified its heroics, installed electricity where the human spirit once ran free? What has it cost?

(W.O. Johnson 1971: 58)

An Italian operatic aria topped the British hit parade, solely because the BBC chose it as their title music for World Cup '90. Who could have predicted that Luciano Pavarotti would emerge as the man of the tournament. Which club side does he play for?

(Letter from friend, 1990)

The effect of television upon sport has been a point of debate for over 30 years, some arguing that television has made sport, some that sport has been ruined, others merely content to bear witness to the unholy alliance. Johnson acknowledged a range of television-inspired changes: the intro- duction of commercial time-outs, the shift in PGA golf from match play to stroke play, the morning scheduling of West coast basketball to suit East coast television. But, he argued, one rarely heard these complaints from those within the game and he asserted that the thesis that television had marred sport was usually advanced by a bystander, and not by those within (Johnson 1971: 61). Of course, those who live by the games might be thought to have a vested interest.

McCormack spoke of an unholy alliance, and Klatell and Marcus judge that 'the marriage of the two businesses has produced a hybrid offspring: the television/sports complex which is neither pure television nor pure sports and resembles each parent only in profitable bloodlines'. They agreed that many changes to sports have been caused by television but that, in general, sport has adapted well to these intrusions (Klatell and Marcus 1988: 22–3 and 42). This judgement, though, depends upon what sports represent, and in whose interests they are changing.

Chandler (1988) argues that television sport represents cultural continuity rather than cultural change, and that television has not changed the essence of sports televised or their conduct, but has simply built on commercial foundations laid by sports industry. She asserts that rule changes are nothing new and are not therefore a product of the needs of television, but rather a continuing and consistent manifestation of sport's attempts to adjust to changing times and changing audience needs. She comments that it is all too easy to announce that television producers have changed traditional rules and ruined the game, if one is ignorant of past rule manipulations. Certainly it is true that there have always been rule changes, usually precisely in response to changing circumstances – social change, technological innovation, performance improvement, and so on. The rise of television and sponsorship, though, constitute not simply the current factors, but the most dramatic, restructuring sports and their significances.

Rader (1984: 116) by contrast feels that the new sports drama created by television inexorably threatened the authenticity of the traditional sporting experience and he offers a detailed account of changes in rules, organisation, performance and audience expectation to support his case. He suggests, for instance, that TV ruined boxing by producing a punch-hungry audience, encouraging a TV style of boxer and sacrificing aesthetics for brutality.

From the 1960s, television increasingly prompted a repackaging of sports. Rader acknowledges that television could broaden and deepen the experience of sports, but argues that the medium ultimately trivialised and diluted the traditional sporting experience. Traditional values of sportsmanship, civility, the suppression of the individual ego for a higher cause, play for the joy of the game, all tended to give way to winning at all costs, number one-ism, incivility, self-indulgence and the blatant enlistment of the games on behalf of monetary interests (Rader 1984: 197). Stephen Aris (1990: xi) points out that no medium captures more vividly the excitement and occasionally the poetry of sport. But he asserts that TV not only exalts, it can also trivialise. He says that:

> I regret that sporting heroes are now being asked not only to perform to the limits of their capacity, but are expected to be super-salesmen as well. It seems to me that sport has been hijacked by industry and TV to serve their own very different ends.
>
> (Aris 1990: xii)

It is easy and tempting to adopt a one-dimensional view – that nasty old corrupt business has come along and ruined good old pure sport. But, if television has changed sports, it is a more complex process. Culturally one can suggest a number of shifts. Television has transformed the nature of the lived experience of sporting cultures; it is largely responsible for one-day cricket, for open tennis, for the gradual move towards professionalism of athletics, for the boom in snooker, and for the remarkable popularity of American football in Britain (note that a small but significant number of British people now *play* American football). It can be fairly speculated that it has also transformed the way people live their relation to their experience of sporting cultures; it has changed the way people see sport.

It is only in the wake of television that people at live events come to miss the action replay; and increasingly at major events a giant TV screen is now provided for precisely this purpose (and of course the displaying of adverts). Just as sports which gain television coverage thrive, those that don't can decline – they can come to seem marginal (see Whitson 1983a: 139–54, Tomlinson 1992). Television has extended its own standards of professionalism to sport, so that events that used to be presented with a casual informality are now 'staged' in a more elaborate manner, they now go further in addressing their spectators. Many events now incorporate a commentator who duplicates part of the role of the television commentator.

In particular television has decreased the degree of autonomy of the lived cultures of the sporting world. For whereas in the 1950s in the myriad diverse worlds of lived sporting cultures many different forms existed, shaped largely by small-scale, localised determinants, nowadays the horizon of possibilities for most sports has been determined by the ever-present possibilities of television and sponsorship.

Television sport offers the consistent picture of a nation set in place, a whole complex pattern of class relations being naturalised. Partly this is accomplished by the masking of class and by the de-politicisation of the discourse of sport. But it is accomplished also by the consistency with which a stable, unchanging world, rooted in tradition, in which everyone knows their place, is represented. The royals have their own occasions (e.g. Badminton Horse Trials) as do the aristocracy (Henley) and the upper middle class (Rugby Union at Twickenham), but so does the working class (e.g. the Cup Final and the Rugby League Cup Final). And just as other classes view the spectacle of the monarchy as Ascot, so do the royals attend occasions of popular pleasure such as the Cup Final, the Derby and Wimbledon. What we see represented on these occasions is a cosy consensual de-politicised communality.

The world of sport is a hierarchised one, which in football is summed up in the saying, 'Directors direct, managers manage, and players bloody well play'. On television this appears as a hierarchy without conflict. In the coverage of Derby Day or the Grand National, where extensive coverage is given of the social context of the main race, we see represented a world with its own neat, stable class system: royalty and the aristocracy of owners; the middle class of trainers and bookies; the working class of jockeys and stable lads; and the picaresque lumpen class of hangers-on and gypsies. The tensions embedded in these social relations – stable lad strikes, wage disputes, poor conditions of work – rarely intrude into the representational frame.

The world of sport as seen on TV is a world in which women are subordinate, blacks are not quite full-status Britons, and men are the stars and the primary definers. In this world we are divided, not by class, by race or by gender, but by our individual sporting preferences, our local identity and our club loyalties. We are united by our common individuality, but above all by the constant appeal to our sense of national identity, our Englishness and our Britishness, on that most apparently innocent of sites, the sports field. It is, in short, precisely because the world of sport appears and is represented as being nothing to do with politics that it provides an effective site for the reworking of popular common-sense. The images of maleness and femaleness, individual achievement and national identity it constructs are part of the constant process of treading and retreading the ground of popular common-sense, ordering the field to make possible the construction of more systematic ideological themes.

The new individualism and the new entrepreneurial culture

So how can the changing cultural images of sport be related to more organised ideological trends? The emergence of the so-called 'leisure society' was accompanied by an ideology of affluence, in contradiction to traditional English moral puritanism over hedonism and conspicuous consumption. The increased spending power of young people placed style and fashion in the foreground, prompting talk of a 'consumer society'. Television went colour in 1968, highlighting its more spectacular dimension, and in the process contributed to the society of the spectacle.

But conspicuous consumption in the 1960s and early 1970s was hedonistic – featuring flamboyant fashions, a commitment to leisure as opposed to work, the emergence of an alternative society of drop-outs, with 'sex and drugs and rock and roll' as one slogan. As such it constituted a reaction against moral puritanism, deferred gratification and the capitalist work ethic.

Consumption in the 1980s, at least as far as fitness chic is concerned, constitutes a magical resolution of the contradiction between puritanism and hedonism. This style still foregrounds the notions of looking good and having fun. But looking good now means looking fit and being successful, and this requires hard work and commitment, self-discipline and abstinence – be it in the form of jogging and exercise, aerobics and work-outs, or squash and weight training. Success is important, preparation is essential, and where 1960s' individualism was merely narcissistic, 1980s' individualism is competitive as well.

It is the rise of monetarism as an economic philosophy, and the rise of the new right as a political–moral force and in particular Thatcherism, that

Figure 13.1 'The Official Baked Bean of the Rugby World Cup' advertisement.

has helped produce this reworking of possessive individualism. Representation of sport provided a fertile ground for this reworking. Sport is pre-eminently a realm of competitiveness, cast in individual terms. A major theme of television's representation of sport is the need for hard work, dedication and sacrifice to win through to victory. The global star system produced by television provides a set of evocative role models of the manifest rewards of this new hard-working, committed individualism.

Sport itself is being reshaped in accord with this new dominant economic and moral philosophy. Sports now stress the need to be businesslike and efficient, offer sites for the celebration of corporate capitalism, provide executive boxes and hospitality tents to serve the needs of commercial sponsors, and in general have become prime sites for the construction and reproduction of an entrepreneurial culture. Television has not itself produced this reshaping but, in enabling the rapid growth of sponsorship, it provided the key element in the process.

Appendix

In Chapter 6 I report on the results of a content analysis of television sport in 1980 and 1989/90. In explaining briefly the methodology, I want to sound a note of caution. It was a global analysis, rather than a sample, because, as sport is so seasonal and many minor sports get coverage only at one restricted period, a random sample carries great risks of inaccuracy. Conducting such a huge analysis, half of it in a pre-computer era, was an exhausting task, with its own risks of inaccuracy through tedium. I attempted to monitor the schedules for a calendar year in each case, noting time, date, channel, length, title and sports featured. As it was an unfunded project I was not able to carry out full accuracy checks. In 1980 the ITV figures are derived from a random combination of the schedules for London and the Midlands, whereas in 1989/90 the ITV figures are all from the London schedule. My information was derived from published schedules, which on occasion are altered at the last moment to accommodate the unpredictability of sport. I had hoped to avoid the Olympic period in 1980, but an ITV strike disrupted my plans. Within these limits the figures are, I hope, fairly accurate.

However, there are problems of interpretation. The information about time of day, day of week, month of year and length is all fairly reliable and revealing. It is in assessing time devoted to particular sports that problems arise. Single-sport programmes are straightforward, but a large percentage of air-time is devoted either to magazine programmes like *Grandstand*, or to broadcasts of two or more sports (racing and cricket for example). It is possible from the published schedules to know which sports will be featured, although some may be omitted, but without exhaustive tape monitoring it is impossible to know how time within a programme is allocated on transmission. My total hours figures for sports heavily featured in magazine programmes are inevitably somewhat inaccurate. I have attempted to correlate my figures with other research and have limited my remarks in this book to aspects of the analysis that hold up.

The question of the amount of women's sport is even more complex, as the scheduling of mixed sports like tennis, athletics or gymnastics in itself yields no information about the proportion of time devoted to women's events or performers. In an attempt to calculate a figure, I endeavoured to be generous to broadcasters in assuming that programmes with mixed sports *might* have featured some women's sport, an assumption unlikely to be true. My tentative figures here suggest that, as a proportion of the total, women's sport is getting less exposure than a decade ago, but more research is clearly needed here.

Notes

Note: File numbers beginning with T all refer to files in the BBC Written Archives Centre at Caversham. The abbreviations used in notes referring to BBC Memos are as they appear in the original documents.

1 SPORT, TELEVISION AND CULTURE

1. For discussion of articulation and disarticulation in ideological production see Laclau (1977) and Mercer (1978).

2 NATIONAL EVENTS AND THE AUTHORITY OF THE BBC

1. BBC Memo on 'Outside Broadcasts War-Time Policy', 8/11/39, in Briggs (1970: 107).
2. David Cardiff and Paddy Scannell, 'Social Foundations of British Broadcasting', Open University paper, published in a different version, without this quote, as 'Serving the Nation: Public Service Broadcasting before the War', in Waites (1982).
3. ibid.
4. Television Act 1954, Section 7, 2 & 3 Eliz 2.
5. BBC Memo from Tel OB Manager Orr-Ewing to HTel S., 1/1/47 (T16/130) and BBC Memo from Tel OB Manager Orr-Ewing to HTel S., 5/11/47 (T16/130).
6. BBC Memo from CTel Collins to DHB, 13/4/48 (T16/130) and BBC Memo from CTel Collins, 24/5/49 (T16/130).
7. BBC Memo from HOB to DTel, 31/8/51 (T16/130).
8. BBC Memo from HOB to DTel, 9/10/51 (T16/130).
9. BBC Memo from Mrs Spicer to DTel, 20/10/51 (T16/130).
10. BBC Board Meeting Minutes, 9/3/53 (T16/130).
11. Notes by OB S.J. de Lotbiniere, 8/7/46, BBC (T18/12).
12. *BBC Annual Report*, 1958/59: 22.
13. *BBC Annual Report*, 1964/65: 27.
14. *BBC Annual Report*, 1969/70: 25.
15. *BBC Quarterly*, 4/1 April 1949: 31.
16. BBC Memo from PCEX re TV OBs, 31/3/39 (T16/52).
17. Letter from P.H. Dorte, OB and Film Supervisor, to E.J. Holt, hon. sec. of the AAA, re covering AAA Championships on 19th–20th July, 24/4/46, BBC (T14/1366).

18. BBC Memo: 'Internal Restrictions Affecting Television Outside Broadcasts', by Ian Orr-Ewing, 3/2/49 (T16/128).
19. BBC Memo of 29/3/47, quoted in Briggs (1979: 841).
20. Gerald Cock, *Report on the Conditions for a Post War Television Service*, 1944; see Briggs (1979: 191).
21. BBC Memo from Dorte, OB and Film Supervisor, to Head of Television, 23/4/46 (T16/128).
22. Notes by de Lotbiniere following a discussion on 'The Future of Television Outside Broadcasts', 19/3/52, BBC (T16/128).
23. BBC Memo from de Lotbiniere to CTelP McGivern, 2/1/53 (T14/307/2).

3   PRODUCTION PRACTICES AND PROFESSIONAL IDEOLOGIES

1. For work on the BBC that examines the relationship between practices and structures see Burns (1977) and Schlesinger (1978).
2. For early football coverage, a diagram of the pitch divided in squares was published in *Radio Times*. As well as the commentator, a second voice periodically announced the number of the square the ball was in. This is believed to have given rise to the saying 'back to square one'.
3. *BBC Handbook*, 1948: 52.
4. Quoted in Briggs (1961: 257).
5. *BBC Handbook*, 1939: 64–7.
6. 'The Technique of the Running Commentary', de Lotbiniere in *BBC Quarterly*, 4/1 April 1949: 37–40.
7. BBC Programme Report on AAA Championships, 18/7/47 (T14/1366); see also Crump (1966).
8. BBC Memo from BBC producer Humphrey Fisher to Roger Bannister, 26/9/57 (T14/1367/16).
9. 'Notes on Television Commentary', internal BBC document, 23/1/52 (T16/128).
10. BBC *Camera Report*, 29/1/49 (T14/487).
11. BBC *Viewer Research Report*, 29/9/53 (T14/93/15).
12. BBC *Viewer Research Report* on table tennis: English Open, 29/3/52 (T14/1224/4).
13. BBC Memo from Craxton, 30/3/52 (T14/1224/4).
14. 'Notes on Television Commentary', 23/1/52 (T16/128).
15. 'Cricket Production' internal paper by BBC producer Anthony Craxton, 1952 (T14/307/2).
16. 'The Coverage of Sport on BBC Television', in *Combroad*, July–Sep 1975: 29.
17. BBC Memo from Assistant Head of Outside Broadcasting Middleton to all OB Prods, 26/4/60 (T14/492/493).
18. *Rugby World and Post*, Jan 1991.
19. See Bridgewater (1950: 179–92) for detailed technical discussion of light, lens type and camera position.
20. BBC *Viewer Research Report* on floodlit football between Tottenham Hotspur and Racing of Paris, 29/9/53 (T14/93/15).
21. BBC *Viewer Research Report* on table tennis: English Open, 29/3/52 (T14/1224/4).
22. BBC Memo from Tel OB Manager Orr-Ewing to A.O.Tel, 21/12/48 (T14/1407/4).
23. BBC *Camera Report*, by Dimmock, 3/4/48 (T14/1224/1).
24. 'Cricket Production', op. cit. (T14/1307/2).
25. BBC Memo from CTelP McGivern to HOB Lotbiniere, 8/7/52 (T16/128).

26. BBC Memo from CTelP McGivern to HOB Tel Dimmock, 5/7/56 (T14/1407/14).
27. BBC Memo from Duncalf to Dimmock, 9/7/56 (T14/1407/14).
28. BBC Memo from Head of TV OB Dimmock, 28/6/57 (T14/1407/15).
29. BBC Memo from CTelP Adam to HOB Dimmock, 26/6/58 (T14/1407/19).
30. *The Report on Wimbledon 1958 and Proposals for Wimbledon 1959*, BBC, 11/8/58 (T14/1407/19).
31. BBC Memo from McGivern to HOB Lotbiniere, 14/3/50 (T14/1224/2).
32. See letter from BBC OB producer Berkeley Smith, re Daily Mirror National Table Tennis Tournament, 5/4/50 (T14/1224/3).
33. 'Cricket Production', op. cit.
34. BBC Memo from Raymond Baxter (OBs) to A/AHOB Tel, 20/12/54 (T16/128).
35. BBC Memo from Head of TV Gorham to Tel OB Manager Orr-Ewing, 8/7/46 (T14/1407/3).
36. 'Cricket Production', op. cit.
37. *Television Outside Broadcasts World Cup 1966*, BBC (T14/1426).
38. BBC Notes on meeting to discuss programme, 15/12/48 (T14/487).
39. BBC note on proposed Television Sports Club series, de Lotbiniere, HOB, 20/6/50 (T14/1178).
40. Publicity note for *Television Sports Magazine*, Berkeley Smith, BBC, 1950 (T14/1178).
41. BBC Memo from Wolstenholme to Dimmock, 3/9/51 (T14/1178).
42. BBC Memo from Alec Sutherland, 6/7/51 (T14/1178).
43. Paul Fox, quoted in K. Baily (ed.) *The Television Annual for 1956*.
44. BBC Memo from Sports Organiser TV OBs Jack Oaten to Paul Fox, 30/10/59 (T14/492/493).
45. BBC Memo from OB Organiser to HPP Tel, 9/3/56 (T14/1192/2).
46. BBC Memo from Fox to HOB Tel, 4/5/56 (T14/1192/2).
47. Announcement for *Programme Parade*, 10/9/55 (T14/1182/1).
48. BBC Memo from Paul Fox, Sept 1955 (T14/1182/1).
49. Programme Script for *Saturday Sports Special*, BBC, 10/9/55 (T14/1182/1).
50. BBC Memo from CTelP to HOB Tel, 12/9/55 (T14/1182/1).
51. BBC Memo from Fox to Dimmock, 16/9/55 (T14/1182/1).
52. BBC Memo from CTelP to HOB Dimmock, 31/9/55 (T14/1182/4).
53. BBC Memo from HOB Dimmock to CTelP McGivern, 7/11/55 (T14/1182/4).
54. BBC Memo from AHOB Alan Chivers to *Radio Times*, 23/3/58 (T14/493/1).
55. BBC Memo from Cowgill to Dimmock, 10/4/58 (T14/493/1).
56. Notes on meeting re Saturday sport, BBC, 14/4/58 (T14/493/1).
57. BBC Memo from Cowgill to Dimmock, 21/7/58 (T14/493/1).
58. BBC Memo from Fox to Dimmock, 1/8/58 (T14/493/1).
59. BBC Memo from Senior Planning Asst TV Dennis Scuse to AHOB, 13/1/59 (T14/492/493).
60. BBC Memo from Dimmock (H of TV OBs) to Fox, 13/4/59 (T14/492/493).
61. BBC Memo from Dimmock, 29/8/58 (T14/493/1).
62. Note for *Radio Times*, 22/9/58 (T14/493/2 File 1b).
63. BBC Memo from Cowgill, 24/9/58 (T14/493/2 File 1b).
64. BBC Memo from Fox to Rowan Ayers, *Radio Times*, 7/11/60 (T14/492/493).
65. BBC Memo from Ronnie Noble (editor of *Sportsview*) to General Manager Outside Broadcasting Television, 4/10/61 (T14/492/493).
66. BBC Memo, 1/9/60 (T14/492/493).
67. Based on information in file T14/492/493, '*Grandstand* – General 1959–60'.
68. BBC Memo from Fox to Baxter, 13/11/59 (T14/492/493).

4   BBC v. ITV COMPETITION

1. *Sunday Express*, 29/5/55.
2. *Daily Herald*, 5/3/55.
3. Bill Ward in *Broadcast Special*, 22/9/76, p14.
4. Television Act 1954, Section 7, 2 & 3, Eliz 2.
5. *Sheffield Telegraph*, 12/11/55.
6. *The People*, 13/11/55.
7. *Evening Chronicle*, Manchester, 15/11/55.
8. *Daily Mirror*, 15/11/55.
9. *Manchester Guardian*, 17/11/55.
10. *The Times*, 2/12/55.
11. In 1954, as a water-testing exercise, the ITA asked for applications from interested parties and, among 25, one offered to provide a supply of sport programming (see Black 1972b: 71).
12. See Bill Ward in *Broadcast Special*, 22/9/76, 12–16.
13. *The Star*, 4/6/55, and *Daily Telegraph*, 6/12/55.
14. *Daily Mirror*, 23/8/55.
15. BBC Memo from Sports Organiser TV OBs Jack Oaten to Dimmock, 7/12/59 (T14/492/493).
16. BBC Memo from Fox (*Sportsview* Unit editor) to HOB Tel, 4/3/59 (T14/492/493).
17. BBC Memo from Fox to Dimmock, 11/1/60 (T14/492/493).
18. BBC Memo from Fox to Dimmock, 1/2/60, and BBC Memo from Dimmock to Fox, 5/2/60 (T14/492/T14/493).
19. BBC Memo from Fox to HOB Tel, 7/11/60 (T14/492/493).
20. BBC Memo from Noble (*Sportsview* Unit editor) to GMOB Tel, 23/11/62 (T14/492/493).
21. This latter option is still under periodic discussion, but there are too many entrenched interests for it to be easily achievable.
22. *ITA Annual Report*, 1964/65: 22.
23. *ITA Annual Report*, 1966/67: 22.
24. *ITA Annual Report*, 1967/68: 25.
25. *ITA Annual Report*, 1968/69: 17.
26. *ITA Annual Report*, 1965/66: 23.
27. *The Times*, 16/1/90.
28. *ITA Annual Report*, 1967/68: 25.
29. John Bromley in *The Times*, 16/1/90.
30. *ITA Handbook*, 1971.
31. *The Times*, 17/1/90.
32. *IBA Annual Report*, 1973/74: 17.
33. *The Coverage of Sport on BBC Television*, BBC 1974.
34. *Broadcast*, 31/3/75, p3.
35. *IBA Annual Report*, 1975/76: 14.
36. See Heller (1978) for an interesting discussion of public interest, national interest and the extent of accountability by broadcasters.
37. *Broadcast*, 16/10/78, pp2 & 12.
38. John Bromley in *The Times*, 16/1/90.
39. *The Times*, 18/1/90.
40. *Guardian*, 11/12/89.
41. *Sunday Times*, 17/6/90.
42. ibid.
43. *Rugby World and Post*, Jan 1991.

44. *Broadcast*, 7/4/89.
45. Peter Dimmock in BBC *Annual Report*, 1951.
46. 'The Land Line Technique for TV OBs', *BBC Quarterly* 2(3), 1948.
47. BBC *Annual Report*, 1962/63, on the launch of Telstar.
48. 'Televising the Boat Race', *BBC Quarterly*, 5(2), 1950.
49. Bridgewater (1950).
50. BBC *Annual Report*, 1955/56: 33.
51. BBC *Annual Report*, 1955/56: 35.
52. See Peter Dimmock's account of Today at Ascot, in Andrews and MacKay (1955: 193).
53. BBC *Annual Report*, 1965/66: 16.
54. Geoff Mason, NBC, quoted in *Broadcast*, 9/7/79, pp8–9.
55. *Broadcast*, 6/8/79, p15.

5 SPONSORSHIP AND THE RISE OF THE SPORTS AGENT

1. Tony Moore at British Society of Sports History, one-day conference, 5/7/89.
2. See Nigel Waite, *Sponsorship in the United Kingdom*, Cranfield School of Management, 1976.
3. ibid.
4. *The Economist*, 22/5/82.
5. *Sportscan*, 1982.
6. *Sunday Times*, 15/10/78 and 16/11/80.
7. *Sunday Times*, 12/7/81.
8. BBC Memo from Bill Wright to Cowgill, 15/7/59 (T14/492/493) and BBC Memo from Middleton to *Sportsview* Unit editor re Racing, 9/11/62 (T14/492/T14/493).
9. BBC Memo from Bill Wright to HOBP Tel, 4/4/62 (T14/492/493).
10. This process is far more striking in the USA. See Rader (1984) and Sugar (1980).
11. Annual Conference of Sports Administrators, CCPR, 1975.
12. CCPR Seminar, 'Women in Sport and Recreation', CCPR, 1976.
13. Annual Conference of Sports Administrators, CCPR, 1976.
14. *City Limits*, 21/1/83.
15. *Sunday Times*, 30/9/84.
16. *Guardian*, 14/3/89.
17. *Sunday Times*, 22/3/87.
18. *Evening Standard*, 18/5/83.
19. *Sport and Leisure*, Jan/Feb 1990.
20. *Guardian*, 16/1/85.
21. *Sunday Times*, 17/7/83.
22. *Sponsorship in Sport*, South Western Sports Council, 1974.
23. 'TV's eye on Badminton', by Barry Davies, *Badminton*, Oct 1979.
24. *Observer*, 15/2/87.
25. Amateur Rowing Association Development Plan 1970–1975.
26. 'Sponsorship Opportunities in Rowing', ARA, Dec 1971.
27. Michael Stamford, Chair of the ARA sponsorship committee, in *Sportsworld*, June 1973.
28. ARA Five Year Plan 1975–1980.
29. *Sportsworld*, 29/1/87.
30. *Swimming Coach*, July 1975: 11.
31. *Table Tennis 70*, a survey commissioned by the Coca-Cola Export Company

and the English Table Tennis Association, conducted by Rawes and Partners Ltd.
32. English Table Tennis Association Sponsorship Presentation, April 1972.
33. 'Table Tennis World Championships 1977 Think Tank', 21/9/73.
34. *Guardian*, 18/9/85.
35. *Sportsworld*, 29/1/87.
36. *The Times*, 13/3/84.
37. *Evening Standard*, 10/2/87.
38. See *Guardian*, 18/3/91, for an account of the emergence of sponsored television.
39. See also, on volleyball, MacGregor (1977).

6   TRANSFORMATIONS OF SPACE AND TIME

1. These figures should be treated with particular caution. It is especially difficult to know without exhaustive monitoring whether Olympic Games and Commonwealth Games broadcasts and magazine programmes like *Grandstand* contained women's sports or events (see the appendix).
2. The whole concept of an 'ideal spectator position' raises problems, as Buscombe recognises. The traditional partisan position at football is at the ends of the ground, as opposed to the 'impartial' position on the half-way line, usually taken by the more expensive seats and by the television cameras. Buscombe argues that the half-way position is one of neutrality, but to what extent the association of partisanship with the ends of a ground is a cultural choice rather than one over-determined by economic circumstance is harder to determine.
3. Harry Carpenter, in BBC's *Sports in View* (1964), quoted by Charles Barr in Buscombe (1975: 52).
4. See discussion of the concept of 'hors-champs' – literally, 'outside the field' – in Daney (1978: 38–43).
5. I followed Charles Barr (Buscombe 1975) in counting the time taken for 50 cuts to be made, and also analysed a 10 minute section taken at random from the 1966 World Cup Final, the England v. Argentina match in the 1986 World Cup, England v. West Germany in the 1990 World Cup, and the 1990 FA Cup Final replay. None of the random sections contained a goal, which in itself says something about modern football.

7   ASSEMBLAGE AND FRAMING

1. 'Topping and tailing' is television jargon for the opening and closing statements from a presenter.
2. Note: *World of Sport* ceased to exist in autumn 1985.
3. *Match of the Day*, BBC, 2/12/78.
4. *The Big Match*, ITV, 26/11/78.
5. Assorted examples from BBC and ITV sport coverage 1979–81.
6. ibid.
7. ibid.
8. ibid.
9. *Radio Times*, 28/7/84, p3.
10. *Olympic Grandstand*, BBC1, 1/8/80.
11. See Smith (1975: 18–24), Hall *et al.* (1978: 60–6), Brunsdon and Morley (1978: 58–70) for discussion of media modes of address and populist ventriloquism.
12. BBC, 4/7/90.

13. BBC, 2/10/88.
14. Assorted examples from BBC and ITV sport coverage 1979–81.
15. *Sportsnight*, BBC1, 15/11/78.
16. *World of Sport*, ITV, 24/11/79.
17. *Sportsnight*, BBC1, 21/11/79.
18. *Sportsnight*, BBC1, 31/10/79.
19. *Wimbledon Preview*, BBC2, 22/6/80.
20. ibid.
21. ibid.
22. 1980 *Open Golf Championship*, BBC2, 16/7/80.

8 STARS, NARRATIVES AND IDEOLOGIES

1. David Coleman, as David Hemery won gold for Britain in the 400m hurdles in the 1968 Olympics in Mexico City. Ironically, it was in fact another Briton, John Sherwood, who came third!
2. *Olympic Grandstand*, BBC, 1/8/80, commentary on Tatyana Kasankina, winner of the 1500m at the Moscow Olympics.
3. *Olympic Grandstand*, BBC, 22/7/80.
4. *Olympic Grandstand*, BBC, 26/7/80.
5. Dan Maskell on *Wimbledon 80*, BBC, 30/6/80.
6. Minter v. Antuofermo on ITV, live from Las Vegas, 16/3/80.
7. *Olympic Grandstand*, BBC, 20/7/80.
8. *Olympic Grandstand*, BBC, 21/7/80.
9. *Olympics 80*, ITV, 21/7/80.
10. *Olympics 80*, ITV, 3/8/80.
11. For discussion of sport and masculinity, see Dunning (1986), Kidd (1978), Maguire (1986), Mangan and Walvin (1987), Miller (1989), Tomlinson (1983), and Williams, Lawrence and Rowe (1987).
12. For discussion of sport and femininity there is now an extensive literature. In the context of my own line of argument, see Dunne (1982), Graydon (1980, 1983), J.A. Hargreaves (1986a, 1989), and P. Willis (1982).
13. Commentary on Wimbledon Final Day, *Wimbledon 80*, BBC, 4/7/80.
14. *Grandstand*, BBC, 20/4/80.
15. Wightman Cup, Great Britain v. USA, BBC, 2/11/79.
16. Wightman Cup, Great Britain v. USA, BBC, 3/11/79.
17. ibid.
18. *Olympics 80*, ITV, 20/7/80.
19. *Olympic Grandstand*, BBC, 26/7/80.
20. BBC, 10/5/87.
21. *Olympics 80*, ITV, 26/7/80.
22. *Olympics 80*, ITV, 26/7/80.
23. *Olympic Grandstand*, BBC, 23/7/80.
24. *Olympics 80*, ITV, 1/8/80.
25. *Olympic Grandstand*, BBC, 21/7/80.
26. *Olympics 80*, ITV, 21/7/80.
27. British Grand Prix Motor Cycling, BBC, 10/8/80.
28. *Olympics 80*, ITV, 31/7/80.
29. Channel 4, 12/9/91.
30. *Daily Mirror*, 7/9/91.
31. See Cashmore (1982) for a detailed study of black sportsmen in Britain.
32. *Olympic Grandstand*, BBC, 22/7/80.
33. *Olympics 80*, ITV, 20/7/80.

34. David Wilkie, *Olympics 80*, ITV, 19/7/80.
35. Dickie Davies, *Olympics 80*, ITV, 19/7/80.
36. *Olympics 80*, ITV, 23/7/80.
37. *Olympics 80*, ITV, 23/7/80.
38. *Olympics 80*, ITV, 3/8/80.
39. Europa Cup, BBC, 29/6/91.
40. *Olympics 80*, ITV, 26/7/80.
41. *Olympic Grandstand*, BBC, 26/7/80.
42. *Olympic Grandstand*, BBC, 26/7/80.
43. *Olympics 80*, ITV, 3/8/80.
44. *Olympic Grandstand*, BBC, 1/8/80.
45. BBC, 30/8/91.
46. *Olympic Grandstand*, BBC, 30/7/80.
47. *Olympic Grandstand*, BBC, 25/7/80.
48. Grand Prix, BBC2, 1/6/91.
49. Channel 4, 31/9/88.
50. *Butlins Grand Masters Darts*, ATV, 16/1/79.
51. *Olympics 80*, ITV, 27/7/80.
52. *Match of the Day Special*, BBC, Jim Watt v. Robert Vasquez, 3/11/79.
53. *Olympic Grandstand*, BBC, 27/7/80.
54. *Olympics 80*, ITV, 21/7/80.
55. *Newsnight*, BBC2, 21/7/80.
56. *Olympics 80*, ITV, 27/7/80.
57. *Olympic Grandstand*, BBC, 29/7/80.
58. *Newsnight*, BBC2, 23/7/80.
59. *Olympics 80*, ITV, 3/8/80.
60. *Olympic Grandstand*, BBC, 22/7/80.
61. *Olympic Grandstand*, BBC, 1/8/80.
62. *Olympic Grandstand*, BBC, 23/7/80.
63. *Olympics 80*, ITV, 3/8/80.
64. *Royal Ascot*, BBC1, 17/6/80.
65. *Grandstand*, BBC1, 20/4/80.
66. *TV Times*, 28/3/87.
67. See Pearson (1988) for a similar analysis of television baseball.
68. *Olympics 80*, ITV, 23/7/80.
69. *Olympic Grandstand*, BBC, 22/7/80.
70. *Olympics 80*, ITV, 23/7/80.
71. All quotations in this paragraph are from *ITV News*, 26/7/80.
72. *Olympics 80*, ITV, 1/8/80.
73. *Olympic Grandstand*, BBC, 1/8/80.
74. *Olympic Grandstand*, BBC, 1/8/80.
75. *Olympics 80*, ITV, 1/8/80.
76. See Deem (1986), Green, Hebron and Woodward (1987), Griffin *et al.* (1982), K.F. Dyer (1982), J.A. Hargreaves (1985), Pannick (1984), Theberge (1981), Wimbush and Talbot (1989).
77. See Neale (1982), S. Johnston (1985), Tomlinson (1988), and Jarvie (1989b). The BFI Education Department has a study pack and slide set analysing the film.

9   THE CASE OF ATHLETICS

1. *Running*, April 1985, p82.
2. *Guardian*, 11/11/80.

3. *Observer*, 12/8/79.
4. *The Times*, 3/10/80.
5. *Running*, May 1985, p102.
6. *Evening Standard*, 12/10/85.
7. Alan Pascoe, *Sunday Times*, 3/2/85.
8. *Running*, Sept 1985, p19.
9. ibid.
10. *Running*, April 1986, p6, May 1986, p48.
11. *Running*, Nov 1985, p32.
12. *Guardian*, 10/1/85.
13. *Guardian*, 11/2/86.
14. *Sunday Times*, 21/7/85.
15. *Guardian*, 1/11/85.
16. *Running*, Dec 1985, p12.
17. *Running*, Dec 1985, p3.
18. *Sunday Times*, 22/9/85.
19. *The Times*, 24/10/85.
20. *Guardian*, 2/2/85.
21. *Guardian*, 15/2/85.
22. *Running*, Jan 1986, p5.
23. *Running*, July 1985, p21.
24. Mary Decker married British discus thrower Richard Slaney and is now often referred to as Mary Slaney; for the sake of clarity I have used Decker throughout.
25. A 50 minute programme, *Take the Money and Run*, about this race and the television coverage of athletics was broadcast on Channel 4 on 2 June 1986 as part of the series *Open the Box*, produced by Beat Ltd and the British Film Institute. I worked on the programme and this section owes much to discussion and debate during its production.
26. Figures are based on my own analysis of the transmission on ITV.
27. *Running*, Sept 1985, p5.
28. *Guardian*, 22/7/85.
29. *Running*, April 1985, p11.
30. *Star*, 4/1/85.
31. *Running*, April 1985, p59.
32. *The Times*, 24/7/85.
33. *Running*, Sept 1985, p7.
34. *Daily Mail*, 24/7/85.
35. *Guardian*, 25/7/85.
36. *Guardian*, 20/7/85.
37. *The Times*, 14/8/89.

10   THE ROAD TO GLOBALISATION

1. *Independent on Sunday*, Stephen Aris, 15/7/90.
2. See Whannel (1985) for a more detailed discussion, derived from a paper given at the conference on 'The Third World: Development or Crisis', in Penang, Malaysia, in November 1984. I would like to thank the Consumers' Association of Penang for giving me an opportunity to take a distanced look at western sport.
3. *Broadcast*, 21/11/77.
4. All these phrases were noted during a conference in Calgary in 1987 on 'The

Olympic Movement and the Mass Media', attended by television executives, sport agents, journalists and academics. Several documentaries made for Channel 4 by Flashback Television (*Going for Gold* 1986, *Selling the Games* 1987, *The Games in Question* and *Running the Games* 1988) offer an invaluable look at the internal working of the Olympic movement.

5. *Guardian*, 20/8/80.
6. *Television Weekly*, 20/6/83.
7. ibid.
8. *Independent on Sunday*, 15/7/90.
9. See, for a review of the situation, *Sponsorship and its Effects*, from the Global Media Commission of the International Advertising Association, September 1988.
10. *Adweek*, 17/6/86.
11. *Television Week*, 4/7/91.

11   FIELD OF REPRESENTATIONS

1. *Daily Mirror*, 8/5/82, p9.
2. But see Lenskyj (1986) for a more wide-ranging discussion of sport and sexuality.
3. *Standard*, 11/3/83, p13.
4. Guinness, White Horse and Sporty advertisements in various colour supplements, 1983–1985.
5. Holiday Inn advertisement, 1986.
6. *Sunday Times*, colour magazine, 1984.
7. *Running*, May 1987.
8. Milk advertisement on ITV during 1987.
9. *Observer*, colour supplement.
10. Advertisement screened on ITV during 1984.
11. Slogan of all-woman dance troupe, in *Sport and Leisure*, July/Aug 1987.
12. John Russell, marketing director of Peugeot-Talbot, at press conference for the Peugeot-Talbot Games, 17/7/85.
13. *Time*, 30/6/86.
14. *Sunday Times*, 17/4/83.
15. Pakistan International Airlines advertisement, 1986.
16. *Guardian*, 8/8/84.
17. Mention should be made of some notable exceptions: Patricia Mordecai, who was the studio director of LWT's *World of Sport* for many years; Patricia Pearson, a football director with Granada; Elaine Watts, part of the original Cheerleader team; and, most visibly, Helen Rollason, BBC's first regular female sports presenter.

12   AUDIENCES AND PLEASURES

1. AGB/SportsWatch/BARB figures, in *The Independent*, 5/4/89.
2. Collett installed special television sets, which also contained a camera to record the audience, into people's homes. The resultant tapes show people reading, hoovering, playing flutes, and almost everything else imaginable, whilst supposedly 'watching television'. Only some of the time do we give the screen our full attention. Extracts from the extraordinary tapes can be seen in a programme in the series *Open the Box*, produced by the British Film Institute and Beat for Channel 4 in 1986.

3. For diverse examples of such work, and discussion of it, see Hobson (1982), Morley (1986), Simpson (1987), Collett and Lamb (1986), Gray (1987), James Lull (1988, 1990), Moores (1990), Morley and Silverstone (1990).

Bibliography

Abrahams, H. (1961a) *50 Years of AAA Championships*, London: Carborundum.
—— (1961b) 'Winning back athletic crowds', *World Sports*, London.
Alt, J. (1983) 'Sport and cultural reification: from ritual to mass consumption', *Theory, Culture and Society*, 1(3), London.
Anderson, B. (1983) *Imagined Communities*, London: Verso.
Andreff, B. and Nys, L. (1987) *Le Sport et la télévision*, Paris: Dalloz.
Andrews, E. and MacKay, A. (1954) *Sports Report*, London: Heinemann.
Annan Report (1977) *Report of the Committee on the Future of Broadcasting*, London: HMSO (Cmnd 6753).
Anthony, D. (1980) *A Strategy for British Sport*, London: Hurst.
Aris, S. (1990) *Sportsbiz: Inside the Sports Business*, London: Hutchinson.
Barnett, S. (1990) *Games and Sets: The Changing Face of Sport on Television*, London: British Film Institute.
Barthes, R. (1967) *Elements of Semiology*, London: Jonathan Cape.
—— (1973) *Mythologies*, London: Paladin.
—— (1974) *S/Z*, London: Hill & Wang.
—— (1975) *The Pleasures of the Text*, London: Jonathan Cape.
Bateman, D. and Douglas, D. (1986) *Unfriendly Games: Boycotted and Broke*, Glasgow: Mainstream.
BBC (1974) *The Coverage of Sport on BBC TV*, London: BBC.
—— (1976) 'Public opinion about the television and radio coverage of the 1974 World Cup', *Annual Review of Audience Research Findings* 2, London: BBC.
Bennett, T. (1981) 'Popular culture: defining our terms', in Unit 1 of *Popular Culture*, Open University Course U203, Milton Keynes: Open University.
Birrell, S. and Loy, J. (1979) 'Media sport: hot and cool', *International Review of Sport Sociology* 14(1).
Black, P. (1972a) *The Biggest Aspidistra in the World*, London: BBC.
—— (1972b) *The Mirror in the Corner*, London: Hutchinson.
Blofeld, H. (1978) *The Packer Affair*, London: Collins.
Bolla, Patricia A. (1990) 'Media images of women and leisure: an analysis of magazine ads 1964–87', *Leisure Studies* 9(3), Sept, London: E. & F.N. Spon.
Bonney, B. (1980) *Packer and Televised Cricket*, Australia (NSW): NSW Institute of Technology.
Boorstin, D. (1961) *The Image*, London: Penguin.
Bose, M. (1983) *All in a Day*, London: Robin Clarke.
Bough, F. (1980) *Cue Frank*, London: MacDonald Futura.
Bourdieu, P. (1977) *Outline of a Theory of Practice*, Cambridge: Cambridge University Press.

Bourke, S. (1991) 'World Student Games 1991: relationship between sport and sponsorship', London: Roehampton Institute, unpublished 3rd year dissertation.

Bown, G. (1981) '2000 Million Tele-viewers', London: Royal College of Arts, unpublished dissertation, and also Gabrielle Bown's film, *Even Russian Soil Tastes Sweet* and the series *Women at the Olympic Games* (Artemis for Channel 4, 1987).

Boyd-Barrett, O. (1977) 'Media imperialism: towards an international framework', in J. Curran *et al.* (eds) *Mass Communication and Society*, London: Edward Arnold.

Boyle, R. and Blain, N. (1991) 'Footprints on the field: TV sport, delivery systems and national culture in a changing Europe', paper at International Television Studies Conference, London.

Brecht, B. (1964) *Brecht on Theatre* (translated by John Willett), London: Eyre Methuen.

Bridgewater, T.H. (1950) 'TV outside broadcasts', *BBC Quarterly*, Autumn, 5(3), London: BBC.

Briggs, A. (1961) *The Birth of Broadcasting*, Oxford: Oxford University Press.

—— (1965) *The Golden Age of Wireless*, Oxford: Oxford University Press.

—— (1970) *The War of Words*, Oxford: Oxford University Press.

—— (1979) *The History of Broadcasting in the United Kingdom*: Sound and Vision vol. 4, Oxford: Oxford University Press.

Brohm, J. (1978) *Sport – A Prison of Measured Time*, London: Ink Links.

Brookes, C. (1978) *English Cricket*, London: Weidenfeld & Nicolson.

Brunsdon, C. and Morley, D. (1978) *Everyday Television: Nationwide*, London: British Film Institute.

Bryant, J. (1989) 'Viewers' enjoyment of televised sports violence', in L. Wenner (ed.) *Media, Sports and Society*, London: Sage.

Bryant, J., Comiskey, P. and Zillmann, D. (1977) 'Drama in sports commentary', *Journal of Communication*, Summer, USA.

Burns, T. (1977) *The BBC: Public Institution and Private World*, London: Macmillan.

Buscombe, E. (ed.) (1975) *Football on Television*, London: British Film Institute.

Cantelon, H. and Gruneau, R. (1988) 'The production of sport for television', in J. Harvey and H. Cantelon (eds) *Not Just a Game*, Ottawa: University of Ottawa Press.

Cardiff, D. (1980) 'The serious and the popular', *Media, Culture and Society* 2(1), London: Academic Press.

Cardiff, D. and Scannell, P. (1981) *The Social Foundations of British Broadcasting*, Milton Keynes: Open University Press.

Cashmore, E. (1982) *Black Sportsmen*, London: Routledge & Kegan Paul.

CCCS (1982) *Sporting Fictions*, Birmingham: CCCS.

Chambers, I. *et al.* (1977) 'Marxism and culture', *Screen*, Winter, 18(4), London: SEFT.

Chandler, J. (1988) *Television and National Sport*, Chicago: University of Illinois Press.

Chapman, S. (1986) *Great Expectorations: Advertising and the Tobacco Industry*, London: Comedia.

Clarke, A. and Clarke J. (1982) 'Highlights and action replays', in J.A. Hargreaves (ed.) *Sport, Culture and Ideology*, London: Routledge & Kegan Paul.

Clarke, J. and Critcher, C. (1985) *The Devil Makes Work*, London: Macmillan.

Clarke, M. (1987) *Teaching Popular Television*, Northants.: Heinemann.

Coghlan, J. (1990) *Sport and British Politics since 1960*, Brighton: Falmer Press.

Cohen, S. and Young, J. (eds) (1973) *The Manufacture of News*, London: Constable.

Coleman, D. (ed.) (1960) *Grandstand TV Book of Sports*, London: BBC.

Collett, P. and Lamb, R. (1986) *Watching People Watching Television*, Report to the Independent Broadcasting Authority, London.

Colley, I. and Davies, G. (1982) 'Kissed by history: football as TV drama', in *Sporting Fictions*, Birmingham: CCCS.

Collins, M. (1990) 'Shifting icebergs: the public, private and voluntary sectors in British sport', in A. Tomlinson (ed.) *Sport in Society: Policy, Politics and Culture*, Brighton: Leisure Studies Association.

Collins, M. and Jones, H. (1990) 'The economics of sport: sport as an industry', in A. Tomlinson (ed.) *Sport in Society: Policy, Politics and Culture*, Brighton: Leisure Studies Association.

Comiskey, P., Bryant, J. and Zillmann, D. (1977) 'Commentary as a substitute for action', *Journal of Communication*, Summer, USA.

Cosgrove, S. (1986) 'And the bonny Scotland will be there: football in Scottish culture', in A. Tomlinson and G. Whannel (eds) *Off The Ball: The Football World Cup*, London: Pluto.

Coward, R. (1977) 'Class, "culture" and the social formation', *Screen*, Spring, 18(1), London: SEFT.

Coward, R. and Ellis, J. (1977) *Language and Materialism*, London: Routledge & Kegan Paul.

Crawford Report (1925) *Report of the Broadcasting Committee*, London: HMSO (Cmnd 2599).

Critcher, C. (1971) 'Football and cultural values', *Working Papers in Cultural Studies*, 2, Birmingham: CCCS.

—— (1979) 'Football since the war', in J. Clarke *et al.* (eds) *Working Class Culture*, London: Hutchinson.

—— (1986) 'Radical theorists of sport: the state of play', in A. Tomlinson (ed.) *Leisure and Social Relations*, Brighton: Leisure Studies Association.

—— (1987) 'Media spectacles: sport and mass communication', in C. Cashdan and M. Jordin (eds) *Studies in Communication*, Oxford: Blackwell.

Crump, J. (1966) *Running Round the World*, London: Hale.

Cunningham, H. (1980) *Leisure in the Industrial Revolution*, London: Croom Helm.

Daney, S. (1978) 'Le Sport dans la télévision', *Cahiers du Cinéma* 292, Paris.

Davis, D. (1960) *The Grammar of Television Production*, London: Barrie & Rockliffe.

De Bord, Guy (1977) *Society of the Spectacle*, London: Practical Paradise.

Deem, R. (1986) *All Work and No Play: The Sociology of Women and Leisure*, Milton Keynes: Open University Press.

Digance, J. (1986) 'Cycling on TV', London: Goldsmiths College dissertation.

Dimmock, P. (1964) *Sports in View*, London: BBC.

Duncan, M. C. and Brummett, B. (1989) 'Types and sources of spectating pleasure in televised sport', *Sociology of Sport* 6(3), Sept, USA.

Duncan, M. C. and Hasbrook, C. A. (1988) 'Denial of power in televised women's sports', *Sociology of Sport* 5(1).

Dunne, M. (1982) 'Introduction to some of the images of sport in girls' comics and magazines', in C. Jenkins and M. Green (eds) *Sporting Fictions*, Birmingham: Birmingham University PE Dept and CCCS.

Dunning, E. (1986) 'Sport as a male preserve: social sources of masculine identity', *Theory, Culture and Society* 3(1), London.

Dunning, E. (ed.) (1971) *The Sociology of Sport*, London: Frank Cass.

Dyer, K.F. (1982) *Catching up the Men*, London: Junction.

Dyer, R. (1978) 'Entertainment and utopia', *Movie* 24, London.

—— (1979) *Stars*, London: British Film Institute.

Dyer, R., Lovell, T. and McCrindle, J. (1977) 'Soap opera and women', in the Edinburgh International Television Festival Programme.

Easthope, Anthony (1989) 'A kiss on the pink', *Plural*, Winter, 2, London.

Elliott, P. (1972) *The Making of a TV Series*, London: Constable.

Evans, H.J. (1974) *Service to Sport – The Story of the CCPR*, London: Pelham.

Featherstone, M. (1990) 'Global culture: an introduction', *Theory, Culture and Society* 7(2–3), London: Sage.

Fejes, F. (1981) 'Media imperialism: an assessment', *Media, Culture and Society* 3(3), London: Academic Press.

Fiske, J. (1983) 'Cricket/TV/culture', *Metro* (Media and Education Magazine) 62, Australia.

Garnham, N. (1977) 'Towards a political economy of culture', *New Universities Quarterly*, Summer.

—— (1978) *Structures of Television*, London: British Film Institute.

—— (1979) 'Contribution to a political economy of mass communication', *Media, Culture and Society* 1(2), London: Academic Press.

Geraghty, C., Simpson, P. and Whannel, G. (1986) 'Tunnel vision: television's World Cup', in A. Tomlinson and G. Whannel (eds) *Off The Ball: The Football World Cup*, London: Pluto.

Gibson, A. (1976) *A Mingled Yarn*, London: Collins.

Gilroy, P. (1987) *There Ain't no Black in the Union Jack*, London: Hutchinson.

—— (1990) 'Frank Bruno or Salman Rushdie', *Media Education* 14, Bracknell.

Glendenning, R. (1953) *Just a Word In Your Ear*, London: Stanley Paul.

Golding, P. (1977) 'Media professionalism in the third world: the transfer of an ideology', in J. Curran *et al.* (eds) *Mass Communication and Society*, London: Edward Arnold.

Goldlust, J. (1987) *Playing for Keeps: Sport, the Media and Society*, Australia: Longman.

Goodhart, G.J. *et al.* (1975) *The Television Audience*, London: Saxon.

Gramsci, A. (1971) *Prison Notebooks*, London: Lawrence & Wishart.

Gratton, C. and Taylor, P. (1986) *Sport and Recreation: An Economic Analysis*, London: E. & F.N. Spon.

—— (1987) *Leisure in Britain*, Letchworth: Leisure Publications.

Gray, A. (1987) 'Behind closed doors: video recorders in the home', in H. Baehr and G. Dyer (eds) *Boxed in: Women and Television*, London: Pandora.

Graydon, J. (1980) 'Dispelling the myth of female fragility' *Action (British Journal of Physical Education)* 11(4) July, London.

—— (1983) 'But it's more than a game, it's an institution', *Feminist Review*, Spring London.

Green, E., Hebron, S. and Woodward, D. (1987) *Leisure and Gender*, London: Sports Council.

Green, T. (1972) *The Universal Eye*, London: Bodley Head.

Griffin, Christine, *et al.* (1982) 'Women and leisure', in J.A. Hargreaves (ed.) *Sport, Culture and Ideology* London: Routledge & Kegan Paul.

Gruneau, R. (1983) *Class, Sports and Social Development*, Massachusetts USA: University of Massachusetts Press.

—— (1988) 'Modernisation or hegemony: two views on sport and social development', in J. Harvey and H. Cantelon (eds) *Not Just a Game*, Ottawa: University of Ottawa Press.

—— (1989) 'Making spectacle: a case study in television sports production', in L.

Wenner (ed.) *Media, Sports and Society*, London: Sage.

Gruneau, R. and Albinson, J. (eds) (1976) *Canadian Sport: Sociological Perspectives*, Canada: Addison-Wesley.

Guttmann, A. (1984) *The Games Must Go On: Avery Brundage and the Olympics Movement*, New York: Columbia University Press.

Hall, S. (1972) 'The determinations of news photographs', *Working Papers in Cultural Studies* 3, Birmingham: CCCS.

—— (1973) *Encoding and decoding the TV message*, CCCS Stencilled Paper, Birmingham: CCCS.

—— (1975) *TV as a medium and its relation to culture*, CCCS Stencilled Paper, Birmingham: CCCS.

—— (1977) 'Culture, media and the ideological effect', in J. Curran *et al.* (eds) *Mass Communication and Society*, London: Edward Arnold.

—— (1980a) 'Cultural studies: two paradigms', *Media, Culture and Society* 2(1), London: Academic Press.

Hall, S. *et al.* (1978) *Policing the Crisis*, London: Macmillan.

Hall, S. *et al.* (eds) (1980b) *Culture, Media, Language*, London: Hutchinson.

Halstorf, A. H. and Cantril, H. (1954) 'They saw a game: a case study', *Journal of Abnormal and Social Psychology*, XLIX, USA.

Hargreaves, J.A. (ed.) (1982) *Sport, Culture and Ideology*, London: Routledge & Kegan Paul.

—— (1985) 'Playing like gentlemen while behaving like ladies', *British Journal of Sports History* 2(1), London: Frank Cass.

—— (1986a) 'Where's the virtue? Where's the grace? Social production of gender', *Theory, Culture and Society* 3(1).

—— (1986b) 'Victorian familism and the formative years of female sport', in J.A. Mangan and R. Park, *From 'Fair Sex' to Feminism*, London: Frank Cass.

—— (1989) 'The promise and problems of women's leisure and sport', in C. Rojek (ed.) *Leisure for Leisure*, London: Macmillan.

Hargreaves, J.E. (1986) *Sport, Power and Culture*, London: Polity.

Heath, S. and Skirrow, G. (1977) 'Television: a World In Action', *Screen* 18(2), London: SEFT.

Heller, C. (1978) *Broadcasting and Accountability*, London: British Film Institute.

Hobsbawm, E. and Ranger, T. (eds) (1983) *The Invention of Tradition*, Cambridge: Cambridge University Press.

Hobson, D. (1982) *Crossroads: The Drama of a Soap Opera*, London: Methuen.

Hoch, P. (1972) *Rip Off The Big Game*, USA: Anchor.

Holt, R. (1989) *Sport and the British: A Modern History*, Oxford: Oxford University Press.

Horne, J., Jary, D. and Tomlinson, A. (eds) (1987) *Sport, Leisure and Social Relations*, London: Routledge & Kegan Paul.

Howell, D. (1983) *Report on Sponsorship*, London: CCPR.

—— (1990) *Made in Birmingham: The Memoirs of Denis Howell*, London: Queen Anne Press.

Ingham, A. and Hardy, S. (1984) 'Sport, structuration, subjugation and hegemony', *Theory, Culture and Society* 2(4).

Ingham, R. (ed.) (1978) *Football Hooliganism – The Wider Context*, London: Interaction Inprint.

Jarvie, G. (1986) 'Dependency, cultural identity and sporting landlords', *Journal of British Sports History* 3(1), London: Frank Cass.

—— (1989a) 'Culture, social development and the Scottish Highland gathering', in D. McCrone *et al.* (eds) *The Making of Scotland*, Edinburgh: Edinburgh University Press.

—— (1989b) 'Chariots of Fire, sporting culture and modern Scotland', *Cencrastus* 38, Edinburgh.

—— (1991a) *Highland Games: The Making of the Myth*, Edinburgh: Edinburgh University Press.

Jarvie, G. (ed.) (1991b) *Sport, Racism and Ethnicity*, London: Falmer.

Johnson, R. (1979a) 'Histories of culture/theories of ideology', in M. Barrett *et al.* (eds) *Ideology and Cultural Production*, London: Croom Helm.

—— (1979b) 'Three problematics: elements of a theory of working-class culture', in J. Clarke *et al.* (eds) *Working Class Culture: Studies in History and Theory*, London: Hutchinson.

Johnson, W. O. (1971) *Super Spectator and the Electric Lilliputians*, Boston, USA: Little, Brown and Co.

Johnston, B. (1952) *Let's Go Somewhere*, London: Cleaver Hume.

Johnston, B. (ed.) (1966) *Armchair Cricket*, London: BBC.

—— (1975) *Armchair Cricket*, London: BBC.

Johnston, S. (1985) 'Charioteers and ploughmen', in M. Auty and N. Roddick (eds) *British Cinema Now*, London: British Film Institute.

Jones, S. (1986) *Workers at Play: A Social and Economic History of Leisure 1918–39*, London: Routledge & Kegan Paul.

—— (1989) *Sport, Politics and the Working Class*, Manchester: Manchester University Press.

Jordin, M. and Brunt, R. (1986) 'Constituting the television audience', International Television Studies Conference Paper, London: ITSC.

Kidd, B. (1978) 'Sports and masculinity', in M. Kaufman (ed.) *Beyond Patriarchy*, Toronto, Canada: Oxford University Press.

—— (1984) 'The myth of the ancient games', in A. Tomlinson and G. Whannel (eds) *Five Ring Circus*, London: Pluto.

Klatell, D. and Marcus, N. (1988) *Sports for Sale: Television, Money and the Fans*, Oxford: Oxford University Press.

Kramer, J. (1979) *The Game: My Forty Years in Tennis*, London: Andre Deutsch.

Kumar, K. (1977) 'Holding the middle ground', in J. Curran *et al.* (eds) *Mass Communication and Society*, London: Arnold.

Laclau, E. (1977) *Politics and Ideology in Marxist Theory*, London: New Left Books.

Laker, J. (1977) *One Day Cricket*, London: Batsford.

Langer, J. (1981) 'Television's personality system', *Media, Culture and Society* 3(4), London: Academic Press.

Lashley, H. (1990) 'Black participation in British sport: opportunity or control', in Frank Kew (ed.) *Social Scientific Perspectives on Sport*, London: BASS.

Lawrence, G. and Rowe, D. (eds) (1987) *Power Play: The Commercialisation of Australian Sport*, Sydney, Australia: Hale & Iremonger.

Lenskyj, H. (1986) *Women, Sport and Sexuality*, Toronto, Ontario: The Women's Press.

Lewis, J. (1983) 'The encoding/decoding model: criticisms and redevelopments for research on decoding', *Media, Culture and Society* 5(2), London: Academic Press.

Lovell, A. (1975) 'The Searchers and the pleasure principle', *Screen Education*, Winter, 17, London: SEFT.

Lovell, T. (1980) *Pictures of Reality*, London: British Film Institute.

—— (1981) 'Ideology and Coronation Street', in R. Dyer *et al.* (eds) *Coronation Street*, London: British Film Institute.

Lovesey, P. (1979) *The Official Centenary History of the AAA*, London: Guinness Superlatives.

Lowenthal, L. (1961) *Literature, Popular Culture and Society*, Palo Alto, California: Pacific Books.

Lull, J. (1990) *Inside Family Viewing: Ethnographic Research on TV's Audience*, London: Routledge.

Lull, J. (ed.) (1988) *World Families Watch Television*, London: Sage.

McCormack, M. (1984) *What They Don't Teach You at Harvard Business School*, London: Collins.

Macfarlane, N. (1986) *Sport and Politics – A World Divided*, London: Willow.

McFarline, P. (1977) *A Game Divided*, London: Hutchinson.

MacGregor, B. (1977) 'Volleyball and the media', *Volleyball Magazine*, 8 April.

McIntosh, P. (1952) *Physical Education in England since 1800*, London: Bell.

—— (1979) *Fair Play*, London: Heinemann.

McIntosh, P. *et al.* (1957) *Landmarks in the History of Physical Education*, London: Routledge & Kegan Paul.

McRobbie, A. (1991) 'New times in cultural studies', *New Formations* 13, London: Routledge.

Maguire, J. (1986) 'Images of manliness (late Victorian and Edwardian Britain)', *British Journal of Sports History* 3(3), London: Frank Cass.

—— (1988) 'Race and position assignment in English soccer: ethnicity and sport', *Sociology of Sport Journal* 5: 257–69.

Malcolmson, R. (1973) *Popular Recreations in English Society 1700–1850*, Cambridge: Cambridge University Press.

Mangan, J.A. (1981) *Athleticism in the Victorian and Edwardian Public School*, London: Cambridge University Press.

Mangan, J.A. and Park R.J. (eds) (1986) *From 'Fair Sex' to Feminism*, London: Frank Cass.

Mangan, J.A. and Walvin, J. (1987) *Manliness and Morality: Middle Class Masculinity in Britain and America*, Manchester: Manchester University Press.

Marcuse, H. (1955) *Eros and Civilisation*, USA: Beacon.

Marles, V. (1984) 'The public and sport', *BBC Broadcast Research Findings*, London: BBC.

Mason, T. (1980) *Association Football and English Society 1863–1915*, London: Harvester.

—— (1988) *Sport in Britain*, London: Faber & Faber.

Masterman, L. (1980) *Teaching about Television*, London: Macmillan.

Mercer, C. (1978) 'Culture and ideology', in A. Gramsci (ed.) *Red Letters*, London.

Mewshaw, M. (1983) *Short Circuit*, London: Collins.

Miller, T. (1989) 'Sport, media and masculinity', in D. Rowe and G. Lawrence (eds) *Sport and Leisure*, Australia: Harcourt Brace Jovanovich.

Mitchell, L. (1981) *Leslie Mitchell Reporting*, London: Hutchinson.

Moores, S. (1990) 'Texts, readers and contexts of reading: developments in study of audience', *Media, Culture and Society* 12(1), Jan, London: Sage.

Morley, D. (1980) *The Nationwide Audience*, London: British Film Institute.

—— (1981) 'Critical postscript to the Nationwide project', *Screen Education* 39, London: SEFT.

—— (1986) *Family Television: Cultural Power and Domestic Leisure*, London: Comedia.

—— (1991) 'Where the global meets the local: notes from the sitting room', *Screen* 32(1), Glasgow.

Morley, D. and Silverstone, R. (1990) 'Domestic communication – technologies and meaning', *Media, Culture and Society* 12(1), Jan, London: Sage.

Morris, B. and Nydahl, J. (1985) 'Sports spectacle as drama: image, language and technology', *Journal of Popular Culture* 18(4), Spring, USA.

Morse, M. (1983) 'Sport on television: replay and display', in E.A. Kaplan (ed.) *Regarding Television*, USA: AFI.
—— (1985) 'Talk, talk, talk – the space of discourse in television', *Screen* 26(2), March–April, London: SEFT.
Mulvey, L. (1975) 'Visual pleasure and narrative cinema', *Screen* 16(3), London: SEFT.
Murdock, G. and Golding, P. (1974) 'For a political economy of mass communications', in R. Milband and J. Savile (eds) *The Socialist Register*, London: Merlin.
—— (1977) 'Capitalism, communications and class relations', in J. Curran *et al.* (eds) *Mass Communication and Society*, London: Edward Arnold.
Neale, S. (1982) 'Chariots of Fire: images of men', *Screen* 23(3/4), London: SEFT.
Nordenstreng, K. and Varis, T. (1978) 'International flow of television programmes', in J. Caughie (ed.) *Television: Ideology and Exchange*, London: British Film Institute.
Nowell-Smith, G. (1978) 'Television–football–the world', *Screen* 19(4), London: SEFT.
O'Neil, T. (1989) *The Game Behind the Game*, New York: Harper & Row.
Pannick, D. (1984) *Sex Discrimination in Sport*, London: Equal Opportunities Commission.
Parente, Donald (1974) 'A History of TV and Sports', USA: Ph.D. thesis.
—— (1977) 'The interdependence of sports and television', *Journal of Communication*, Summer, USA.
Parry, S.J. (1984) 'Hegemony and sport', *Journal of the Philosophy of Sport* X, 71–83, London.
Paterson, R. (1980) 'Planning the family', *Screen Education* 35, London: SEFT.
—— (1990) 'A suitable schedule for the family', in A. Goodwin and G. Whannel (eds) *Understanding Television*, London: Routledge.
Paulu, B. (1961) *British Broadcasting in Transition*, London: Macmillan.
Pearson, Roberta E. (1988) 'Take me out to the ballgame: narrative structure of TV baseball', paper for ITSC Conference, London.
Peters, R. (1976) *Television Coverage of Sport*, Birmingham: CCCS.
Pilkington Report (1962) *Report of the Committee on Broadcasting*, London: HMSO (Cmnd 1753).
Pilsworth, M. (1980) 'An "imperfect art": TV scheduling in Britain', *Sight and Sound*, Autumn, London: British Film Institute.
Potter, J. (1989) *Independent Television in Britain vol. 3: Politics and Control 1968–80*, London: Macmillan.
—— (1990) *Independent Television in Britain vol. 4: Companies and Programmes 1968–80*, London: Macmillan.
Poulantzas, N. (1973) *Political Power and Social Classes*, London: New Left Books.
Powers, Ron (1984) *Supertube: The Rise of Television Sports*, USA: Coward McCann.
Rader, B.G. (1984) *In Its Own Image: How TV has Transformed Sports*, New York, USA: Free Press.
Real, M. (1975) 'Superbowl: mythic spectacle', *Journal of Communication* 25, USA.
—— (1989) *Super Media*, London: Sage.
Redhead, S. (1986) *Sing When You're Winning*, London: Pluto.
Reich, K. (1986) *Making It Happen: Peter Ueberroth and the 1984 Olympics*, Santa Barbara, California: Capra.

Robertson, R. (1990) 'Mapping the global condition: globalisation as the central concept', *Theory, Culture and Society* 7(2–3), London: Sage.

Rojek, C. (ed.) (1989) *Leisure for Leisure*, London: Macmillan.

Ross, G. (1961) *TV Jubilee*, London: W.H. Allan.

—— (1972) *A History of Cricket*, London: Arnold Barker.

—— (1981) *The Gillette Cup*, London: Macdonald Futura.

Rowe, D. and Lawrence, G. (1989) *Sport and Leisure: Trends in Australian Popular Culture*, Australia: Harcourt Brace Jovanovich.

Scannell, P. (1990) 'Introduction', *Media, Culture and Society* 12(1), London: Sage.

Schiller, H. (1971) *Mass Communication and American Empire*, Boston: Beacon.

Schlesinger, Philip (1978) *Putting Reality Together*, London: Constable.

Schramm, W. (1964) *Mass Media and National Development*, London: Stanford University Press.

Sendall, B. (1982) *Independent Television in Britain vol. 1: 1946–62*, London: Macmillan.

—— (1983) *Independent Television in Britain vol. 2: 1958–68*, London: Macmillan.

Shulman, M. (1973) *The Least Worst Television in the World*, London: Barrie & Jenkins.

Simpson, P. (1987) *Parents Talking Television*, London: Comedia.

Smith, A.C.H. (1975) *Paper Voices*, London: Chatto & Windus.

Snagge, J. and Barsley, M. (1972) *Those Vintage Years of Radio*, London: Pitman.

Spence, J. (1988) *Up Close and Personal*, New York: Atheneum.

Sugar, B.R. (1980) *The Thrill of Victory (Inside ABC Sports)*, New York: Hawthorn Books.

Sugden, J. and Bairner, A. (1986) 'Northern Ireland: sport in a divided society', in L. Allison (ed.) *The Politics of Sport*, Manchester: Manchester University Press.

Talbot, G. (1976) *Permission to Speak*, London: Hutchinson.

—— (1973) *Ten Seconds From Now: A Broadcaster's Story*, London: Hutchinson.

Talbot, M. (1979) *Women and Leisure*, London: Sports Council/SSRC.

Taylor, P. (1986) *The Smoke Ring: Tobacco Money and Multinational Politics*, London: Bodley Head.

Telecine (1978) 'Sport et télévision', *Telecine* 229, June, France.

Theberge, N. (1981) 'A critique of critiques: radical and feminist writings on sport', *Social Forces* 60(2), Dec, USA.

Thomas, H. (1977) *With an Independent Air*, London: Weidenfeld & Nicolson.

Thompson, E.P. (1978) *The Poverty of Theory*, London: Merlin.

Tomlinson, A. (ed.) (1981a) *Leisure and Social Control*, Brighton: Brighton Polytechnic.

—— (ed.) (1981b) *The Sociological Study of Sport*, Brighton: Brighton Polytechnic.

—— (1983) 'Reproducing gender ideologies: physicality, masculinity and sports', Symposium on Gender, Leisure and Cultural Production, Canada: Queens University, Kingston.

—— (1988) 'Situating Chariots of Fire', *British Society of Sports History Bulletin*, no. 8.

—— (1989) 'Whose side are they on? Leisure Studies and Cultural Studies in Britain', *Leisure Studies* 8(2): 97–106, London: Leisure Studies Association.

—— (ed.) (1990) *Consumption, Identity and Style*, London: Comedia.

—— (1992) 'Shifting patterns of working class leisure: the case of knurr-and-spell', *Sociology of Sport* (forthcoming).

Tomlinson, A. and Whannel, G. (eds) (1984) *Five Ring Circus*, London: Pluto.

—— (1986) *Off the Ball*, London: Pluto.

Trevor-Roper, H. (1983) 'The invention of tradition: the highland tradition of

Scotland', in E. Hobsbawm and T. Ranger (eds) *The Invention of Tradition*, Cambridge: Cambridge University Press.
Tunstall, J. (1977) *The Media are American*, London: Constable.
Ueberroth, P. (1985) *Made in America*, New York: William Morrow.
Vinnai, G. (1976) *Football Mania*, London: Ocean.
Wagg, S. (1984) *The Football World*, London: Harvester.
Waites, B., Bennett, T. and Martin, G. (1982) *Popular Culture: Past and Present*, London: Croom Helm.
Wakelam, H.B.T. (1938) *Half Time*, London: Thomas Nelson.
—— (1954) *The Game Goes On*, London: Sportsmen's Book Club.
Walvin, J. (1972) *The People's Game*, London: Allen Lane.
—— (1986) *Football and the Decline of Britain*, London: Macmillan.
Wedlake, G.E.C. (1973) *SOS: The Story of Radio Communication*, London: David & Charles.
Wenner, L. (ed.) (1989a) *Media, Sports and Society*, London: Sage.
—— (1989b) 'The Super Bowl pre-game show: cultural fantasies and political subtext', in L. Wenner (ed.) *Media, Sports and Society*, London: Sage.
Wenner, L. and Gantz, W. (1989c) 'The audience experience with sports on television', in L. Wenner (ed.) *Media, Sports and Society*, London: Sage.
Whannel, G. (1982) 'Narrative and television sport: the Coe and Ovett story', in C. Jenkins and M. Green (eds) *Sporting Fictions*, Birmingham: CCCS.
—— (1983a) *Blowing the Whistle*, London: Pluto.
—— (1983b) 'Sit down with us: TV sport as armchair theatre', in Sue Glyptis (ed.) *Leisure and the Media*, London: Leisure Studies Association, Conference Papers 16.
—— (1985) 'Television spectacle and the internationalisation of sport', *Journal of Communication Inquiry* 2(2), Summer, School of Journalism and Mass Communication, University of Iowa, USA.
—— (1986a) 'The unholy alliance: notes on television and the re-making of British sport', *Leisure Studies* 5, London: E. & F.N. Spon.
—— (1986b) 'The head to head that had to happen: TV sport and entrepreneurship', International Television Studies Conference, London.
—— (1986c) 'Televising sport: the archaeology of a professional practice', *Leisure: Politics, Planning, People vol. 5: The Media and Cultural Forms*, Brighton: Leisure Studies Association.
—— (1988) 'Human billboards', *Sport and Leisure*, Nov–Dec, London: Sports Council.
—— (1988) *Sport on 4*, London: Channel 4.
—— (1989) 'History is being made: Television sport and the selective tradition', *The Olympic Movement and the Mass Media*, Calgary, Canada: Hurford.
—— (1991) 'Grandstand, the sports fan and the family audience', in J. Corner (ed.) *Popular Television in Britain: Studies in Cultural History*, London: British Film Institute.
Whitson, D. (1983a) 'Pressures on regional games in a dominant metropolitan culture: shinty', *Leisure Studies* 2(2), May, London: E. & F.N. Spon.
—— (1983b) 'Sport and hegemony', *Sociology of Sport Journal* 1: 64–78.
—— (1986) 'Structure, agency, and the sociology of sport debates', *Theory, Culture and Society* 3(1).
Wiggins, D. (1989) 'Great speed but little stamina: the historical debate over black athletes, *Journal for the History of Sport* 16(3), USA.
Williams, B. (1977) 'The structure of televised football', *Journal of Communication* 27.
Williams, C.L., Lawrence, G. and Rowe, D. (1987) 'Patriarchy, media and sport',

in G. Lawrence and D. Rowe (eds) *Power Play*, Sydney, Australia: Hale & Iremonger.

Williams, D. (1957) *Clear Round*, London: Hodder & Stoughton.

—— (1968) *Show Jumping*, London: Faber & Faber.

Williams, R. (1973) 'Base and superstructure in Marxist cultural theory', *New Left Review* 82, Nov–Dec, London.

—— (1974) *TV Technology and Cultural Form*, London: Fontana.

—— (1977) *Marxism and Literature*, Oxford: Oxford University Press.

—— (1980) *Problems in Materialism and Culture*, London: Verso.

Willis, B. (1979) *Diary of a Cricket Season*, London: Pelham.

—— (1981) *The Cricket Revolution*, London: Sidgwick & Jackson.

Willis, P. (1982) 'Women in sport in ideology', in J.A. Hargreaves (ed.) *Sport, Culture and Ideology*, London: Routledge & Kegan Paul.

Wilson, N. (1988) *The Sports Business*, London: Piatkus.

Wimbush, Erica and Talbot, Margaret (eds) (1989) *Relative Freedoms*, Milton Keynes: Open University Press.

Wolstenholme, K. (1958) *Sports Special*, London: Sportsmen's Book Club.

Wren-Lewis, J. and Clarke, A. (1983) 'The World Cup – A political football?' *Theory, Culture and Society* 1(3), London.

Index